AOL®

COMPANION

2nd Edition

AOL®
COMPANION
2nd Edition

Jennifer Watson

An International Data Group Company
Foster City, CA • Chicago, IL • Indianapolis, IN • New York, NY

AOL® Companion, 2nd Edition

Published by

MIS:Press, an imprint of IDG Books Worldwide, Inc.

An International Data Group Company

919 E. Hillsdale Blvd., Suite 400

Foster City, CA 94404

www.idgbooks.com (IDG Books Worldwide Web site)

Library of Congress Catalog Card Number: 98-072470

ISBN: 0-7645-7501-5

Printed in the United States of America

10 9 8 7 6 5 4 3 2 1

1B/RW/QY/ZY/FC

Distributed in the United States by IDG Books Worldwide, Inc.

Distributed by Macmillan Canada for Canada; by Transworld Publishers Limited in the United Kingdom; by IDG Norge Books for Norway; by IDG Sweden Books for Sweden; by Woodslane Pty. Ltd. for Australia; by Woodslane (NZ) Ltd. for New Zealand; by Addison Wesley Longman Singapore Pte Ltd. for Singapore, Malaysia, Thailand, Indonesia, and Korea; by Norma Comunicaciones S.A. for Colombia; by Intersoft for South Africa; by International Thomson Publishing for Germany, Austria, and Switzerland; by Toppan Company Ltd. for Japan; by Distribuidora Cuspide for Argentina; by Livraria Cultura for Brazil; by Ediciencia S.A. for Ecuador; by Ediciones ZETA S.C.R. Ltda. for Peru; by WS Computer Publishing Corporation, Inc., for the Philippines; by Unalis Corporation for Taiwan; by Contemporanea de Ediciones for Venezuela; by Computer Book & Magazine Store for Puerto Rico; by Express Computer Distributors for the Caribbean and West Indies. Authorized Sales Agent: Anthony Rudkin Associates for the Middle East and North Africa.

 is a trademark under exclusive license to IDG Books Worldwide, Inc., from International Data Group, Inc.

 is a registered trademark of IDG Books Worldwide, Inc.

Credits

Acquisitions Editors
Juliana Aldous
Nancy Stevenson

Development Editor
Ellen L. Dendy

Technical Editor
Susan Glinert

Copy Editor
Timothy Borek

Project Coordinator
Tom Debolski

Book Designer
Kurt Krames

Graphics and Production Specialists
Linda Marousek
Hector Mendoza
Dina F Quan
Mark Yim

Quality Control Specialists
Mick Arellano
Mark Schumann

Proofreader
Mary C. Barnack

Indexer
Ty Koontz

About the Author

Jennifer Watson is one of America Online's foremost teachers, sharing her knowledge with beginners and insiders alike. Her invaluable compilation of keywords, prepared and shared with America Online's membership, became the top-selling *AOL Keywords* by MIS:Press, Inc. (now in its third edition). As the founder of The VirtuaLeader Academy — an online training center for AOL's volunteers, partners, and employees — she teaches the leaders of the online community how to make AOL come alive. Jennifer lives in Ann Arbor, Michigan, with Kippi, her Alaskan Malamute companion.

To David Marx, for his dedicated and invaluable contributions to this book. If I'm the "front cover" companion, he's the "under cover" companion. I look forward to his move to front (and shared) covers before long.

Welcome! Are you alone? If not, walk quietly to the other side of that row of books you're standing near, or sneak off inconspicuously to an empty room with a comfortable chair. I have some secrets to share with you.

First, I'm not simply a book that someone named a *Companion*. I'm a real, honest-to-goodness, thinking, and feeling companion. My name is Jennifer, and I've poured myself into this book to help you with America Online. I'm here to explain and demonstrate not simply how to use America Online, but how to make it *work for you*. There are many online resources and offline books that can (and will) show you how to use America Online's many features, but none that focus solely on how to get the real power out of these features for yourself. This is, in essence, a collection of tips, tricks, and secrets that I've collected over the years. This is the stuff you hastily flip pages for in other books, the stuff you wisely take notes about so you won't forget, and the stuff you proudly pass on to your friends. Now it's all in one place.

I have another secret. You and I are not really alone. Inside are over a dozen of *my* companions, those who are happily accompanying us on our journey through America Online. Their collective experience, knowledge, and wisdom enrich this collection immeasurably. I will introduce each one to you in turn as we go along.

Is This Book for You?

I've taken special care to make the tips and tricks in the *AOL Companion* as nontechnical and easy to read as possible. I want members of all levels have the opportunity to make the best use of the information. This also keeps the book up to date for a longer period. Do keep in mind, however, that America Online is growing quickly and things do change. If you notice that something no longer works, or you have a better way to accomplish it, please let me know! E-mail me at screen name: *Jennifer.* I read my mail daily, and though I can't guarantee a response I will do my best to reply or forward it to one of my companions. All comments and suggestions are welcome!

Using This Book

I debated even including this section. The *AOL Companion* is so easy to use, I don't think there is much that won't be obvious to you already. But for the sake of completeness, let me give you a few tips to help you get the most out of your *AOL Companion.*

- The tips and tricks in the *AOL Companion* are sorted into eight chapters, organized in the order that I anticipate you prefer reading them. Even so, you're welcome to skip around as much as you like.

- Every tip is introduced by a *TipBar*. At the left end is the tip's title, with some helpful information at the opposite end: a complexity rating, a money-saving indicator, and a computer compatibility note (don't worry, most tips work on all computers). See the following diagram for the TipBar key.

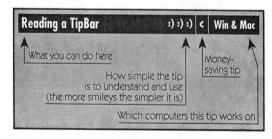

The TipBar is easy to use.

- Each tip title is clear and straightforward, designed to help you quickly and easily locate exactly what

you need. Keep an eye on the subtitles below the
TipBar — they can often clue you in on some of the
more esoteric and fascinating aspects of the tip.

- Graphics and illustrations are included within the
tip whenever they seem appropriate. And as this is a
multiplatform book, I've noted in the caption when
screens are views from Windows AOL software or
Mac AOL software.

- As most of you are likely to be using the latest revision of the AOL software, version 4.0, you should
assume that the tips are intended for this software
unless otherwise noted. If you are unable or unwill-
ing to use the latest version, a fair number of these
tips apply to older versions as well. Do, however,
consider upgrading if at all possible.

- At the bottom of a tip, you may notice I've indicated
the name and screen name of the contributor. These
are my own companions — community leaders
from around America Online who represent years of
combined experience. These folks are a wealth of
information; adding their voices made the book
much richer. You'll find my musings on them scattered throughout the book.

- There are also three appendixes at the back that
describe emoticons (smileys), shorthands, netiquette, and a whole slew of America Online jargon
and terms.

- Remember the table of contents and index are great
for finding exactly what you need!

- Your *AOL Companion* is purposefully compact so
that you can tuck it next to your monitor. It travels
well, too!

- Many of the tips contain lists of tricks and related
tips. Read them carefully for useful and unique ways
of doing things. There are some "hidden" gems
lurking in the lists, plus a few "secrets" thrown in to
keep you on your toes.

Your *Companion* in life

Wondering what to do with all the tips in this book? Allow me to show you my vision of life both *with* this book (let's call that *Companion*ated) and *without* the book (*Companion*less). A bit idealistic? Perhaps — but what is life for but to dream?

*Companion*ated: Through the peal of ringing bells, we see John. He is standing forlornly in his college graduation cap and gown — he has no job lined up yet. While searching for work, he spies a want ad from America Online, Inc. Recalling all the great things he's heard about it, he decides to apply. Like a good college graduate, he does his homework first and picks up a copy of the *AOL Companion* book (why thank you, John!). After a few futile tries on his own, he cracks open the *Companion* for help in locating AOL software. The *Companion* mentions there could be software pre-installed on his computer and, sure enough, he finds it after some searching. Impatiently he attempts to sign on only to realize the software doesn't recognize his modem. After some wild — and unsuccessful — guessing, he troubleshoots the modem with tips from the *Companion*. After also learning to disable call waiting, he successfully signs on. He encounters a problem as he enters his credit card to register, but a call to Member Services (number courtesy of the *Companion*) solves that dilemma. In no time, he's online soaking up the information that lands him the job. John — 1: Life — 0.

*Companion*less: John fruitlessly spends his time trying to find AOL software, not realizing he had it all along. He gives up when the first college loan statement arrives, settling for a job at the fast-food chain around the corner. John — 0: Life — 1.

OK, so perhaps I'm idealistic. But you'll find down-to-earth examples of the tips and tricks all throughout the *Companion*. And watch for "Companion Confessions" at the end of each chapter for a *revealing* look at how I've put this information to work for me on a daily basis.

One More Confession Before You Delve In

I must confess something else. I'm terribly ticklish. And I can feel your fingers on my spine . . . the book spine, that is. But the more you use me, the easier it will become. I'm here for you. Open me, bend me, fold me, highlight me. Set me by your computer or keep me in your bathroom. Read me from cover to cover, or skip around in me as you please. Don't be shy.

I have many more secrets, but I'll save them for later. Meanwhile, we have an adventure awaiting us.

Your Companion,

Jennifer O;>

Now, let the tips begin!

ACKNOWLEDGMENTS

The *AOL Companion* is the result of many minds and hands, working together in rhythm. My heartfelt thanks go out to:

David ("Dave") Marx, who contributed to this collection selflessly, offering his ideas and time generously. He read every word I wrote (except the ones about him) and helped polish my prose. Thank you, David, for smoothing my rough spots so nicely.

Ben Foxworth, who fed me tips and tricks throughout our years of companionship. Your contributions to this edition — both acknowledged and unacknowledged — are invaluable.

George Louie, my companion of many years, who co-authored the VirtuaLingo Glossary with me and contributed his knowledge and advice on several other topics in this book. Thank you, George, for sticking with it when it got bumpy.

My other 11 companions, Sue Boettcher, Becky Fowler, Genevieve Kazdin, Maria Therese Lehan, Adrienne Quinn, Brendan Rice, Brian Thomason, Kate Tipul, Bob Trautman, Kimberly Trautman, and Bradley Zimmer, who contributed unconditionally to this collection. Thank you, friends — I'm truly blessed.

All the Cadre in The VirtuaLeader Academy for giving me the chance to learn about you and your experiences online, and for your patience while I was off adventuring with the newfound knowledge. Thank you in particular to Shelley Sheahan and Varian, my two trusted and loyal assistants — without them I'd never have been able to finish this book.

My editors at IDG Books Worldwide, Ellen Dendy, development editor, and Juliana Aldous, acquisitions editor, for believing in me even though I was the new kid on their block. And thanks also to copy editor Tim Borek and project coordinator Tom Debolski. Thanks to Susan Glinert, the technical editor, for catching my lapses into the past that would have otherwise gone unchecked and confused the heck out of everyone. Thanks also to the rest of the dedicated team at IDG Books Worldwide who did so much behind the scenes to put this book to your hands.

Last and most important, I want to thank you. Without you, there would be no *AOL Companion.* I love to thank you personally, too! So please send your thoughts and ideas about the *AOL Companion* to screen name: *Jennifer.*

CONTENTS

CHAPTER 1

ACCESSING AMERICA ONLINE

Step 1: Initializing modem
Step 2: Dialing 1-800-AOL-TIPS
Step 3: Connecting to the AOL Companion

Welcome! You've got mail! And that's not all . . . you've just accessed a secret cache of America Online tips and tricks. Imagine megabytes of priceless information, streams of valuable shortcuts, and gems of rich advice. And a thoroughly modest and down-to-earth companion to guide you through it all — me!

Like the genie of the lamp, I can open your eyes and show you a whole new world. But I'm not limited to granting three wishes; there are over 150 individual tips in this book, plus hundreds more tricks and secrets scattered throughout. These tips can help you save time and money, make your online experience more enjoyable, introduce you to new people, and show you how to make the most of your America Online adventure.

But before you dive in, you need a good understanding of America Online itself. Allow me, as your companion, to give you a tour. Hop aboard the magic carpet and get ready for the ride of your life.

What Is America Online?

Most folks will tell you America Online is an online service you can use with your personal computer. Others may say it is a way to use e-mail and to get to the Internet. And still others may claim it is one of the best ways to meet people in the '90s. Yes, America Online is all that.

But when you get right down to it, it is really what *you* make of it that matters most.

With over 12 million members, America Online certainly clocks in as the largest online service. It is large in more than membership, too: there are hundreds of areas, each with original content and quality services. All the areas, or *forums*, are organized into 19 *channels*, and cover just about every topic under the sun. And, of course, there's full access to the Internet — e-mail, World Wide Web, the gamut. It is a full-service pump on the information superhighway, at a self-service price.

If you're not yet a member of America Online, don't worry. The very first tip in this chapter — "Finding AOL Software" — will help you get started. Once you're online, the rest of the tips and tricks in this chapter will head you in the right direction, whether you're new or experienced.

Now about that "mail" you received at the start of this chapter — it looks like it is from someone by the name of Jennifer . . .

A Letter from your Companion

Hi there!

If we're going to be together for the next 300 or so pages, we should get to know one another. Allow me to begin: I usually go by Jennifer Watson (as is noted on the cover of your book, I hope), though I will answer to "Angel" on my good days. I detest being called anything other than "Jennifer," such as "Jen" or, worse yet, "Jenny."

I live in beautiful Ann Arbor, Michigan, with my dog Kippi, an Alaskan Malamute who was surely royalty in a former life. I work in my "cockpit," a collection of desks arranged in a circle around me, each stacked high with hutches and shelves holding computers, monitors, and assorted and sundry hardware (plus a few stuffed animals). I also surround myself with books of all types, of course. When I travel, which is often, I usually bring along as many "toys" as will fit in my tiny car, including my "Pet Powerbook" (I prefer Macs), which I appear with in my photo (see Figure 1.1).

Figure 1.1 Jennifer and her Pet Powerbook.

But my real home is online, with my friends, family, and colleagues. I've been on America Online since I returned from a year-long trip to Japan in 1992. Never content to be a bystander in life, I got involved by volunteering to help in chats. But that wasn't enough. I had to know more, do more, be more. I learned as much as I could about America Online in those early years by researching and writing articles and guides, helping book authors get the word out, compiling lists of online information, training volunteers like myself, and even helping America Online take off. These days I am happily involved in coordinating The VirtuaLeader Academy, an amazing place that helps volunteers, partners, and staff with their work online (see keyword: VLA). I also love to share my knowledge and experiences by writing books, such as *AOL Keywords, 3rd Edition*, also published by MIS: Press, and the *Official America Online Tour Guide* published by The Coriolis Group.

(continued)

Though no one can do everything and be everywhere, I think I'm now qualified to say I'm one of the most experienced and "widely traveled" folks on America Online. I'm delighted to be your companion on your journey through this book, and onward to your adventures online. :)

Now, how about you? I can't read your mind, but I will read your e-mail. Reply with a note to screen name: *Jennifer* and tell me what you think!

Jennifer O;>

Finding AOL Software :) :) :) | ‹ | Win & Mac

. . . or how to get the goods

Desperately seeking software? If you aren't on America Online yet, or cannot access it for some reason, don't despair — AOL software can be found everywhere! First, check that you haven't received an AOL software sign-on kit in the mail, be it at home or at the office. America Online distributes these generously. Look for them also at a local software store, office supply store, bookstore, or even grocery. Sign-on kits can often be found shrink-wrapped with magazines or attached to the back of relevant books (but please avoid the temptation to sneak the disk and leave the magazine or book without its goodies). You'll also find AOL software bundled in CD collections, software, modems, and computers. And don't forget software conventions and trade shows. You can also get software from America Online's BBS — use a standard telecommunications program (settings: 8 data bits, no parity, 1 stop bit, up to 14.4 Kbps) and dial 1-800-827-5808. If all else fails, call 1-800-827-6364 or 1-703-893-6288 (Canada and overseas) to request a sign-on kit.

If you're already on the AOL service but need to upgrade or for some reason get a version of AOL software other than what you're currently using, you have more options. The first is to use keyword: UPGRADE to download the latest software and get helpful information and tips on using it. For more information, see the section on upgrading your software near the end of this chapter.

If you are unfamiliar with keywords, they can take you directly to an area without having to worry about navigating through menus or windows. To use a keyword, sign on and type the keyword (the word that appears after *keyword:* in all capital letters) in the long, white box on your toolbar at the top of the screen and click the **Go** button. You can learn more about keywords in Chapter 3. In addition, my book *AOL Keywords* provides a terrific resource for finding the latest AOL keywords.

If you don't need the AOL software immediately, or want to give it to a friend, use keyword: FRIEND (surprise surprise!) and request that a sign-on kit be sent via snail mail. Finally, if you need an older version of the AOL software, go to keyword: GET 30 (for Windows and Mac AOL software v3.0), keyword: GET 25 (for Windows AOL software v2.5), or keyword: GET 27 (for Mac AOL software v2.7). Note that these keywords only work on their corresponding platform.

Don't copy AOL software from a friend's computer. The installed program is customized for each member, making it impossible for you to establish your own account. You'll also lack important settings needed by the Windows and Mac operating systems. On the other hand, you can borrow a disk or CD from a friend, provided you don't need registration numbers (which only work once).

Contributed by Brian Thomason
(screen name: JBThomason)

Connecting to AOL   :) :)   Win & Mac

. . . or how to avoid the busy signal blues

Reaching out and touching someone used to be a little simpler. You picked up the phone, hoped the party line wasn't in use, and dialed that favorite restaurant for reservations (and you got right in, of course). Life's not as simple as it once was. More often than not it seems as though the phone is busy. Even when you get an answer, that barrage of static from an answering modem is never as pleasant as the folks down at the Chopstick House. But

there is always a fortune cookie at the end of the meal —
take your pick:

- *When one door closes, another one opens* . . . to a
  new local access number. In most cities, there are
  several local access numbers (also called *POPs*, or
  points of presence) available to get you signed on
  to the AOL service. New numbers are being added
  all the time. Be sure to check out the tip "Finding
  Local Access Numbers" in this chapter. Online, visit
  keyword: PULSE OF AOL for announcements of new
  numbers, too!

- *Today you will find your fortune through.* . .
  Internet service providers (ISPs) and local area networks (LANs). If a local access number isn't available, consider using an ISP or the LAN at work or
  school (if it has an Internet gateway). ISPs and LANs
  are a convenient way of connecting and are useful
  even if you have a local access number. You access
  the AOL service by connecting to your ISP or LAN
  and then signing on using your AOL software and its
  TCP/IP settings. You can even save money this way
  using the "bring your own access" pricing plan. See
  the tips "Using Internet Service Providers" and
  "Choosing a Pricing Plan" for more information.

- *Your lucky number is.* . . an 800/888 access number. America Online provides several toll-free, *surcharged* numbers. If you don't have a local access
  number, you know that calling over to the next town
  or county is as cheap as calling China. Though there
  is a fee for the toll-free numbers, it can be significantly cheaper than an intrastate call. More information on these toll-free numbers is in the tip
  "Using 800 Access Numbers."

Contributed by Brian Thomason
(screen name: JBThomason)

. . . or how to get to the Yellow Brick Road

Can you imagine Dorothy trying to get to the Emerald City
without the infamous Yellow Brick Road? Not likely, huh?
Local access numbers are your yellow brick road to
America Online, and it starts in the Munchkin Village at
keyword: ACCESS. Search the list for your area code
and/or city, and presto, you have your ruby slippers.

Alas, to get to this keyword, you need to actually be
online *at the time*. And usually if you need a new number
you can't get online at all. Here are the Good Witch of the
East's top five ways to get access numbers offline:

1. Click **Setup** on the Setup & Sign On screen, select
   the "Add numbers from the list of access numbers"
   option, and click **Next** to input your area code. Now
   just choose the access numbers you want from the
   Select AOL Access Phone Numbers window and
   click **Add** to add them to your software. If you are at
   a hotel and need to use a dialout string first, highlight the access number in the list, click **Edit**, and
   then enable the number to reach an outside line.

2. Call America Online at 1-800-827-6364 or 1-703-
   893-6288 (Canada or overseas), from 6:00 a.m. to
   4:00 p.m. Eastern Time, seven days a week.

3. Phone the network: AOLnet is at 1-888-AOL-NETS or
   1-888-265-8005. SprintNet is at 1-800-473-7983
   (automated) or 1-800-877-5045 (voice).

4. Check an older version of the AOL software lurking
   on your hard drive and salvage the numbers.

5. Call someone else who will look one up for you.

If you are having difficulties connecting with a local
access number, report it at keyword: ACCESS. America
Online and the access companies rely on such reports to
track troublesome network modems and to evaluate
capacity at various access numbers. If nothing else
works, try clicking your heels together three times and
reciting, "There's no place like AOL." It is worth a try.

Contributed by Ben Foxworth (screen name: BenF7)

Using 800 Access Numbers   :) :) :) | ¢ | Win & Mac

. . . or how to save the people you love money

Now what happens if you're stuck in Kansas and the Yellow Brick Road to Emerald City Online doesn't even exist? Many communities still don't have local access numbers, meaning you need to make a toll call to reach any access number. That can quickly add up to a telephone bill that is as out of control as a tornado.

To avoid paying an exorbitant amount for access, America Online offers "800" access numbers — for a fee. At the time of this writing, the charge is 10 cents per minute, which can be cheaper than a call to Topeka. Currently there are two numbers: 1-800-716-0023 and 1-888-245-0113. Both are accessible from the United States, Puerto Rico, and the U.S. Virgin Islands at speeds up to 28,800 *bits per second* (bps). There is also a special 800 number for Canadian residents at the rate of 20 cents per minute. The surcharges appear with your other AOL service charges at keyword: BILLING. The price may go up, and the numbers may change, but chances are good these special access numbers will always exist. Check keyword: ACCESS for the latest information.

One more thing: dial A-O-L before you make a call to save the people you love money. I may have the slogan wrong, but I am on the right path. America Online offers a long-distance plan for their members at only 9 cents a minute (at the time of writing). It is a bit cheaper than the 800 or 888 number at 10 cents a minute. Just be sure to dial out-of-state — in-state long distance rates are higher. You can get more information at keyword: LD.

Note that the fees for 800 numbers and any special long-distance calling plans are assessed whenever you use them, even during your free trial period with America Online. If you don't feel safe on a Yellow Brick Road that's paved in gold, there is a rainbow on the horizon. Internet service providers may offer more affordable access with monthly flat fee rates. See the following tip, "Using Internet Service Providers," for the details.

Contributed by Brian Thomason
(screen name: JBThomason)

Using Internet Service Providers :) :) | ¢ | Win & Mac

. . . or how to ride the rainbow connection

Somewhere over the rainbow, connections fly. This may seem like a dream to veteran America Online members, but it is possible for many these days. Internet service providers are providing surprisingly fast connections. In the simplest terms, an ISP is a company that has invested in the hardware needed to connect to the Internet, and for a fee you can get there, too. This can mean faster connections to America Online, or simply a connection in the first place if you have no local access number. Most ISPs charge reasonable monthly fees, making it an affordable alternative if you sign up for America Online's reduced "bring your own access" rates.

ISPs range from the national to the local — you've likely heard of AT&T Worldnet, but probably not Meg's Internet, Inc. They are found around the world, in major metropolitan areas like New York City and in small, rural communities like the Catskill Mountains. To find out if you have an ISP in your area, check the phone book under *Computer Online Services*, *Internet Providers*, or any variation. Other places where you'll find information on local ISPs are nearby universities, the business or computer sections of your local newspaper, or through a listing of ISPs (available online by using keyword: FILE-SEARCH and searching on "Internet Service Providers"). The World Wide Web is also a good sources of ISPs. Try searching for them at http://www.yahoo.com (the Internet is discussed in greater detail in Chapter 7).

Once you establish an account with an ISP, you can connect to America Online through *TCP/IP*, a feature already built into your AOL software. Rather than explain exactly how to configure here (and risk confusing you when the AOL software changes), use keyword: HELP if you need assistance. Once configured, just log in to your ISP with your modem, using the software they've provided. Now connect to America Online with your AOL software, piggybacking onto the connection you've already established to your ISP.

Contributed by Kate Tipul (screen name: KMTipul)

Speeding Up Your Connection :) **Win & Mac**

. . . or how to chat at the speed of light!

They say speed kills, but on America Online you need all the speed you can get! All those wonderful graphics and files come to you one bit at a time. Fortunately, fast modems are available and affordable . They're always a sound investment (you can "window shop" at keyword: MODEM SHOP).

Most members connect via modem using AOLnet — America Online's own network — at speeds up to 56,000 baud. See keyword: ACCESS for numbers in your area.

Regardless of the access number's speed, you can only go as fast as your modem. X2 and K56flex modems are the fastest currently available, but the new *56KITU* standard is expected to go into effect in September 1998, resolving the rivalry between X2 and K56flex. The manufacturers of X2 and K56flex modems offer free upgrades to 56KITU for all those who have purchased their 56K modems and promise that the upgraded modems will still be compatible with X2 and K56flex access numbers.

The quest for speed extends beyond conventional modems and AOLnet. You can access the AOL service via the Internet using the TCP/IP protocol at the full speed of your Internet link. Ask your ISP — many offer ISDN connections at speeds up to 128,000 baud (refer to the tip "Using Internet Service Providers"). On corporate or university networks you can connect at even higher speeds. And still revving their engines are cable modems, which America Online has been testing for years. They can deliver data 200 times faster than conventional modems via your local cable television system. Watch for all of this at keywords: MODEM and CABLE MODEM.

Try the following tips to tune up your modem's performance when accessing America Online:

1. Optimize! Make sure your exact make and model modem has been selected in **Setup** (on the Setup & Sign On screen) and visit keyword: MODEM for more info.

2. Purge your Web browser cache! Most versions of AOL software save the Web pages you visit on your hard disk, taking up memory. It pays to clean house every so often. You'll generally find a "Purge Cache" in your Web Preferences (under the **My AOL** button in the toolbar).

3. Another drag on speed is your computer itself — upgrade your RAM for a real performance boost at a very reasonable price. Also maintain your hard disk, which gets cluttered with e-mail and downloads. There's plenty of advice on achieving peak performance at keyword: COMPUTING.

Despite everything you do, at times AOL still crawls to a standstill. It's not your fault, it's due to America Online's popularity. The answer is simple, if frustrating: sign on when the traffic thins out, during the day or late at night.

Contributed by Dave Marx (screen name: Dave Marx)

Meet Dave

My friend Dave Marx started using computers back when Bill Gates did, on much the same equipment. Go figure! His early journalism training lead to a career in broadcasting and music production, and he's zigzagged from technical titles to writing, producing, and back again. Computers were never far away, though. He joined America Online back when it was young, and found his online community among those who volunteer to help make it a better place. He spent more than a year as a Tech Live Advisor, assisting AOL members with their technical and software problems. For the past three years he has worked with me in The VirtuaLeader Academy, which teaches the preparation and presentation of content to AOL's community leaders (volunteers), partners, and staff. Dave's contributions are invaluable, online and offline, and I consider him my partner in many of my adventures.

(continued)

> In his spare time he holds down a full-time job with a major market broadcaster, as engineering supervisor and coordinator of information technologies. His writing credits include contributions to *AOL Keywords*, also published by MIS:Press.
>
> Thank you, David, for all you've given me!

Disabling Call Waiting :) :) :) | Win & Mac

. . . or how to make your Aunt Jeanne happy

If your phone line has the call waiting option, Aunt Jeanne has the power to knock you offline. Ironically, by the time you realize someone's calling, your favorite aunt has probably hung up! This is a frustration and a mixed blessing, of course. To be sure your online session is uninterrupted you can set your AOL software to disable call waiting while you're signed on.

To disable call waiting on the AOL software version 4.0 (both Windows and Mac), follow these steps:

1. While offline, click **Setup** on the Setup & Sign On screen.

2. Select the location you want to change from the Connection Locations list (if you don't see this, click **Expert Setup** first) and click **Edit**.

3. Look for a check box marked "Dial *70 to disable call waiting." Enable it (click once on the box) and a small "x" appears to let you know call waiting will be turned off when you dial America Online.

If you're using version 3.0 or below, you can still disable call waiting. Look for a check box marked "Disable Call Waiting" or something similar in your Setup.

There's also a way to enter the actual command that disables call waiting. The most common code used by local phone companies is *70, which comes preset in the AOL software. If you use rotary dial or your phone company uses a different code, you're free to change it. When you change the code, be sure to leave a comma after the code number — it tells your modem to pause a second while your phone company processes the code.

Many folks would consider it rude to hog the phone, especially if a number of people share that number, so be sure everyone agrees that you may disable call waiting, and when. In a busy household the cost of a second phone line for your modem may pay a big "peace dividend."

Oh, by the way, call waiting gets turned back on automatically when you sign off. So, assuming you actually stay off your computer for a few minutes at a time, Aunt Jeanne (and the rest of the world) can now get through.

Contributed by Dave Marx (screen name: Dave Marx)

Quieting Your Modem Speaker :) :)   Win & Mac

. . . or how not to wake up your spouse at 3 a.m.

Can you get rid of those annoying sounds when you sign on to America Online? You bet! The methods vary depending on your computer and the version of AOL software you use, but here's the path to peace and quiet.

On Windows AOL software version 4.0:

1. Click **Setup** on the Setup & Sign On screen.
2. Click the **Connection Devices** tab.
3. Highlight your modem from the list and click **Edit**.
4. You can now select your noise tolerance level from the **Speaker Volume** menu.

On Windows AOL software version 3.0 (and lower):

1. Click **Setup** on the Setup & Sign On screen.
2. Click **Setup Modem** and then **Edit Commands**.
3. Look for the **Setup Modem String** box, find the ^M in the string of text, and insert **M0** (that's a zero) immediately before it.
4. Click **OK** and then select **Custom Modem Profile** from the Choose Modem list.

On Mac AOL software version 3.0:

1. Click **Setup** on the Setup & Sign On screen.
2. Choose **Modem Configuration**.
3. Change the volume control slider as you like.

If your software differs at all from what I describe above, your best bet is to locate your modem command strings within the AOL software and use the step 3 directions for Windows version 3.0 above.

Now, I'd like to put in a word for not turning off your sounds. Once you get used to them, they give you feedback on how your connection is progressing. Sounds can tell you when an access number isn't cooperating (the cacophony of screeches gives it away). Plus you don't have to be watching the screen to know if you connect — just listen while you make that sandwich or fold clothes!

Contributed by Dave Marx (screen name: Dave Marx)

Troubleshooting Modems   :) | Win & Mac

... or how to make your modem sing

I remember installing my first modem in our home PC about five or six years ago. I was so proud of myself for having the courage to actually take the cover off the computer and dive right into the ominous looking circuit boards, cables, and colored wires. No guts, no glory, right? I popped the modem into the right slot, put everything back just the way I found it, put the cover back on, said a quick "Hail Mary," plugged the phone line in, and tada! It actually worked. Alas, not everyone is so lucky.

These days modems are as common to personal computers as a keyboard and mouse — it is difficult to purchase a new computer without a modem. And with newer technology comes faster modems: up to 56,000 baud, over 20 times faster than my old 2,400 baud modem. Most modems are internal, accessible only through a slot on the back of your computer, though some folks prefer the external kind. Either way there's bound to be some trouble somewhere along the line (no pun intended) — here are some troubleshooting tips:

1. If your modem won't initialize, check your AOL software setup located on the Setup & Sign On screen. You may need to reconfigure your modem to work with the AOL software, or set it up using a different configuration if you have just installed a new modem. Use the Auto Detect feature (select **Setup** and then **Connection Devices**) in Windows AOL 4.0, or click **Setup** and then **Configure a New Modem** in Mac 4.0. If you're using an older version of the AOL software, click **Help** for directions. When in doubt about your modem type, always choose Hayes Compatible Basic or Hayes Compatible Extended. Confirm that the port selected matches the location of your modem. If you're not sure, check the manual that came with your modem.

2. If your modem reports no dial tone, make sure your phone line is connected from the wall jack to the proper jack on the back of your computer (it might be labeled "Line," "Jack," or "To Wall"). External modem users should check the modem cable for a loose connection between the modem and computer. Also, external users want to be sure the modem's power cord is plugged in and the modem is turned on. Still no dial tone? Unplug it from the modem, connect it to a phone and check for a dial tone.

3. If your modem dials and screeches yet doesn't connect to anything, the access number may either be busy, temporarily out of service, or not an access number at all. Double-check the access numbers, change them if incorrect, and try additional ones if necessary. If the number is correct and you continue to have connection problems, report this number at keyword: ACCESS.

4. If the AOL software is unable to open the communications port, this means that the modem is already in use by another program, such as a fax application. Close the other program and try again.

5. If the AOL software freezes at the Request Network Attention screen, there may be a temporary problem with the access number. Choose another number and try again. Alternatively you could have the

wrong network selected for the access number —
double-check your settings and try again.

6. If the AOL software freezes at the Checking
Password screen, try signing on as Guest. If that
works, you may need to delete the files in the
Organize directory (use File Manager or the
Windows Explorer to locate the Organize directory
inside the America Online directory and throw all
files inside). If that doesn't work, or you're using a
Mac, you may need to delete and reinstall the
software.

If after all of this you're still having trouble with your
modem, don't rip it out of the computer and throw it out
the nearest window, however therapeutic it may seem.
Call Technical Support at 1-800-827-3338 or 1-800-827-
6364. If you can get online, try keyword: MODEM HELP
for even more information, updated drivers, and help
with those blazing high-speed modems.

Contributed by Kate Tipul (screen name: KMTipul)

| Keeping Track of Time | :) :) :) | ¢ | Win & Mac |

. . . or how to monitor your AOLcohol levels

Most America Online services and online features are free
of surcharges, but that doesn't mean you should sit in
front of the monitor all day. If you do, you'll miss that
appointment to have your dog manicured, forget to pick
the kids up from school, or soak up too many monitor
emissions and take on that eerie "computer green"
pallor. You wouldn't want your keys to the information
superhighway taken away, would you?

So how do you know whether you've been online for
one hour or ten? If you can't tell, we suggest using keyword: COFFEE. Seriously though, check keyword: CLOCK.
You can also select the **My AOL** icon on the toolbar and
then select **Online Clock** (using AOL software version
4.0), or click the clock button in the version 3.0 toolbar.
America Online will tell you the date, time, and how long
you've been online (see Figure 1.2).

Figure 1.2 The online clock can be your best friend, or your worst enemy (view from the Mac).

If you elect to pay an hourly fee to America Online, keyword: CLOCK (as well as keyword: BILLING) is of particular importance to you. Keep an eye on your current usage to make sure your America Online bills aren't larger than your mortgage, telephone, and electric bills combined. If they are, consider switching your pricing plan, also at keyword: BILLING (see the next tip for more details). More importantly, you should also consider a 12-step group (try keyword: ADDICTION).

*Contributed by George Louie
(screen name: NumbersMan)*

Choosing a Pricing Plan :):):) ¢ Win & Mac

... or how to determine if the price is right

When it comes to paying for America Online, you have a choice. No, that doesn't mean you can decide not to pay at all, but rather that there are five different pricing plans from which to choose. Do you know which one is best for you? If you pick the right one, you could get cash and prizes (OK, maybe you just save a few bucks). Let's find out which price is right — what's behind our doors, Bob?

- Door number one: The monthly *unlimited usage* plan at $21.95 each month, at the time of writing. If you're online more than ten hours a month, this plan saves you money. For even more savings, there is an option to buy a full year's unlimited use at $239.40, a little over an 8 percent discount off the monthly rate. (Oooooooh.)

- Door number two: The *light usage* plan at $4.95 a month (with three free hours) and the *limited* plan at $9.95 a month (with five free hours). The light usage plan is the better buy with additional hours at $2.50, compared to $2.95 on the limited plan. (Ahhhhhhh.)

- Door number three: The "bring your own access" plan at $9.95 a month for *unlimited usage*. If you access America Online via an Internet service provider (ISP) rather than dial direct through an access number, you can save half off the regular unlimited rate. A real deal if you already have an ISP, and it could save you a few dollars to go out and get one just for this. (Wow, dude.)

Speaking of games, note the $1.99 per hour surcharge for premium games is on top of any connection charges. Another surcharge is the $6.00 per hour (or 10 cents per minute) charge for dialing in on the 800/888 access numbers. As with all hourly charges on America Online, you're charged by the minute not the full hour.

The best way to pay for any plan is with a major credit card — there are other options, but they incur additional charges. Also, discounts are offered for select groups (for instance, AARP members receive a 10 percent discount on the unlimited usage monthly plan — use keyword: AARP, click **Member Benefits**, and then choose **AARP Online** to apply).

Be sure to check out keyword: BILLING for further details on all pricing plans!

Contributed by Bradley Zimmer
(screen name: Bradley476)

Understanding Billing   :) :) | ¢ | Win & Mac

... or how to think like an accountant

Let's face it, America Online is selling a service and they want our money. In the "old days," it used to be far too easy to rack up a big bill in online charges. Some of my friends reported bills over $1,000 (yes, that is just for a month). Thankfully, big bills are mostly a thing of the past now that America Online offers more pricing options. If you're not familiar with their pricing plans, visit keyword: PRICING now to get the lowdown.

Once you get a handle on how much you're paying, keep an eye on your bill. Unlike other service companies where you don't get the bill until the end of your billing period, you can check your bill at any time on America Online. Do note that while charges won't appear on your bill for your current online session until you sign off, America Online generously shows you how much time you spent during each session upon sign off to help you keep track. Watch for it on the Sign Off screen.

Here are some more billing tips, picked up from my grand-a-month friends:

1. If you find it is too easy to overspend on America Online, you can call them and request that a cap be placed on your account.

2. You can change your pricing plan in midstream with enough advance notice. Know the plans and use the one that best fits your online habits.

3. Know your billing date, determined by the day of the month on which you first signed up to the service. For example, my first sign-on date was 8/8/92, so each billing cycle ends on the eighth of each month, when a new one also begins. This is the date you'll be billed (is there room on that credit card?).

4. If you discover a discrepancy in your bill, report it at keyword: CREDIT.

5. Learn how to offset your bill with credits and rewards in the next tip, "Accessing AOL for Less."

Accessing AOL for Less   :) :) | ¢ | Win & Mac

. . . or how to avoid bankruptcy

Let me guess: you've just received your America Online bill? While that new skylight where you went through the roof after reading it lends unique character, something tells me you'd like to keep that roof over your head, right? Relax — there are ways to save money and get your

America Online bill down to a reasonable level. Here are my top ten ways to lower that bill:

1. Be sure you're using the best pricing plan. If you have a high bill, I strongly suggest an unlimited usage pricing plan. Alternatively, if you spend less than ten hours online each month, the light or limited usage plan is a money-saver. See keyword: PRICING and the tip "Choosing a Pricing Plan."

2. Consider using an Internet service provider (ISP). Not only will this give you a local access number (a big savings right there if you're using the 800 number), but you can change your pricing plan to "bring your own access" at half the price.

3. Reduce hidden charges like communication surcharges (toll calls or 800/888 access — see the tips earlier in this chapter) and premium services (newspaper archives, special games, and so on).

4. If you have children or others who use your account, set your parental controls so they cannot rack up big bills. You may even want to set these on your own screen names to "control" your spending.

5. Earn rewards for being a good America Online citizen. *AOL Rewards* is a program that encourages you to give your opinions about a variety of products and services (think surveys). In return, you accumulate points that can cover monthly service fees or earn merchandise (you can even get a brand new computer for a mere 209,500 points). You can also earn points for buying certain products, using the AOL VISA card, or winning contests. Check it out at keyword: AOL REWARDS.

6. Bring along your friends. At the time of writing, you can make $20 for each friend of yours that signs on to America Online and stays online for more than 90 days. They must use a special America Online sign-up kit that you send them in order to get the twenty bucks, however. And though you're limited to 12 sign-on kits a month, you might actually be able to turn a tidy profit if you have a lot of friends. See keyword: FRIEND for details.

7. Consolidate and downsize! If you have more than one account in your household, or have other family members also using America Online, consider consolidating your accounts. Remember: you can have up to five screen names on every account — room for everyone! Sharing an account is especially practical if you don't sign on often. Keep in mind that you cannot move screen names from one account to another (so somebody has to give up their names), and you cannot both be signed on at the same time if you're using the same account.

8. If you enjoy America Online, like to help others, and have been online for some time, consider volunteering to help out your favorite forum. They may be able to offset your costs in return for your assistance. This is by no means guaranteed, however, and I urge you to volunteer only if you are truly interested in helping out.

9. Use the resources available on America Online to save money in other arenas, such as investing or shopping. I know I've personally saved hundreds, perhaps thousands, of dollars over the years buying my computers and drives from the AOL Classifieds.

10. Alternatively, get a hobby that isn't online. I'm not one to talk, but I do feel a healthy, balanced life has some offline activities too. Rediscover the joys of sunshine.

Now just imagine: If you can save money on America Online, maybe you can afford to patch the roof. Not to mention feed the family, pay the rent, fix the car, avoid bankruptcy, finish school, start a business, and maybe even buy a small country.

Using the Guest Account   :) :)   Win & Mac

. . . or how to get a guest pass to AOL

Do you start to feel the pangs of online withdrawal the moment you're gone for more than a day? Do you wonder how you'll be able to check your e-mail or stay in touch with your online pals? The Guest feature built into the AOL software makes it easy to get online without having to resort to the "have AOL disk, will travel" mindset. So if you're visiting Great Aunt Edna over the weekend and don't want to miss a single thing online, just make sure she has a modem and a copy of the AOL software installed on her computer. What? You say Great Aunt Edna isn't a member of America Online? Well, this would be a perfect time to sign her up!

To sign on as a guest on any computer with the AOL software installed, simply select **Guest** from the Select Screen Name drop-down menu on the Setup & Sign On screen, and then click **Sign On**. Soon after a dialog box appears — type in your screen name and password and click **OK**. That's it!

A couple of things to keep in mind about Guest access: Since you're not signing on from your own computer, you won't have access to features like Favorite Places, Personal File Cabinet, Download Manager, preferences or creating/deleting screen names. However, rest assured that any Parental or Mail Controls remain in place on their screen names. The Guest feature is also handy for those of us who have multiple accounts to sign on without having to close and start up a different America Online application for the other account.

And just as in real life, it's always a good idea to use common sense and etiquette when you are a guest on someone else's computer. This means not downloading any files to their computer without their knowledge or permission, closing any applications or windows you may have opened, and not changing their preferences or messing with their files. More etiquette pointers are in the "Traveling with AOL" tip. Don't forget to send Great Aunt Edna some virtual flowers for her hospitality!

Contributed by Kate Tipul (screen name: KMTipul)

| Traveling with AOL | :) :) | ¢ | Win & Mac |

. . . or how to see the world in 33.6 Kbps

Are you going on the road? America Online will be waiting for you when you arrive at your destination! Whether you're carrying a laptop or using a friend's desktop, using America Online on the road couldn't be simpler.

You already have your AOL software installed on your laptop computer, right? Wherever you go, from Arizona to Zambia, all you need to reach America Online is a telephone line and a new local access number! Keywords: ACCESS and INTERNATIONAL ACCESS have the details.

You say you don't have AOL software installed on the laptop? You can have the software installed on as many computers as you want. Get an AOL software installation disk or download an installer, run the setup program, and supply your current screen name and password when you first sign on. It's that simple!

I suggest you do your homework in advance:

1. Research the access numbers and install them in Setup (accessed from the Sign On screen) while you're still at home. See the tip "Finding Local Access Numbers" in this chapter.

2. Check with your hotel to be sure your room's phone has a modem port. If not, they may have a hospitality desk where you can plug in.

3. Compare the cost of access. America Online's 800/888 surcharged access numbers may be cheaper than the hotel's rates for local calls if your sessions are short (see "Using 800 Access Numbers").

4. Before you unpack, set up your computer and try to sign on (don't forget to modify your Setup to dial 8 or 9 for an outside line.) If there's a problem, ask for help from maintenance, request a different room, or even consider another hotel.

5. Bring a 12-foot telephone extension cord, a spare telephone cord, and a little 3-plug electrical outlet strip. Trust me!

6. Consider an antitheft cable and lock for your expensive equipment. One less thing to worry about!

Being a Good Guest: You can sign on to your account using your friend's computer and AOL software. See the previous tip "Using the Guest Account" for details.

If your friend doesn't have the AOL software installed, but she has a modem and she's willing, bring an America Online software disk and install the AOL software. You can install the software with your own account information by supplying your screen name and password when you first sign on. You could also recruit your friend by helping her set up a new AOL account for herself. Then you can be her guest. (You can get $20 from AOL for signing up your friends — go to keyword: FRIEND and order disks. Have them sent to your home address and bring them with you when you visit. If you use the disk that came in *Computer Wonk* magazine, you won't get the $20.) Bring whatever personal files you may need on floppy disks, or send yourself e-mail with those files to download at your destination.

You can build a portable Favorite Places list before you leave home by dragging items from your Favorite Places list to a window for new mail (click the **Write** button on the toolbar) or a new file (select **File** and then **New**).

A few words on etiquette:

1. Your friend probably has one phone line, don't hog it. Use Auto AOL (FlashSessions) and read offline (see the tip "Reading Mail Offline" in Chapter 4).

2. Ask yourself why you're chatting online while you have a friend standing nearby, glaring at you.

3. Clean up your mess — don't leave your software and files behind on her disk (or desk).

4. Plan ahead and bring any files you may need on a floppy disk. Don't forget a few blank disks so you can save everything you need when you leave.

5. Buy your friend antivirus software and install it before you sign on (see the tip "Preventing Viruses" in Chapter 6).

Contributed by Dave Marx (screen name: Dave Marx)

Using Payphones with Dataports :)   Win & Mac

. . . or how to change to SuperModem in seconds

Imagine yourself in an airport. Suddenly the need to sign on to America Online seizes you in a kryptonite grip. You rush to the nearest pay booth with a dataport. You tear open your briefcase and bring out your laptop. There's just one problem: You can't figure out how to sign on from the pay phone.

Before your manners turn less than mild, read this tip and learn the trick:

1. First things first — does the phone have a dataport? Look for a standard phone jack on the front, side, or bottom of the pay phone. They won't hide it so well that you need to rip the phone off the wall, however. If there is no dataport, try other pay phones. I've been able to find at least one pay phone with a dataport in most major airports and even in major hotels (great for conventions).

2. If the pay phone lets you dial directly from your modem, you can skip the rest of this tip. How will you know? Check the instructions printed on the phone, if provided.

3. If you aren't so lucky as to find a pay phone that makes things easy for you, it is time to get down and dirty with your modem. First you need to modify your modem setup commands to tell your modem to respond immediately to the information America Online sends after dialing.

   • Using Windows, click **Setup** on the Setup & Sign On screen and click the **Connection Devices** tab. Select the modem you use from the list, click **Edit**, and then click **Edit Commands**. Jot down the information in the Setup Modem String field in the event you make a mistake. Somewhere in that string you may see the letter *X* with a number after it — if you see it, make a note of the number (usually a *4*) and change it to 1. If you don't see it, just type **X1** to the very end of the string.

- On a Mac, navigate your way to the modem string and edit it in the same manner. Be sure to note what change you made — you'll want to put it back to normal when you get home.

4. Now create a new locality. Return to your Setup & Sign On screen, click **Setup**, and click **Add Location**. Name your new location **Pay phone**, select the custom connection option, and go to the next screen. Type in **Pause** as the name, verify you will connect using your modem, type a comma (,) in the number field (don't include anything else, not even your access number), and click **OK** (see Figure 1.3).

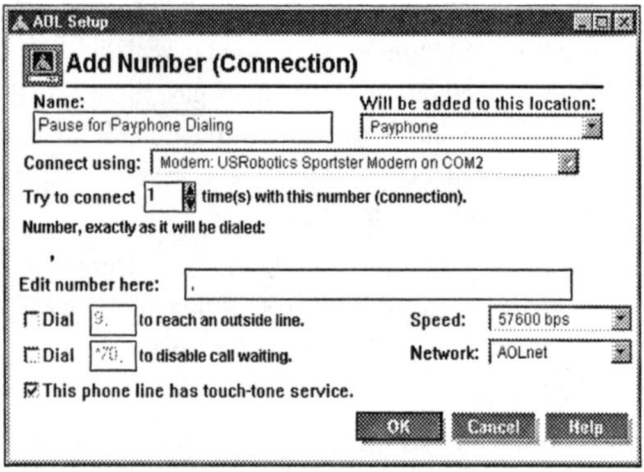

Figure 1.3 Adding a "pause" for manual dialing (view from Windows).

5. Prepare your laptop for sign-on. Select the Pay phone location you just created from the **Select Location** pull-down menu on your Setup & Sign On screen and type your password into the entry field so it's ready to go. Now plug your modem into the pay phone's dataport and dial a local access number on the phone's keypad (be sure to pay for it with coins or a calling card, too). Immediately after dialing, click **Sign On**. If your timing is right, your modem picks up the line and responds just as America Online answers. If your modem picks up too late and misses the tones, try again — click

Sign On earlier in the process, this time just as you begin dialing the number.

It may take a few tries, but persistence pays off. Good luck and enjoy your flight — by bird, plane, or pay phone!

Contributed by Bradley Zimmer
(screen name: Bradley476)

Staying Safe Online   :)   Win & Mac

. . . or how to avoid the big bad wolf

America Online's membership is larger than some countries. While we'd all like to think that an online environment would be a place where "we could all just get along." While it is ideal in many respects, we do still have to keep an eye out for hazards. Just as you wouldn't give your PIN for your ATM card out to a total stranger or even someone you thought was a friend, you should never give out your PIN's online equivalent: your password.

For lack of a better word, "phishers" (as in *phishing* for information) take great pride in getting members to reveal passwords, credit card information, and other private information. The disguises they "wear" are oftentimes ingenious. Who wouldn't think someone named *AccessCtrl*, *Bi11gRep 2*, or *AccountRep9* or any thousands of similar names wouldn't be legitimate? Well, some of them are — but no one from America Online will ever ask you for your password or billing information. These fake requests come in the form of e-mail (discussed in Chapter 4) or Instant Messages (discussed in Chapter 5). The requests are often very urgent in nature, going so far as to say your account will be deleted if you do not respond immediately. Some will say a certain sector of our database was wiped out and your help would be greatly appreciated to rebuild the information. Report any and all of these requests to keyword: I NEED HELP.

The hackers are even more ingenious than just plain, outright asking for it. They will send you e-mail with attachments for downloading. The file may promise the Playmate of the Month/Chippendale screen saver, the

latest version of America Online, or even ways to access
America Online for free — what they don't tell you is that
they are going to access your account for free. There is a
very simple solution: never download and run a file from
someone you don't know. The file, in all probability, is
what we call a *password sniffer* and can run without
your knowledge — they contain no viruses, so no virus
software will pick it up. Most password phishers capture
your password when you type it, or copy portions of files
from your hard disk, and then send that information out
in e-mail that you won't be able to detect. The next thing
you know, you can't get online because someone else is
using your account and good name for less-than-honor-
able purposes.

How did you get tricked into accepting that file? Say
JILL sent you the e-mail. Well, you've known *Jill* all her
life, but do you see anything different between these two
names? *JILL* and *JILL*? Aha. The one I use as my example
above is actually *JLLL* and the other is *JiLL*. Although they
are completely different names, when typed with mixed
capitalization and, with certain fonts, they look alike.
How do you get around this? Send *JiLL* a new e-mail
(don't click Reply — use a brand new, separate form)
and ask her if she sent you a file. If so, great! Enjoy! If not,
forward the original e-mail to the screen name: *TOSFiles*
or *TOSFiles1* (or 2 or 3) — use keyword: NOTIFY AOL
when in doubt).

While this all sounds dreary and troublesome, it actually happens very rarely. The idea is to keep alert and use
your judgment. Also make your children aware (besides
using parental controls at keyword: PARENTAL CON-
TROL) of these issues. Caution children not to give out
their real names, ages, home address, or telephone number. If they have profiles, be sure that they are very vague.

Last but not least, I recommend you visit keyword:
NEIGHBORHOOD WATCH for tips and tools from America
Online. Just about everything you need to ensure a safe
and fun online experience is found here, from parental
and mail controls to virus and password protection. But
like seatbelts, you have to understand and use them
before they will work for you. If you ever have or suspect
problems, don't hesitate to notify America Online.

The best tip of all is to use your common sense. There are plenty of good folks out there and a few not-so-good. Oh, no! That sounds like life. Well, it is life. Just be cautious as your mother always warned you, and never take candy from a stranger.

Contributed by Brian Thomason
(screen name: JBThomason)

| Updating Screen Names   :) :) :) | Win & Mac |

. . . or how to guard your good name

Do you have AOL software installed on more than one computer? If you do, you've no doubt run into the problem where if you create or delete a screen name on one computer, the other computer doesn't reflect this change.

What to do? Well, in the old days, you could reinstall your AOL software on the second computer and sign on as a New User to force the software to update. But now there's a much simpler, less painful solution. Just sign on with your second computer, use keyword: NAMES and select **Update Screen Names on My Computer** in the list box. America Online will automatically update your software's list of screen names. You can see the list of names without signing off by selecting **My AOL** from the toolbar, choosing **Preferences**, and clicking the **Passwords** button.

There is also a less obvious benefit to updating your screen names list now and then, even if you only own one computer. When hackers compromise an account, they often create a screen name for themselves to hide the fact that they've scammed you. They then use this screen name for password scamming and other nasty things that can get your account terminated. If you periodically update your screen names at keyword: NAMES, you can tell if any unauthorized person created a screen name on your account. If this ever happens, you need to get "unscammed" right away! Just call America Online at 1-800-827-6364 and explain your situation.

Once you've gotten yourself unscammed, be sure to sign on to your master account screen name and delete any screen names you don't recognize. Otherwise, the hacker(s) could still continue to use those screen names. Also, immediately change the password for each of your legitimate screen names. For more information, see the "Staying Safe Online" tip in this chapter, as well as the "Creating More Screen Names" tip in Chapter 2.

Originally contributed by Bill Rayl (screen name: AMAZN Bill) and updated by Brian Thomason (screen name: JBThomason)

| Switching Screen Names | :) :) :) | Win & Mac |

. . . or how to change names on the run

Aolville (February 29) —Johnny Doeboy, alias "Mouseman99," was seen leaving the scene of the crime last night. Officers pursued him, only to watch him disappear before their astonished eyes — the street where the Mouseman had fled was empty but for a boy. They questioned the boy, who gave his name as "Johnyboy99," but he claimed to have seen no others. Authorities are still on the lookout for this suspect.

Sound unbelievable? Once changing screen names on the run was impossible — you had to sign off, dial your access number again, and sign back on. If you had any sort of problems accessing America Online, this could take a while. But no longer! AOL software version 4.0 lets you switch screen names without signing off.

The next time you're online, take a peek under the **Sign Off** menu — besides an option to actually sign off (imagine that), **Switch Screen Name** is there, as well. Select it and give it a spin. A list of all the screen names on your account appears, along with a small envelope icon (if it is "lit," that name has mail) and the parental control settings for each name.

To make the screen name swap, highlight the screen name you want to switch to and click **Switch** (or just double-click the screen name). All windows associated with your old screen name close (to keep things orderly and private) and a small window appears to let you know how long you were online. Click **OK** to continue. If you haven't stored your passwords, another small window appears and requests your password — type it in carefully (you only get two tries, just like a regular sign-on). Give it a few moments and voila!

There are a couple drawbacks: you can't switch screen names while signed on as a Guest, and if you've got two accounts you can't switch between them.

But for all other purposes, this new feature is one of the best introduced with version 4.0.

Contributed by Bradley Zimmer
(screen name: Bradley476)

Getting Help   :) :) :) | Win & Mac

... or how to reach a helping hand

Need help? It's hard to find a more helpful community anywhere than on America Online. Whether you need help with AOL software and services, surfing the Internet, using your computer, schoolwork, or those rotten apples that disrupt your chat rooms and then run off (refer to the earlier tip), you'll be hard-pressed to miss the helping hands America Online and its membership extend to their fellow members. Here are some of the best help resources:

- Keyword: HELP takes you to AOL Member Service, where you can find help with all your America Online-related questions and needs (see Figure 1.4). You'll even find links to live online help if you click the **Ask the Staff** buttons. AOL Technical Support can also be reached at 1-888-265-8006 for AOL Windows, 1-888-265-8007 for AOL/Mac software, and 1-800-265-8010 for AOL/DOS software assistance from 6 a.m. to 4 p.m. Eastern Time. You can get help with your AOL service bill at 1-888-265-8003. For more phone numbers, check keyword: CALL AOL.

Figure 1.4 Help is just a keyword away (view from the Mac).

- At keyword: COMPUTING you'll find every kind of help on anything related to using your computer and computer software — from hardware to multimedia, and beyond!

- Keyword: ASK-A-TEACHER (formerly the Academic Assistance Center) offers targeted academic help for students in elementary school, junior high school/high school, and even college and beyond. Thousands of volunteer teachers are on duty to help scholars over the educational rainbow.

- One of my favorite help areas is keyword: DOWNLOAD 101, which guides you through the process of downloading software and files to your computer.

- Another winner is AOL INSIDER. Meg is there to help us get the most out of our America Online experience and introduce us to some of the people behind the scenes.

- Beginners are pointed toward keyword: QUICK START for lessons, explanations, and much more!

- Keywords: MODEM and ACCESS can answer just about any question about getting connected.

- If you're in a chat room and folks start disrupting things, who are you gonna call? Click the handy **Notify AOL** button on the chat window, and summon help.

- Many of America Online's chat rooms are staffed by volunteer hosts who help make your chat experi-

ence a pleasure. Visit keyword: COMMUNITY CEN-
TER to learn more about them and the art of chatting online.

- A quick visit to keyword: NEIGHBORHOOD WATCH
  will bring you all sorts of information on dealing
  with every type of online unpleasantness.

In short, wherever you go on America Online, look for
help resources. They're provided by caring folks who
want your time online to be rich and rewarding!

Contributed by Dave Marx (screen name: Dave Marx)

Checking Your Version :) :) :) **Win & Mac**

. . . or how to look the under the hood

Just as you know the make and model of your car, you
should also know what version of the America Online
software you use. While it happens rarely, for both your
car and the AOL software, things break, are recalled
(upgraded in computer terms), or sometimes you just
want to fancy things up a bit. For example, imagine
putting a Volkswagen engine in a Trans Am. It would be as
much a mistake as trying to run RealAudio through the
Mac AOL software v2.7. So let's first take a look at deter-
mining what year Trans Am — I mean which version of
Mac AOL software — you're currently using. (Oh! And if
you don't know whether you have a Mac-compatible or
Windows-based computer, now would be a good time to
read the manual that came with the computer.)

If you're running Windows, launch America Online
and go to the **Help** menu, and then choose **About
America Online**. There's also a little-known trick that
will give you additional information about your copy of
Windows AOL software. While you have the About
America Online window open, press **Ctrl+R**. This not
only tells you which version of Windows AOL software you
have, but the revision, as well. Those tiny little revision
numbers help ensure that you have the latest and greatest
version.

If you're on a Macintosh, launch America Online and
go to the **Apple** menu — usually represented by a small

Apple icon in the upper left-hand corner — and choose the **About America Online** menu item. A window with the version clearly stated appears. If you see the words *preview* or *beta*, this is a good time to upgrade. You don't even need to run the Mac AOL software to determine its version. You can also select the America Online icon from the Finder, and select **Get Info** from the Finder's **File** menu.

Contributed by George Louie
(screen name: NumbersMan)

Upgrading Your Software   :) :) | Win & Mac

. . . or how to keep up with the joneses@aol.com

The AOL software is constantly being improved and upgraded. Change is so rapid, in fact, that even as a brand new version is released, the AOL software developers are already working on the next version.

Why all the upgrades, you ask? Simple: America Online knows you don't want to miss one single, extraordinary thing introduced in this new online frontier of ours. You demand the latest and greatest technology, and they do their best to provide it. Recent features like integrated Web browsers, slide shows, and new sound technology make being online a true multimedia experience. And with the release of America Online version 4.0 come more goodies — don't miss the party just because you didn't know you were invited.

So how do you know if you need to upgrade to a newer version? First check your software version using the previous tip. Now go to keyword: UPGRADE and note the version currently available. If the versions don't match, it's time to upgrade.

Before you upgrade, read the information at keyword: UPGRADE and learn about the new software. If you have an early model computer, you may need to upgrade the hardware on your computer or modem before you can install and use the latest AOL software. Be sure you also know which version of the software you need — there are often different versions depending on your computer (PowerMacs or 68K non-PowerMacs) or your operating system (Windows 95 or Windows 3.1). If you aren't sure, check your computer or the manual that came with it.

A note about beta software: America Online usually offers a preview version of their upcoming AOL software shortly before it is introduced. You may hear friends talking about it and it is easy to get confused about which version is which. The current, or *golden master*, version of the AOL software is always found at keyword: UPGRADE; any beta versions available are at keyword: PREVIEW. Preview software changes frequently and may not be stable. If you choose to preview it, keep a copy of the current version until the preview goes "golden."

Upgrading to the latest AOL software from a previous version is a simple and automatic process. Go to keyword: UPGRADE, download the software, and relax while the software installs itself. Provide information when prompted (such as which copy of the AOL software from which you'd like to transfer your screen names and preferences). All your artwork, favorite places, personal file cabinet contents, and offline mail are automatically transferred to your new version.

Upgrading to version 3.0 from an older version takes just a few more steps. First determine which version you need, initiate the download, and make a note of the download's location on your hard drive. You'll need to know where it is going so you can run the installation program when the download is complete. Depending upon the speed of your modem the download could take a while — you can choose the **Sign Off When Finished** button on your download dialog box and walk away. Consider also printing out the complete installation instructions at keyword: UPGRADE to have them handy when you're ready to install. Even so, installation is not difficult — usually you only need to double-click (or run) the file you downloaded, which is why it's important to remember where you put it. Like version 4.0, many of your personal files and settings are transferred to the new version, unless you request they not be.

Once you've upgraded, you may be tempted to delete your old version from your hard drive. Wait! Did you transfer all your files and settings over? If you did, double-check that they are really there. Are there any downloads you want to keep? Check in your Download directory on Windows and in your Online Downloads folder on the Mac.

If you ever need help with upgrading, there are plenty of knowledgeable people at keyword: UPGRADE who are happy to help you. And if the thought of downloading and installing anything makes you the least bit nervous, request a copy of the software on floppy disk or CD-ROM through the Upgrade area. So what are you waiting for? The party is about to begin!

Contributed by Kate Tipul (screen name: KMTipul)

Companion Confessions

If you turned to this page first (tsk tsk), you probably have a preconceived notion about what to expect here. But I'll bet I surpass even your expectations. You see, you wouldn't have read about John yet (he's in the preface), or about how I intended to reveal myself here. Truly though, this isn't juicy stuff. But it is hot. This is where I share my pains from online foibles, and the joys that come from finding solutions. All using, you guessed it, the tips from this book. In fact, I'd love to hear how you use the tips — mail and regale me with details of your adventures at screen name: *Jennifer*.

1. **Finding AOL software.** While I was living in Japan six years ago, I decided to wanted to start my own America Online account (my first was through work). Trust me when I say that Japan is one of the toughest places to find AOL software, though I'm sure it is much easier these days. It took flying back to the States, driving to Boston, and attending the MacWorld convention to secure a sign-on kit; but I found it! (OK, so I was going anyway.) In the years since then, I've needed AOL software desperately, and knowing where to find it has saved me several times over. I admit to buying books and magazines just to get the bundled AOL software.

2. **Understanding billing and accessing AOL for less.** Considering that I once had an America Online

bill over $500 (please don't ask), I can't really say that I'm an expert at keeping costs down. But I did learn how to check my bill regularly, and I used all the ways to save money on it. All the legal ways, of course. I would have even joined a support group if I thought that doing so would have helped. Did you know that the quickest way to get your bill is to use the abbreviated keyword: BILL? And that it is even faster if you add it to your software as a shortcut? Chapter 3 will fill you in how to do this.

3. **Using the guest pass.** I am a terrible guest. If I'm somewhere, it is almost always as a guest. I leave windows open and don't close them. I zip about constantly, rarely staying in one place for long. I make loud sounds at all hours, and I'm always talking to someone no one can see. Sounds dreadful, eh? Seriously, though, I use the Guest slot in my software a lot because it lets me move more fluidly through my online tasks. This is my solution to a problem most people don't have — too many screen names on different accounts.

4. **Traveling with America Online**. I love to travel and I get to do it often. In my journeys I have discovered just about every idiosyncrasy of hotel phones, modems, and access numbers. I have a modem survival kit (though I forget and leave it at home more often than not) with all the goodies mentioned in this chapter. I've also discovered the importance of getting access numbers before you travel, or at least bringing the list of access tips along when I've forgotten to do that. This book is a part of my survival kit (surprise surprise).

CHAPTER 2

PERSONALIZING AMERICA ONLINE

While I lived in Japan, the thing America was best known for (besides Marilyn Monroe, blue jeans, and baseball) was its great diversity. Tall people, short people, big people, small people, dark people, light people, nice people, mean people, good people, and bad people. I often heard it remarked that the only thing we Americans have in common is how different we are. So it is only fitting that America Online recognize our individuality. Both your AOL software and your online experience are easily customized to your needs. If you want to hear "When the Saints Go Marching In" upon signing on to America Online, you can (but I don't recommend it).

It all begins with a *screen name*. Chances are if you're this far into the book, you've already started your account with America Online and chosen a screen name. If so, and you don't like it, don't worry — in this chapter you learn how to add screen names you *do* like. If you haven't yet started your account, you may have an advantage. The first tip in this chapter helps you select a screen name you'll be proud of for years to come.

Learn to protect that good screen name with a secret password. From there, you can create more personas, set your preferences, customize your sounds, show your style, organize your desktop, control your access, avoid advertising, record your journeys, create a member profile, set up reminders, track your stocks, customize your news, and learn more about *your* America Online. Whew! See what I mean? There's more, too. You have a lot of control on America Online, and the tips and tricks in this chapter show you how to wield it wisely and responsibly.

So grab your passport, bring along the *AOL Companion*, and let's get down to it.

Choosing a Screen Name   :) :) :) | Win & Mac

. . . or how to play the name game

Years ago when I was born, my parents handed me a name; I didn't have any choice in the matter. Now that I'm all grown up, I get to pick my own name. Online, that is. In some ways, my decision is simpler and, in other ways, it is more difficult. Having the choice means having to make a decision.

If you've yet to sign on to America Online, make a list of screen names you'd like to use. You may not get your first, second, or even fifth choice, but chances are you'll get one you like. In the excitement of signing on for the first time, I accepted the screen name that America Online first gave me — *User5429*. Yeah, it was as unique as any screen name, but it's not what I'd want printed on the capstone when my time ends.

I'll never be able to remove that *master screen name* from my account; master screen names are permanent and can only be deleted by canceling your entire account. But at least I have four more slots for screen names that I can use, and so do you. So if you've already picked a bad screen name, don't worry too much about it (see the tip "Creating More Screen Names" later in this chapter).

I know you want to sign on soon, so here are some more quick screen name pointers:

- Your screen name must start with a letter and can be up to ten letters and/or numbers in length. I've heard rumors that screen names as long as 16 characters may one day be possible. Keep an eye out!

- Be careful not to pick a name that violates the Terms of Service, otherwise you may have to create a whole new account. You can assume that anything vulgar or suggestive is inappropriate. See keyword: TOS for more information on the Terms of Service.

- Be sure to capitalize and space the name exactly as you'd like it to appear. If you type the name with all

UPPERCASE letters when creating it, your screen name is stuck that way forever. The only exception is the first letter of a screen name, which is always shown capitalized when on America Online.

Finding the right name can be tricky. You don't want to be known as *Smit342199* or *User5429*. What would people call you? Smit or User? Besides, it is hard for you and your friends to remember a name like that. Rather than accept the names America Online offers, get creative and choose a name that really means something to you and others. Here are some more tips to the perfect name:

- You can bet that your first name isn't available unless it is really unique — Jennifer was extraordinarily lucky to get her screen name. If you're really set on using your own first name, try different spellings of it. Vary the number of consonants or interchange similar-sounding vowels. Also consider using a middle name or nickname in conjunction with your first name.

- You may also want to try using another word before your preferred name, such as *Mr, Ms, Miss, Miz, La, Le, Its, Itz, TheNew, Super, Big, Little,* or *Lil.* Or try one of these words that will work anywhere in a screen name: *Kid, Girl, Boy, Woman, Man, Gal, Guy, Bud, Lady, Lord, Madam, Sir, Mom, Dad, Sr, Net, Cyber, Web,* and *No1.* Another option is to use a title related to your field or hobby, such as *CEO, Dr, DDS, Chef, Poet,* or *Writer.*

- Speaking of hobbies, these work well for names when you want to avoid using your own name for one reason or another. Think about what you spend most of your free time doing or what you'd really rather be doing. Like first names, chances are the name of the hobby alone is already taken. Try adding in words like *Lover, Master, Fan, Crazy, Nut, Star, Ace, Best, First, Last, Love2, Like2,* and *Max.*

- Try incorporating more details of your life (the ones you don't mind the world knowing) into your screen name. Good choices are your state, hometown, alma mater, favorite color, or favorite team.

- If you must use numbers, try those that mean something to you like your birth year or birth date. Don't use anything you've ever had as a PIN or password.

Contributed by George Louie
(screen name: NumbersMan)

Protecting Your Password   :) :) | ¢ | Win & Mac

. . . or how to keep your account secure

Imagine yourself standing in a dark alley, facing a poorly made but sturdy-looking wooden door. You rap quickly on the door. Hearing a rasping noise, you observe a small square of wood slide open and a pair of sneaky eyes looks down upon you. "Password?" you hear a voice growl. Your stomach turns cartwheels as you try desperately to remember the correct response. Just as you are opening your mouth to speak, a well-manicured hand covers your mouth and you hear a soft "Shhh!" in your right ear. "Remember, never give your password out to anyone . . . ANYONE!"

If you've been online for any length of time, you've no doubt seen the admonitions to not divulge your password to anyone. They are serious, and you'll be warned again in the *AOL Companion*. Remember, your password is the key to your account. With it, anyone can sign on; protect it fiercely. Don't share it with anyone — not your spouse, parents, kids, or friends. If you must give it to someone (say you are in traction in the hospital following a Web surfing accident and you simply have to read your e-mail), change it afterwards as soon as possible.

Here are some more helpful password tips:

1. Change your password often and regularly at keyword: PASSWORD (see Figure 2.1). A good password is a combination of letters and numbers that is not easily guessed. Don't use any information from your profile, any of your names (or your spouse's names), or anything commonly found in a dictionary. I recommend using eight characters — the longer it is, the harder it will be to guess. An eight-digit random password is over 1,600,000 times

more difficult to crack than a four-digit password. And definitely don't use anything like *god*, *password*, *12345678*, a PIN number, your phone number, or your screen name for your password. Also avoid spelling your name, screen name, or other easily guessed words backwards.

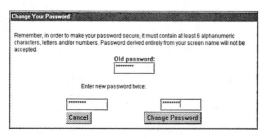

Figure 2.1 Changing your password is simple (view from Windows).

2. If you're stuck trying to come up with a good password, use the U.S. Government's method: Take the first letter of each word in an eight-word sentence. Another method is to use a word that is easy to remember and insert numbers into it such as *SUMM3ER*. (Important: Do not use any passwords you see used as examples.)

3. Try to avoid writing down your passwords. Commit them to memory and enter them each time you sign on. I don't recommend using the password storage option built into your AOL software. Anyone who has access to your computer (family members, co-workers, and so on) then has access to your account.

4. No one should ever ask for your password, including AOL employees. If someone does ask, use keyword: I NEED HELP immediately and report it. If you accidentally give it out, change it right away at keyword: PASSWORD and then report the incident.

If you forget your password (it happens to the best of us), just call AOL Member Services at 1-800-827-6364 and request help. Don't be shy and don't delay. Be prepared to verify your identity.

Contributed by Ben Foxworth (screen name: BenF7)

Setting Locations :) :) ¢ | Win & Mac

. . . or how to live nomadically

Some people just can't stay put. They carry their laptops with them and use America Online all over the place—work, home, or in cities to which they travel. As you might imagine, local access numbers at work may be different than at home, and certainly are different in other cities. Even if your computer stays in one place, you may use multiple access methods (different local access numbers, TCP/IP connection, and so on). Luckily, there is a feature that allows for various setups for it all: *Locations*.

Locations contain the information the AOL software needs to connect your computer with the America Online host computer. It records your modem type, your local access numbers, dialing prefixes, and other access preferences like disabling call waiting.

The real tip here is that you can create separate locations for each location and/or use. To create a new location in the AOL software, begin by clicking **Setup** on the Setup & Sign On screen. Follow the steps to give your new Location a name and then fill in the access information as suits your needs. If you get stuck, consult your offline help resources under the **Help** menu in the AOL software. Here are some useful tips for AOL software v4.0:

1. The name of your new Location appears up in the Select Location menu on the Setup & Sign On screen, so choose wisely. You might consider the simple (*Home #2*, *Work*, *My Local ISP*, *My Laptop*, and so on) or the specific (*Ann Arbor*, *On The Road*, *The Yacht*, and such). Pick one you can recognize later.

2. You can have as many access numbers within a Location as you like, and vary the number of redial attempts for each. I recommend keeping the number of redial attempts low, or you may wind up redi-

aling a busy number over and over when you could have simply tried another number. Add more numbers or more Locations that you can switch between instead. You can change the order of numbers in a location by selecting and dragging them elsewhere within the list.

3. You can get a helpful menu of options by clicking with the right button in Windows, or holding down the Control key while clicking on the Mac.

Using My AOL	:) :) :)	Win & Mac

. . . or how to make AOL your AOL

America Online is ready to use right out of the box. Yet there are so many ways you can put your personal imprint on it and, to borrow a phrase, make it work for you! That's the premise of *My AOL*.

Are you a new member? My AOL will take you by the hand and walk you through the process of creating a profile, adding screen names and passwords, setting your preferences, creating a Buddy List, and more! It's slick and easy to understand.

It will show you how to make America Online fetch your stock listings, keep you abreast of your online friends, and send you the news you want to read.

You can also learn how to use *Automatic AOL* (FlashSessions), create your own Web page with Personal Publisher, explore the AOL service and the Internet with *Road Trips*, control your children's use of America Online with Parental Controls, and more. A recent addition to My AOL is a comprehensive Preferences Guide. It explains every one of your preferences in the AOL software and how to make them work best for you.

This is a great one-stop jumping-off place for accessing and learning about the many ways you can get the most out of America Online's customizable features. You'll find that many of the functions we detail in this chapter are accessed through My AOL, and I recommend you become familiar with it before you proceed further.

Here's my tip: Use My AOL to learn how to use Favorite Places, and then use Favorite Places to save your favorite My AOL tips and features in a My AOL folder.

You can find My AOL on your toolbar. The first selection on the drop-down menu takes you to keyword: MY AOL, which walks you through all the customizable features. The menu also contains direct links to Set Up AOL (more help with customizing), Preferences, My Member Profile, Screen Names, Passwords, Parental Controls, the Online Clock, Buddy List, Personal Publisher, Stock Portfolios, Reminder Service, and News Profiles.

Contributed by Dave Marx (screen name: Dave Marx)

Creating More Screen Names :) :) :) | Win & Mac

. . . or how to have a split-personality disorder

Now why in the world would you want more than one screen name? You only have one mailbox sitting in front of your house. Why clutter up the street or your computer and make things complicated, right? Not necessarily.

People create multiple screen names for many reasons. Probably one of the most common is that one account may be used by more than one person. Having a screen name for each person who uses that account allows everyone to have their own online identity, to receive their own e-mail, to create their own favorite places, to maintain their own Personal Filing Cabinet, to have a unique profile, and to have their own Buddy List. For example, on my family account I use the first (master) screen name, my sister Kim and her husband Chad use another screen name, my aunt Jeanne has a screen name, and I have a slot reserved for my father who I hope will one day be persuaded to get online.

Those who like to keep their accounts to themselves also find additional screen names useful. Extra names can help you stay organized, for example. A writer friend of mine prefers to keep her posts to various writing-related message boards (like those at keyword: NOVEL) and her correspondence with other writers all organized under one screen name. She uses a different screen name for sending and receiving e-mail with her weaving friends, and yet another for her volunteer work. The advantage of having different screen names for specific online activities is greater than simply e-mail and message board posts. It also allows my friend to have a Buddy List just for her weaving friends, a Favorite Places list of all her favorite writing Web pages, and a Personal Filing Cabinet filled only with e-mail from her volunteer work.

Another reason for creating a separate screen name for yourself is anonymity. If everyone knows all your screen names — your co-workers, your mom, the guys in the HO Railroad club, and so on — you lose the chance to go peeking into chat rooms or post to message boards without being recognized. You can create a separate screen name for those opportunities.

To create additional screen names, go to keyword: NAMES and select **Create a Screen Name** (see Figure 2.2). You must be signed on with your master screen name in order to create other new screen names. Just type the name you want (see the tip "Choosing a Screen Name" at the start of this chapter for ideas). If the screen name you want is unavailable, you are told so and asked to select a different screen name. If the screen name is available, you are asked to supply a password for that screen name and to type it in twice to verify that you entered it correctly. When typing passwords, asterisks (*) replace the actual letters so no one peeking over your shoulder sees your password. Passwords must be at least four characters in length. See the "Protecting Your Password" tip in this chapter for further information.

To delete a screen name that is no longer in use, go to keyword: NAMES and select **Delete a Screen Name**. Once a screen name is deleted, it is placed on an inactive list where it will remain for about six months. You can restore it during this time period by selecting **Restore a Screen Name**. Just be sure you have a free slot on your account (remember you are limited to five screen names per account) and that you know the password. If you forget your password, call Customer Service at 1-800-827-6364.

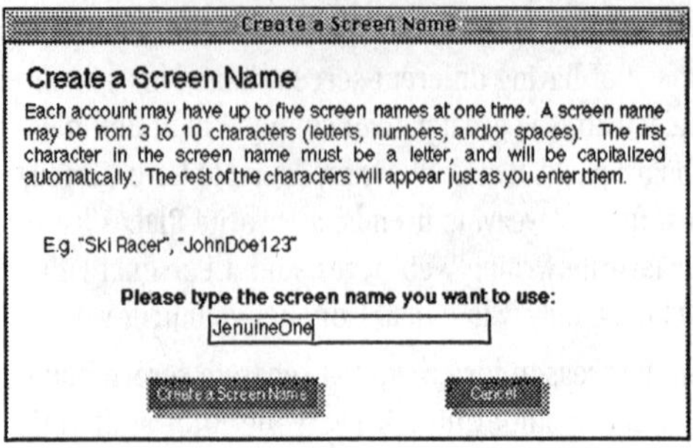

Create a Screen Name

Each account may have up to five screen names at one time. A screen name may be from 3 to 10 characters (letters, numbers, and/or spaces). The first character in the screen name must be a letter, and will be capitalized automatically. The rest of the characters will appear just as you enter them.

E.g. "Ski Racer", "JohnDoe123"

Please type the screen name you want to use:

JenuineOne

Create a Screen Name   Cancel

Figure 2.2 New screen names made fast and easy (view from Mac).

I recommend using all five screen names you are entitled to on your America Online account. If all five slots are in use, it is more difficult for someone to create a screen name without your knowledge. See the tip "Updating Screen Names" in Chapter 1 for information about "hackers" and your account.

Setting Your Preferences   :) :)   Win & Mac

. . . or how to get AOL software well done

"And how would you like your AOL software, sir? Broiled? Sauteed with a splash of wine? Steamed?"

Oh, the choices we face in life! AOL software is no exception — there is a raft of "preferences" available for customizing your AOL software. Fortunately, if you do nothing, "House Style" will satisfy most people. However, there are a lot of good reasons to look at your preferences "menu" and order exactly what you want.

Start by accessing your AOL software preferences, either online or offline. Click the **My AOL** icon on the toolbar and select **Preferences**. There are a lot of choices, aren't there? You can control the behavior of chat rooms, turn sounds on and off, determine how much hard disk space the AOL software will use for various functions, control the appearance of your Web browser, make choices about your file downloads and e-mail, and a good bit more.

Throughout this book you'll find suggestions regarding particular preferences. What I suggest for now is to examine all the choices available in your preferences, and make preliminary choices. They're easy to change later as you gain experience.

Recommended preferences for everyone:

1. Make a beeline to **Mail preferences** to set up your Personal Filing Cabinet and then check your Personal Filing Cabinet preferences, too. On the Mac, these preferences are found under **Filing Cabinet**. (Mail and the Personal Filing Cabinet are discussed in more detail in Chapter 4.)

2. Head up to **Download preferences**. If you don't understand your choices, visit keyword: DOWNLOAD 101 and read Chapter 6.

3. Beware of Passwords preferences. It allows you to password-protect your Personal Filing Cabinet (generally a good thing), but it also eliminates the need to enter your password when you sign on (a major security risk). Don't leave your account unlocked! (See "Protecting Your Password" for more details.)

Preferences for Windows AOL software members:

1. Go to **General preferences** and disable **Display Channels at Sign On**. The Channels window takes forever to load when you sign on. When you know where you want to go when you sign on, keywords and your Favorite Places are better ways to get there. You can still access the Channels window when you want, by clicking the remote control icon in your toolbar or using keyword: CHANNELS.

2. If you have an old, slow computer and/or an old, slow modem, and you use an older version of AOL software, such as AOL 3.0 for Windows, visit **Multimedia preferences**. You can achieve much greater speed by disabling graphics and sounds. You also have similar choices in **World Wide Web preferences** to speed up your Web surfing (see Chapter 7 for more information on the World Wide Web).

Preferences for Mac AOL software members:

1. If you have limited hard disk space, limit your Art Database in the **Graphics preferences** (on Windows) or the **General preferences** (on the Mac). Just select an appropriate size from the list — you can go as low as one megabyte.

2. If you save a lot of mail, visit the **Personal Filing Cabinet preferences** and enable the automatic deletion functions as you like. Not only will this keep your Personal Filing Cabinet clean, but this automatic housekeeping keeps things running at peak performance. I also suggest you compact your Personal Filing Cabinet once a month or so with the button available here — it will keep the size of your Personal Filing Cabinet down to a minimum.

3. Note that if you are using the guest name, you won't be able to access your preferences. Sign off, select another screen name (it doesn't matter which one — you don't need to sign on), and then edit your preferences. The modified preferences will be in effect when you return again as a guest.

Contributed by Dave Marx (screen name: Dave Marx)

Customizing Your Sounds   :)   Win & Mac

... or how to make AOL software sing

If your computer could talk, what would it say? Perhaps, "Oh, you really know how to push my buttons," or maybe even, "What are you staring at, buddy?" What fun that would be! Alas, lacking this witty repartee, most of our computers only utter a few blatant beeps and impotent dings. Thankfully, America Online takes us one step closer to some semblance of computer coherence with its preinstalled sounds. If your computer has a sound card, you can hear these sounds — even customize them:

- When you sign on to America Online, the first sound you hear is "Welcome."

- When you sign off of America Online, the last sound you hear is "Goodbye."

- When you have e-mail waiting for you, you hear "You've Got Mail."

- When someone sends you an Instant Message, you hear the Instant Message chime (a bit like a wimpy doorbell).

- When you download or upload a file, "File's Done" tells you that the file has finished.

- When a buddy arrives, you hear a door open. And when a buddy leaves, you hear a door shut.

Each of these event-associated sounds comes with the AOL software. On PCs, the sounds are known as WAV files and are stored in your AOL software directory. On the Mac, they are stored within the AOL software itself.

But what if you don't like these sounds? Elwood Edwards (the voice of America Online) sounds great, but if you're going to hear him everyday you may as well marry the guy. Would you rather hear your three-year-old's voice greet you as you sign onto America Online, and hear Humphrey Bogart whisper good night as you sign off? Does that Instant Message chime drive you crazy when you have five Instant Message conversations at once? Yes, you can customize all your sounds.

Just perform the following steps to customize America Online sounds for your platform:

- Under Windows 95, select **Settings** from the Start menu, **Control Panel**, and finally **Sounds**. You'll see a list of all the events on your computer for which you can enable or disable sounds. Each enabled sound has a little cone-shaped speaker icon next to it. If you select a sound, you can preview/play the sound, see the name of the WAV file, change the sound, and even browse around for a new sound for that event. The sounds associated with America Online are: `Buddy In, Buddy Out, File's Done, Goodbye, IM` (Instant Message), `Welcome,` and `You've Got Mail`. To change any of these, first highlight the event you want to change and then select a new WAV file for it by browsing through your sound files and selecting one (or by typing the name of the file, including the path to that file into the **Name:** box). You may also select **(None)** to turn off the sound for that event. When you've finished changing your sounds, click **Apply** and then the **OK** button. You don't need to be running the Windows 95 version of the AOL software in order for this to work, but you can do all of this while still connected to America Online.

- On Windows 3.1 you do much the same as you do for Windows 95. Open the **Main** program group in the Windows Program Manager, find and open the **Control Panel,** and then double-click **Sound**. Now associate individual event sounds with the sound you prefer as directed for Windows 95.

- On the Mac, you'll need to use an application that allows you to replace sounds in other programs. Agent Audio by Clixsounds works great! You can download it online by going to keyword: FILE-SEARCH, clicking **Download Software**, and searching on **Agent Audio**. Agent Audio is shareware and includes complete documentation. Just remember that you need to install the sound in your system, not in the America Online application itself.

Keep your sounds short and sweet, and don't be afraid to try out new things. You can always change them back.

Hearing AOL Talk   :) :)   Mac only

... or how to make your Mac curse

America Online already beeps, chips, creaks, and groans — it may even utter stranger noises if you've customized your sounds in the previous tip. But what if you could listen to e-mail from Aunt Jeanne, or hear an article about environmental reform? Macintosh members using version 3.0 and 4.0 can do just that!

Thanks to the foresight of Macintosh developers and the AOL software developers who took advantage of it, you can convert text to speech in America Online. Just highlight any text you want to hear and press **Command +H**, or select the **Edit** menu and then **Speak Text**. Your Mac reads aloud the selected text. It will even call out the names and functions of buttons — just hold down the **Control** key and move your mouse over a button in the active window. Music to your ears?

If you don't hear anything, make sure your sound is turned up. Still nothing? Make sure you have some text for it to speak (you need to highlight the text by clicking and dragging with your mouse) and then select **Speak Text** from the **Edit** menu again. When you're ready to restore the peace, just select **Stop Speaking** from the **Edit** menu (or press **Command + .**).

You can customize what you hear by selecting **My AOL** in the toolbar and then choosing **Preferences**, and then **Speech**. You can choose a new voice (hint: experiment with the **Test** button). If you want to hear all text that appears in a chat room (including your own), enable the **Speak incoming messages in chat rooms** option here first.

Okay, so this is fun and a bit weird, but what can you use it for? Here are some ideas:

1. Relieve your eyes. If you have trouble reading the computer screen, speech may make America Online considerably more enjoyable for you.

2. Multitask. You can have AOL software read your mail while you're playing backgammon or knitting. Consider the possibilities.

3. Keep up with ongoing conversations. Turn speech on during a slow chat and then go do something else. As soon as you hear your computer talking, you know to pay attention to the conversation again.

Setting Your Style   :) :)   Win & Mac

. . . or how to transform your image in seconds

Step over, Henry Higgins. Now America Online can give anyone style. With AOL software version 3.0 and 4.0, you can transform your text with different sizes, styles, colors, and even fonts — all faster than you can say "the r-r-r-rain in Spain falls stays mainly in the plain." How, you ask? I'll tell you. Normally an image consultation would cost you a pretty penny, but in the altruistic spirit of *My Fair Lady*, I'll share everything I know here. (Did you notice how short this section is?)

But seriously, let's begin by creating your personal image palette. Start by opening a new file (**Ctrl+N** in Windows, or **Command+N** on the Mac). Notice the row of buttons near the top of the window? I like to call this bar "The Stylinator." Across it are a variety of style options that differ if you're using Windows or the Mac, but always include text color, background color, text size, text style (bold, italic, and underline), and justification (left, right, and center).

Type either your real name or your screen name (whichever one you most identify with) into the new file you opened. Now select the text you just typed by high-lighting it with your mouse and experiment with colors, sizes, and styles — use the buttons in The Stylinator at will. Try a light background color under a dark text color. Or colored italics. Find something that suits your person-ality (or at least the version you want to share), and at the same time, make sure it is legible and clear. Now save this palette (select **Save** from the **File** menu) and try out your new styles on the world. If you hit on a scheme that seems to really work, use it consistently to build your online image. By George, you've got it!

You can save your styles as defaults in your prefer-ences. Just select **My AOL** from the toolbar and then select **Preferences**. Then choose **Font**. Select the fonts, styles, and colors you want. Now whenever you type text in America Online, it shows up automatically in your pre-ferred style. On Mac AOL, you can even have different set-tings for chat and mail windows.

If you elect to change your font, note that others won't see it if they don't also have the font installed on their computer. So either choose a common font (like Helvetica or Times), or expect it to be for your eyes only.

Organizing Your Desktop :) :) | Win & Mac

. . . or how to keep AOL software in line

You don't have to spend much time on America Online before you notice how many windows pile up on your screen. The newest windows bury the older windows until you can't find anything at all. Large windows like the chat rooms can hide almost everything else onscreen. Similar windows (like multiple Instant Messages) stack up one over the other, obliterating the earlier conversation. Bringing order to this chaos isn't easy, but the AOL software and your operating system (whether Windows or Mac) do provide tools that can help you get organized.

One way to manage the screen clutter problem is to get a larger "desk." The expensive route is to buy a new computer monitor. If you have a 14-inch monitor, a 17-inch monitor will amaze you with its capacity. Another route is to change the screen resolution of your existing monitor. The typical 14-inch monitor is set to display 640×480 pixels. That means the screen display is made up of 640 dots horizontally, and 480 dots vertically. By changing your resolution to 800×600 or more (refer to your Windows or Mac manual if you need help learning how to do this), you'll pack more stuff into the same space. The only problem is, onscreen elements, including text, shrink a bit, and you may find yourself suffering from eyestrain. When you graduate to a 17-inch monitor, that same 800×600 is easier to read because it is enlarged to fit the bigger screen.

If limiting yourself to available desktop space makes you feel claustrophobic, stretch out! A hidden feature in the Windows AOL software lets you expand your virtual desktop space and navigate it using horizontal and vertical scrollbars. To make more space on your virtual desktop, just drag a window partially off-screen into the lower right-hand corner. As soon as you do this, vertical and horizontal scrollbar(s) appear allowing you to move over and view the window, thereby increasing your total desktop space. You can keep moving windows off-screen to continue expanding your space. Mac users can also enjoy this expanding desktop trick by downloading and installing the Virtual Desktop utility by Ross Brown (available by searching at keyword: FILESEARCH).

Learn how to manipulate your windows. Your operating system (both Windows and Mac) has a tutorial in its Help section that will teach you how to manipulate the size, shape, and placement of your windows. You'll find that America Online makes all these capabilities available, too.

Your AOL software also adds some additional features. On Windows AOL software, you have options to **Remember Window Size and Position**, **Remember Window Size Only**, and **Forget Window Size and Position**, each under America Online's **Window** menu. On the Mac AOL software, the **Window** menu options include **Remember Placement**, **Forget Placement**, **Clean Up Windows**, and **Close All Except Front**. They are all straightforward and work just as they sound.

My first attempts at organizing my desktop focused on dragging the newest windows around the screen to uncover the older ones, and closing the ones I didn't need. That only took me so far. Minimizing windows is the key. In Windows, you can minimize by clicking the minus button in the upper right-hand corner of a window. On the Mac, double-clicking or triple-clicking the window's title bar will do the trick (check your **Window-Shade** or **Appearance** control panel if it doesn't).

The ability to set a window's size and placement is the most powerful tool at your disposal with AOL software. When a particular window seems too large and/or badly positioned, resize it and/or drag it to a unique place onscreen. Then select **Remember Window Size and Position** (or **Remember Placement** on the Mac, which will "remember" size, as well). Whenever you open that window in the future, it displays exactly the way you want. Now, one-by-one, open all the types of windows you use at the same time and start resizing, positioning, and "remembering" all of them. Now you're treating your virtual desktop just as you would your office desk — a place for everything and everything in its place. Don't forget to leave some blank desktop space. You'll need to drag things like your newest Instant Message onto that space, so the older ones aren't hidden.

Contributed by Dave Marx (screen name: Dave Marx)

Customizing Your Toolbar   :) :) :) | Win & Mac

... or how to put a tool belt on your computer

Do you wish you had a tool for everything and everything in its place? I sure do. I get organizers and sorters and bins and shelves in the hopes it'll cure my tendency towards disorganization. The same goes for my computer. Over the years I've gotten all sorts of utilities designed to keep things organized. I'd often wish America Online would get on the bandwagon and offer more tools for their own software. Like Dave says in a previous section, the windows can really pile up when you're online. What I needed were more places to put my tools. America Online introduced the toolbar with software v3.0, but it was stubbornly rigid — no room for customization. Happily, the new toolbar in AOL software v4.0 is everything I wanted and more: feature-rich, flexible, customizable, and it even looks better hanging up there on my screen.

So you can imagine I use the toolbar a lot, and I do. I've figured out all the ways to customize it to my liking — I've even unraveled the hidden features within it.

My toolbar trade secrets:

1. Save some screen real estate by getting rid of the cute icons in the toolbar — text takes up less room. Icons can be disabled by choosing **My AOL**, **Preferences**, **Toolbar**, and then **Text Only**.

2. Location is everything. Windows users have the option of moving the toolbar to the bottom of their screen, and Mac users can unanchor the toolbar entirely and move it anywhere they please. Set these options in your **Toolbar preferences**, too.

3. Add your own icons. Just drag a Favorite Place heart from the corner of a window to the toolbar, pick an icon from the list that automatically pops up for you, give your new icon a label, and presto!

4. Need more room for your icons? You can remove any icon on the purple background (including **Quotes**, **Perks**, and **Weather**). In Windows, click the icon with your right mouse button and select **Remove from toolbar**. On the Mac, drag the icon to your Trash on the desktop (it needs to be visible in the background). You'll find even more on toolbars in Chapter 3.

| Taking AOL Shortcuts | :) :) :) | Win & Mac |

. . . or how to start in second gear

Remember the shortcuts you took as a kid? Through the yards, between the fences, and behind the buildings? Not only did they save you time, they were invariably more exciting. You can do the same thing with America Online!

The simplest shortcut is to add America Online to your **Start** menu (Windows 95) or your **Apple** menu (Mac). In Windows 95, the America Online installation program usually asks if you want to place a shortcut in the Start menu. If it doesn't, or you want to do it later, simply locate the icon for America Online in **My Computer** or **Windows Explorer** and drag it right over to the top of the **Start** menu. If you're using a Mac, highlight (click once) the America Online application and select the **Apple** menu, **Automated Tasks**, and then **Add Alias to Apple Menu**. If that doesn't work, just put an alias (select **America Online** and press **Command+M**) in your Apple Menu folder in the System folder.

Another shortcut is to start up the AOL software automatically upon booting — this works with both Windows and Mac software. You can even have specific files open up within America Online all ready for you to use each time it does this. The second shortcut, for Mac users, allows you to create templates for certain things you use a lot, like e-mail to the family or a virtual diary.

Here are the "secret" directions for the first shortcut: getting your computer to launch the AOL software automatically after booting:

- Using Windows 95, open **My Computer**. Then select the **Windows** directory, then the **Start Menu** directory, then the **Programs** directory, and finally the **StartUp** directory. Any file or application you place in the StartUp directory will be automatically opened upon booting your computer. If you have an icon for AOL software on your desktop, you can drag it right into the **StartUp** directory. Otherwise, find America Online within **My Computer** and copy it to your **StartUp** directory. You can also access your **StartUp** menu and copy a shortcut to your AOL software to it through **Windows Explorer**.

You can even have a file automatically open within America Online — perhaps a To Do list — by adding its name to the end of the program item's command line. On Windows 95, you access the AOL command line by navigating to the America Online directory in **Windows Explorer** or **My Computer**, highlighting the AOL software icon and then selecting **Properties** from the **File** menu. To have the AOL software and your To Do list launch, for example, the command line might be something like this:

```
"C:\AMERICAONLINE 4.0\AOL.EXE"
MYTODO.TXT.
```

- Using Windows 3.1, locate your **Startup** program group in the **Program Manager**. Now either drag your AOL software icon to the **Startup** program group, or create a new program item with the **New** option under the **File** menu. You can edit the command line just as you would in Windows 95 to get a file to open up with the AOL software.

- Using the Mac, simply make an alias of your AOL software (use **Command+M**) and drag the alias to your **Startup Items** folder (located in your **System** folder). As with Windows, you can have a file open within America Online at the same time — just place the file or an alias to it in the **Startup Items** folder.

How about creating templates? Macs let you save any file as a *stationary pad*, which is a fancy way of saying it is a copy instead of the original. Stationary pads are a great way to create e-mail templates to send to your colleagues, complete with addresses, subject line, and opening and closing remarks filled in. To convert a file to a stationary pad, just save an America Online file or Compose Mail window as you normally would. Now go to the desktop, find it, and highlight it. Press **Command+I** (or choose **Get Info** from the **File** menu) and click the **Stationary Pad** check box at the bottom. Now each time you open the file, whether from the desktop or within America Online, a copy is automatically made for you, for you to edit and send as e-mail if you wish, without messing up the original.

Windows users, you aren't forgotten. You can create templates, too, though you need to use AOL software add-ons. See Chapter 8 for more information.

Keeping Off Mailing Lists   :) :) :)   Win & Mac

. . . or how to avoid the P.O. box blues

Who needs more junk mail? Granted, one person's junk is another's treasure, but you know what I mean. At least three different kinds of junk are found on America Online: postal junk, which your letter carrier delivers; junk e-mail, which arrives in your mailbox; and the merchandise offers that appear when you sign on to AOL service. America Online provides ways to cope with all of them, all in one place — keyword: MARKETING PREFERENCES. Unfortunately, finding Marketing Preferences can be hard, unless you're a whiz with keywords, or if you happen to visit My AOL. (How to use keywords is discussed in detail in Chapter 3).

Like nearly every business these days, America Online maintains and sells its postal mailing list to other businesses, which may fill your mailbox with valuable or worthless merchandise offers. We're talking about "snail mail" here — from the U.S. Postal Service, not the junk mail you receive via e-mail. America Online does not distribute the screen names of its members and works hard to protect its members from unwanted e-mail (see Chapter 4 for more information on e-mail).

As with any other reputable business (and in compliance with the law), America Online will take you off its postal mailing list. Information on removing yourself from America Online's mailing list is at keyword: MARKETING PREFS, along with information on removing yourself from many other mailing lists via the Direct Marketing Association (for both mail and telephone soliciting). Take some time to explore this area and set your preferences. Be sure to set them on all your screen names, too.

And yes, Virginia, you can even get rid of those merchandise offers that hit you when you sign on! See the next tip, "Avoiding Online Ads," for the details.

Contributed by Dave Marx (screen name: Dave Marx)

Avoiding Online Ads	:) :) :)	Win & Mac

. . . or how to skip the commercials

The television remote control contributed more to our society than a generation of couch potatoes. Remote controls gave us greater control over what we saw and when we saw it. We can now skip the Pistons game when they're losing and avoid sexually explicit scenes when we're nervous. Best of all, we can skip the commercials with one click of the remote control. One click is all it takes to dismiss America Online's advertisements, as well. Every window has a close box or **No Thank You** button, after all. But wouldn't it be better to not get advertisements in the first place?

Marketing Preferences (at keyword: MARKETING PREFS) gives you control over not only the kinds of pop-up adds you want to receive, but also whether you want them at all. To disable them entirely, select **Tell Us What Your Pop Up Preferences Are** and click the last box. Simple, but overlooked by many.

You don't need to be on your master screen name to disable pop-up advertisements, but you will need to set your preferences for each screen name you use.

To learn more about avoiding advertisements in e-mail, see the tip "Blocking Mail" in Chapter 4.

Contributed by Brendan Rice
(screen name: KUBrendan)

Meet Brendan

Brendan Rice is an honors student studying human biology at the University of Kansas with a plan to practice medicine. He's the recipient of several scholarships and awards, including the U.S. Silver Congressional Medal. His passions are playing the violin, singing, playing tennis and soccer, volunteering with his church youth group, and working with computers. His America Online adventure started around 1993, and these days he's helping out at keyword: HOMEWORK and in The VirtuaLeader Academy. He loves to help people. Thanks, Brendan!

Using Parental Controls   :) :) ¢ | Win & Mac

. . . or how to get an electronic chaperone

If you have children, you know how they can get into things — the cookie jar, the toilet, and, of course, the computer. If you allow or encourage them to use America Online, they can get into trouble on their own. There's a whole lot of talk about safety on the Net — dangers for our kids and teens. We all want to protect our children, but many of us can't sit beside them every time they sign on.

So what is a concerned parent to do? First of all, educate yourself about the dangers your child can encounter and the options you can set to control the things and people your child can access through AOL. Visit keyword: PARENTAL CONTROLS from your master screen name. Read the information there. Decide which access level best suits your child. We all know our own kids best and America Online allows customization to suit each one.

There are basic settings for each age level. **Kids** (ages 12 and younger) are restricted to the Kids Only channel. They are also prevented from sending and receiving Instant Messages or file attachments, as well as accessing member chat rooms. And no premium games that can run up your bill!

Young Teens (ages 13-15) have a little more freedom. And **Mature Teens** (ages 16-17) even more. They can participate in forums offering content that interests them, such as sports or scouting. They are restricted from member chat rooms. And their access to the Web is limited to sites appropriate for their age level.

Take some time to go over the custom controls, too. It is worth the few minutes to read carefully and consider the choices. You may want your youngster to exchange e-mail with relatives but not strangers. Set the controls appropriately and then set mail controls for that account. Think about the best way to use this ability to protect your family while still letting them have their fun.

Don't be put off by scary headlines! Learn what you can do to be proactive in protecting your kids and then do it. You know your child better than anyone. Make his or her online experience the best it can possibly be.

Oh, do sit with the child when he/she is online when you can. There is so much you can do and learn together!

Contributed by Genevieve Kazdin (screen name: GenK)

Understanding Time Zones :) :) :) | Win & Mac

. . . or how to get the best of AOL

Do you know the time? The time zone, that is. Time means everything to computers, and time zones mean everything when you're on America Online with other folks from across the country. Are you correctly interpreting the times on America Online? Have you personalized your time zone for use on America Online?

But I'm getting ahead of myself. Let's back up to your time zone. The four time zones with which most

Americans are familiar are Eastern, Central, Mountain, and Pacific. These are the time zones that spread from east to west starting at the Atlantic Ocean and heading toward the Pacific Ocean. If you're unsure of your time zone, keyword to `http://www.mich.com/~timezone/` and enter your city (or a city near to you).

America Online is headquartered in the Eastern time zone. All times you see on America Online (in e-mail, on message boards, on various text and data pages, on schedules, and so on) are in Eastern Time unless otherwise stated. And yes, America Online switches to Daylight Savings Time.

Many of the scheduled activities on America Online take place between the hours of 8:00 p.m. and 11:00 p.m. Eastern Time. These times best accommodate the greatest number of people in all four of the previously mentioned time zones. Figure 2.3 is a handy chart for your reference — note that during daylight savings time in the summer this chart doesn't work to convert from or to time in Arizona, Hawaii, and the majority of Indiana, which do not apply daylight savings.

Eastern	1:00	2:00	3:00	4:00	5:00	6:00	7:00	8:00	9:00	10:00	11:00	12:00
Central	12:00	1:00	2:00	3:00	4:00	5:00	6:00	7:00	8:00	9:00	10:00	11:00
Mountain	11:00	12:00	1:00	2:00	3:00	4:00	5:00	6:00	7:00	8:00	9:00	10:00
Pacific	10:00	11:00	12:00	1:00	2:00	3:00	4:00	5:00	6:00	7:00	8:00	9:00

Figure 2.3 An Eastern Time Zone conversion table.

If you find it hard to convert to Eastern time in your head, you may consider changing your computer's clock to read Eastern time. I only recommend this if you're a diehard America Online member, though — changing your computer's clock changes the time for all other software on your computer too.

And if you find that e-mail arrives with the wrong time, the culprit is bound to be your own computer and not America Online. Make sure your time is set correctly on your computer, as well as your time zone (and whether it is standard time or daylight savings time).

Contributed by Kimberly Trautman
(screen name: KTrautman)

| Using the Log Manager | :) :) :) | | Win & Mac |

. . . or how to have a recording session

You've clicked the **My Files** button on the toolbar and see an option titled **Log Manager**. What in the world is that? Go ahead and select it. The little screen that appears is divided into sections. Depending on your computer, you'll see different types of logs. On Windows, you have the Chat Log and the Session Log. On the Mac, you have a System, Chat, and Instant Message log. Here's an explanation of each log:

- **Chat log:** You're in a meeting in a chat room with your relatives and you're planning the next family reunion. You want to save a copy of everything uttered, in the event of a squabble over who was going to bring the potato salad. To record a transcript, you open a chat log when you start and you close the chat log when you end. Your entire chat is now saved in a text file (with a .log extension for Windows folks) and you can refer back to it later or send a copy of it to Aunt Sophie, who couldn't make it to your meeting. The Chat Log function works the same on both Windows and the Mac.

- **Session (or System) log:** You need to get online to grab a bunch of information for reading later and then get right back off again — no time for online reading. You need to gather information from message board postings, articles on your favorite sports team, instructions for installing a new piece of software, the lottery results for the past week, and so on. Instead of printing each page and having to wait on each page to finish printing before you can move on to the next page, you can open a session log, click through all the pages you want to read (without actually reading or scrolling through them), close the log, and sign off. Then, at your leisure, read through the log of your session. This is a great tool for those who have limited time on America

Online. And it works the same on both Windows and Mac, with the exception of Instant Messages. Read on.

• **Instant Message log:** You're having a heated debate in Instant Messages with your best friend about ear wax. You want to record everything that is said so you can go over it in detail later and find her argument's weaknesses. Instead of just saving it and risk losing it if you accidentally get signed off, you can open an Instant Message log and capture it all. Though the dedicated Instant Message log is only an option on the Mac, you can still log Instant Messages in Windows — just turn on your session log and click the **Log Instant Messages** check box.

How do you actually get these working? Click the **My Files** button on the toolbar and select **Log Manager**. Just click the **Open Log** button for the log you want to start. Once opened, you'll be given the opportunity to name the file and choose the location where the log will be stored on your hard drive (or floppy drive if you wish). Accept the name given or type in a new one, and click the **OK** button. Your log is now open and ready to receive information. If this is a chat log, just go into your chat room and the chat is automatically recorded into the chat log. If this is a session log, go visit the places with information you want. As you visit those places, the text data is placed in the session log. Note that graphics, headlines, titles, and so forth are not added to the session log, just text.

Here's a tip: Leave the Log Manager window up on your screen to remind yourself that you have a log running (you want to remember to close it when you're done). If you have a log you started yesterday or last week, you can use the **Append Log** button to add information to an already existing log. When you are finished with your log, whether it be a new or appended log, remember to close the log.

To view your log, select **Open** from the **File** menu, and find the log you created. If the file does not open using the AOL software, the file is too large to be viewed by America Online's editor — use a word processor to open it instead.

Creating a Member Profile :) :) :) | Win & Mac

... or how to expose yourself to the world

A screen name tells people who you are at first glance, but what if they want to know more? Well, America Online has made it simple for you to expose as much or as little of yourself to the world as you desire. Introducing the *member profile.*

Every screen name is entitled to have a member profile, but it's not a requirement. If you want to be anonymous, that's fine. If you want to tell the world that you're Jennifer Watson from Michigan and were born on 10/9/68, enjoy writing, reading, exploring, and laughing, and own a Mac and PC on which you do consulting, writing, and training while believing in John F. Kennedy's quote "Leadership and learning are indispensable to each other," that's fine, too. It's up to you. To create your profile, go to keyword: PROFILE and click the **My Profile** button.

One word of caution: Don't tell the world exactly where you live or give them your phone number. Safety online isn't something to be taken lightly. But there's nothing wrong with exposing your inner self!

If you use a Mac, you can put special fields such as "Aspirations" or "Favorite Breakfast Cereal" in your profile. First create a normal profile and save it online. As soon as you can view it online (usually after a minute or so), go back to the profile-editing screen (keyword: PROFILE), copy the text from one of the fields, open a new, blank file, paste the text in, add a return after the text, type your new line, copy the new line and the old text together, and paste everything back into the field from which you originally took it. That's all there is to it — America Online accepts the carriage return characters in your profile! Keep in mind that if you create a new field for your profile, the spaces won't always line up when viewed, but you can get them to line up on your screen, and it'll be close to the others. Try adding a couple of returns and a short line or your favorite smiley, or *emoticon*, in the bottom field (see Appendix A for a list of emoticons).

Contributed by George Louie
(screen name: NumbersMan)

| Setting Up Reminders   :) :) | Win & Mac |

... or how to remember to forget

If you can remember to do this, here's a great tip: Use America Online's free reminder service! Fourteen days before any occasion you choose, America Online can send you e-mail to remind you of, well, anything! You even have an option to get a second reminder four days before the occasion. It's totally free, and strictly confidential! You have your own database, where you can review, edit, add to, and delete your pending reminders online. You can access the reminder service at keyword: REMINDER or just about anywhere in America Online's Shopping channel.

Is there a catch? Well, sort of. The reminder service is operated by America Online's Shopping channel, so it's designed to help folks buy gifts for birthdays, holidays, and similar occasions. That's why the reminders are sent 14 and 4 days in advance. You can't change that, either. Also, when you set up a reminder, there's no space to type in more than a brief text describing the reason for the reminder — it's not a full-blown secretarial service. Finally, the e-mail you receive will promote the activities of America Online's Shopping channel, but that is a small price to pay.

Don't forget:

1. You can enter about 16 characters of text into the **Gift Recipient's Name** box and 20 in the **Occasion: Other** box. With any luck, that'll be enough information to jar your memory.

2. Remind yourself to perform routine maintenance on your computer.

3. "Cheat" the date of the reminder, so that the reminder really arrives on the date you desire, rather than 14 or 4 days prior.

4. Remind yourself to buy this book for all your friends' birthdays and holidays. (Oh, you know we had to throw that in somewhere!)

Contributed by Dave Marx (screen name: Dave Marx)

Tracking Your Stocks :) :) | c | Win & Mac

. . . or how to get a kickin' portfolio

If you run with the Bulls and Bears, America Online is the place for you! At no extra charge, you can get stock quotes and set up and maintain up to 20 different stock portfolios for each of your screen names. It's quite simple to do. Just use keyword: STOCKS to get started.

Now, I'm a simple guy. I guess I could have 20 fantasy portfolios, each with as many as 100 stocks and mutual funds, to test various market strategies, but all I want to know is the current state of my real portfolio, with the number of shares held, purchase price, gain/loss, and market value displayed. When I double-click a portfolio item, I get a detailed report with current market information and company news, and I can display charts summarizing historic performance. If I stay signed on during the day I can leave the portfolio open, and click the **Refresh** button whenever I want a current valuation — well, a 15-minute-old valuation; all stock prices are delayed by at least 15 minutes. Click **Details** to learn the time of the quotation.

Hot stock-tracking tips:

1. If you want to protect your portfolio valuation from prying eyes around the office, create a second portfolio. Omit the shares held and purchase price information — you'll get a report with only the current per-share price.

2. You can readily print a portfolio report, or save it as a text file that can be read by most spreadsheet programs.

3. Since you have to click through three screens to arrive at your portfolio, do as I did and make a favorite place for each of your portfolios. Then they're just a single click away! (Favorite Places are discussed in more detail in Chapter 3.)

4. Remember to buy low and sell high.

Contributed by Dave Marx (screen name: Dave Marx)

Customizing Your News   :) :) | ¢ | Win & Mac

. . . or how to get a personal press

Extra! Extra! A personal edition of the current news can now be e-mailed directly to you. Get your copies now!

Yep, you heard it right. You can get exactly the news you want delivered right to you through your e-mail. And no, America Online doesn't hire a newspaper clipping service and offer it free of charge, though it is practically as good. The service is entirely automated, using the reputable news sources already online: The Associated Press, Business Wire, and PR Newswire. Just let America Online know what kind of news you want to receive. You decide what, how many, and even when. This can save you money! Instead of searching for the news yourself, News Profiles puts it all in one place for fast retrieval. Here's how to set it up:

1. To begin, go to keyword: NEWS PROFILES and click the **Create a Profile** button. Don't confuse this with member profiles, which are discussed earlier in this chapter. Give your news profile a name and indicate the maximum number of stories you want to receive daily, then click the **Next** button.

2. Now, in the next two windows, enter the words or phrases that would appear in the kind of news you want — the first window is for any occurrence of the words, and the second window is for words that absolutely must be present. Be specific. You can even use *wildcards* to help you get exactly the news you seek (you can read more about wildcards in

Chapter 6). A fourth window allows you to list words or phrases you don't want in your stories.

3. Finally, you can designate what news sources are searched for your articles in the fifth window.

4. When satisfied, click **Done** to save your handiwork.

You can change your news preferences at any time by clicking the **Manage News Profiles** button, selecting the appropriate profile, and clicking **Edit**. Note that you can also turn your news on and off by clicking the button at the bottom of this window. It's a good idea to turn your news off if you're going to be away from America Online for a period of time, or just find you're getting more news than you can read. If you are getting too much news, change your news preferences so that they are more specific. Don't worry if it takes some time to get your profile just right. Consider creating multiple profiles; they'll help you specify precisely what you want. You can have up to five profiles per screen name.

The advantages to those who take their news seriously are obvious. How about those of us who enjoy news on the side? Here are some creative uses for the News Profile service:

1. Keep track of articles that mention your own name. While they may not refer to you (unless you're a celebrity or just always getting into trouble), it is fascinating to watch what your namesakes do.

2. Specify America Online as a phrase and observe the flurry of articles. You could almost write a book on it. Hmm, that's an idea.

3. Enter your screen name, pet's names, birth date, or a whimsical phrase. You'll be surprised at what turns up.

Contributed by Brian Thomason
(screen name: JBThomason)

Meet Brian

Brian Thomason is one of the most generous individuals I've had the pleasure of knowing. As a transplant from the south to the Pacific Northwest, Brian works for a major wood products company as a relocation counselor. He counsels transferees and new hires, helping them settle into their new homes. Brian loves to travel, read, surf the Internet, and explore his personal growth. He's a loving uncle, a brother, and a life partner to Curt.

Brian has been on America Online for many years, playing the role of member, observer, and volunteer. After he accepted the offer to become a volunteer host for Digital City Seattle/Tacoma, his online life changed significantly and hasn't been the same since. I met Brian when he joined The VirtuaLeader Academy in November 1996, where he generously gives his time and offers his friendship. Thank you, Brian!

Learning More About AOL :) :) | Win & Mac

... or how to really feed your habit

Feeling overwhelmed by all there is to learn about America Online? Besides the hundreds of tips and tricks I'm sharing with you here, there are all the regular features to understand, plus the mass of content to explore. It would be enough to discourage even our friend Albert Einstein.

But before you sneak off to play with your latest physics problem, let me explain the Law of America Online. It is simple: The more you learn about America Online, the more you'll get out of it. Dazzlingly brilliant, eh? But seriously, if you really want America Online to work for you, it is important to understand how it works. You're on the right track with the *AOL Companion*, but there are other resources you can use.

1. The first resource you're likely to encounter is QuickStart (at keyword: QUICKSTART). Here you can learn about important features quickly and easy. Designed for beginners, QuickStart walks you through each "lesson" step-by-step.

2. AOL Member Services at keyword: HELP also provides valuable lessons in using the service. Just pick your area of interest and click for information.

3. If you learn well from peer advice, Members Helping Members at keyword: MHM is a gold mine. You can ask a question, or just read the answers.

4. Explore the People Connection and learn how to make the most of its unique features at keyword: SHOW ME HOW.

5. If you need to see it to understand it, visit keyword: VISUAL HELP for illustrated help files on everything from using smileys to locating friends.

6. To learn how to download files, check out keyword: DOWNLOAD 101. More tips on using this resource are in Chapter 6.

7. Don't forget the built-in help programs in your software, which often include step-by-step tutorials. Check your **Help** menu, whether online or offline.

Companion Confessions

I get a big kick out of personalizing my things. I have my name on pens, pins, fluffy pink towels, and those Mickey Mouse "ears" you can get at Walt Disney World. I even put my America Online screen name on my U.S. mailbox. So when it comes to personalizing America Online and making it work for me, I'm in the big leagues. Here are some things I've done:

1. **Choosing my screen names.** To me, screen names are the equivalent of my clothing. Now I don't have the worry of running around naked without my screen name, but I do care what I look like when I'm wearing one. My main screen name —*Jennifer* — is what I consider my Sunday best. True to my

personality, however, I don't limit myself to Sundays; I "wear" it any day I please. I waited a long time to get it (you can read the story in Appendix B), and I take good care of it. The same is true of my other screen names. I make lists of potential screen names before I actually try to create one, so I have lots of alternatives. And I'm always careful that a new screen name matches my image (*Jenni4U* just does not work for me).

2. **Changing my passwords.** Every one of my screen names has its own hard-to-guess-and-harder-to-remember-when-I-forget password. I change them all at least once a month, often more frequently. The password creation method I like best is using the initial letters of a sentence, like *tromlb2d* which stands for "the rest of my life begins to(2)-day." I like to sneak in a little positive reinforcement with a password like *piav7ewo* which means "patience is a virtue, especially when online," with the number 7 thrown in for good measure. When you sign on as much as I do, these passwords start to feel like a mantra. I always use both letters and numbers for extra security. I recommend you do the same.

3. **Setting my style**. If you ever write to me and get a reply, you'll notice my text is in a slightly smaller font size than normal. You may also notice at the bottom, below my signature, is a row of books, with information on affiliations and titles alongside them (see Figure 2.4). This is not an imported graphic (which you can do, and we explain how in Chapter 4). This is created entirely with styled text — the "books" are just spaces or equal signs with a different colored background. You'd be surprised at what you can do with styled text.

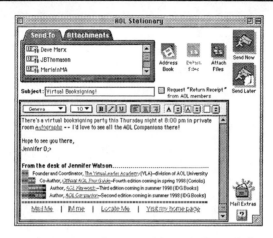

Figure 2.4 Jennifer's virtual bookshelf in styled text (view from Mac).

4. **Creating my profile.** Take a look at the profile for screen name: *Jennifer* the next time you're online. Notice anything different? (Well, besides the fact that I have one and have filled in virtually every field.) At the bottom is my angel smiley. It's my trademark — it works a bit like a signature (you'll notice it also appears in my e-mail). I used the profile tip that you read earlier in this chapter to place it there, below the rest of the text. How do you make smileys? See Appendix A.

CHAPTER 3

NAVIGATING AMERICA ONLINE

Cyberspace . . . the final frontier. These are the voyages of the *AOL Companion*.

Imagine for a moment that you're drifting in a vast void, with no ignition and even less direction. You see many strange new worlds as you float along, but they are out of reach. Finally, you land on a planet by sheer coincidence. You become engrossed in its culture, perhaps even put down roots. But you often dream of those worlds you passed along the way, and wonder what you may be missing. Does this seem familiar? The universe of America Online can seem a lot like that to the newcomer. And if my experiences are any indication, even the old-timers feel this way when they get stuck somewhere.

Your *AOL Companion* has been many things up to this point — a book, an advisor, a group of friends. Well, now it is also a space shuttle capable of navigating the universe at the touch of a button. It is programmed with the information you need to get you exactly where you want to go — from navigating through menus, windows, and buttons to traveling through cyberspace with keywords, shortcuts, and favorite places. There's even data on a black hole we charted at keyword: RANDOM. There's more, and it is entirely under your command.

So, step on up (watch your head) and get settled in the cockpit. My companions and I are right there with you. Think of us as your bridge crew — you're the Captain (but I get dibs on Number One). We're here to relate information, answer questions, and advise you on your best course of action. So, without further ado . . .

Engage!

. . . or how to get off the ground

You have the software and you have the account. Now how do you use America Online to take you places? Get out your ladders so you can climb aboard! Ladders?

Everyone who has America Online also has the ladders. You know, those things with lots of steps that are always falling down. Oh, do you call them menus? Silly me. But they do work a lot like ladders. And, like ladders, you don't need a special knowledge of the service to use them. Chances are good that you're already familiar with them through other programs.

The AOL software comes with several ladders, er, menus. The names differ a bit depending on whether you're using Windows or a Mac, version 4.0 or 3.0, but all the basic elements are there. Within each menu are the various menu items that you can select. Remember, if a word is grayed out, you cannot select it yet (you may need to sign on or do something else first). Here are some tips you may not yet know about menus and their items:

1. In Windows, you can open any menu without using the keyboard. Just hold down the **Alt** key and press the letter underlined in the menu's title. Mac users can install Easy Access (it comes with your operating system) to do pretty much the same thing.

2. On both Mac and Windows, many menu items have *keyboard shortcuts*, too. See the tip on them later in this chapter for more details.

3. The Window menu keeps track of all your open windows. Use it to bring hidden ones to the front.

4. Note the toolbar menus in version 4.0 of the AOL software. Any icon with a small arrow next to it is a drop-down menu. If you are new to version 4.0, look here for many of your favorite v3.0 menus.

5. Find the "hidden" menus in AOL software version 4.0. Menus pop up in certain windows when you right-click with the mouse (Windows) or hold down the **Control** key and click (Mac). So far I've found

menus hiding in Write Mail, Read Mail, Instant Messages, and Chat. How many can you find?

Using the Welcome Window :) :) :) | Win & Mac

. . . or how to cruise at light speed

Just as Wendy stepped through the window and began to fly in *Peter Pan*, so can you with America Online's Welcome window. It is a window of opportunity, a window to the world, and a launch window all rolled up into one. Every time you sign on, the Welcome window opens up with links to your mail, channels, chat, what's new, Parental Controls, Member Services, the Web, and stock quotes. In addition, you are welcomed with current news around the world, current events on America Online, and current weather outside your window, plus more teasers of areas online that are being showcased. Just click any button to fly to that area and get more detailed information. Best of all, no pixie dust is required. Regard the Welcome window as your starting point, with plenty of buttons and links to get you to a virtual Neverland.

Hints and tips on using the Welcome window:

1. Actually pay attention to it! You may be tempted to race in and go directly to your destination, but if you do that you'll be missing all the great scenery and roadside attractions on the way.

2. Clicking any "button" (either a picture or a small blue circle) takes you somewhere. More detail on using buttons can be found in the next tip.

3. Details on what's happening on AOL Today are summarized at the top. Click the picture if you're interested and want to learn more (see the tip "Exploring AOL Today" later in this chapter).

4. If you find something you like on the Welcome window, make a note of its name and keyword (if available). It won't stay on the Welcome window long, and there is no online record that it appeared there.

5. An up-to-date news blurb always appears on the Welcome window, as do the current weather

conditions. When I'm too busy to read the news and check the weather, I stay current by reading it as I stroll through on my way to other places.

6. There's a surprise behind the America Online logo. Click it.

7. If you forget what screen name you're using, you can always double-check it by noting the title at the top of the Welcome window. It always welcomes you by screen name.

8. Understand that the Welcome window changes frequently. As often as every 15 minutes the top news story, the current weather conditions, and the showcased areas are updated. You will not see these updates until you sign off and return again, however.

| Understanding Buttons | :) :) :) | Win & Mac |

... or how to read the charts

Button, button, who's got the button?

Your America Online screen is filled with buttons and icons that are just aching for a click or two from your hungry mouse! Do you know how to recognize all those buttons when you see them? And what do those tiny icons represent on America Online's menus?

Top ten click tips:

1. How do you know it's a button? When you click your mouse on it, the button moves, like a real push button, and bounces back when you release the mouse. Oh, clicking the button should do something, too!

2. Find Buttons Without Making Things Happen, Part 1: Move your cursor over the suspected button, but don't click it. The cursor should turn into a little hand if it is indeed a button.

3. Find Buttons Without Making Things Happen, Part 2: Click a suspected button, but don't release the mouse button. If it's a button it should move "down" and stay down. Keeping the mouse button depressed, slide the cursor off the button and then release the mouse button.

4. Illustrations that are buttons in disguise may change color when you click them.

5. The AOL software has a way of hiding buttons behind graphics and advertisements. Use the tricks just described to test them.

6. When you visit an area of America Online that's new to you, or one that has added new graphics, you may see "bare" buttons — little yellow boxes with tiny green America Online icons in them, with descriptive text alongside the button. Although you can wait until all the artwork has arrived before clicking the buttons, the buttons are active immediately.

7. Balloon help: In some cases, if you move your cursor over a button and let it "hover" for a bit, a tiny text box will appear to describe the function of that button. This is especially true of the toolbar at the top of the screen.

8. At the bottom of many windows, you'll see a tiny row of rectangular text labels. They're buttons, too, and useful ones. Keep your eyes peeled!

9. Recognize and understand list boxes: When you enter a forum and find a box containing a menu of selections, that's called a *list box*. If you single-click a list box item, the background color changes. A double-click will take you to the selection. Most list box items include a little icon (graphic) that should help you understand what you'll get when you select that item. The following table shows some common list box icons and what they represent.

Keep in mind that there are many more icons used to decorate and communicate in list boxes than listed in this table. Unfortunately, sometimes forums do a better job of decorating than communicating. If the forum has left you confused by misapplying these mini-icons, drop them a note.

10. Hypertext links: When you see an underlined word or phrase all in blue it ought to be a hypertext link. Click that word or phrase once and be transported. With luck, the text should accurately describe your destination before you click it.

List Box Icon	Represents
File folder	Another list box and/or a window with buttons. It may take you to another forum.
Document (a single sheet of paper)	Either a text article, an illustration, or both.
Blue globe	A World Wide Web page.
Handshake	A connection to another forum or the Internet.
Single floppy disk	Downloadable file.
Multiple floppy disks	A library of downloadable files.
Document with pushpin	A message board.
Two faces in profile	A chat or conference room.
Rows of seats	An auditorium.

Contributed by Dave Marx (screen name: Dave Marx)

Using the Toolbar   .:) :) :)   Win & Mac

. . . or how to hang up your tool belt

They say that whoever has the most toys wins. The same can be said of tools. And the toolbar that comes with America Online is bound to make you a finalist.

The America Online toolbar is the row of icons and buttons immediately below your menu bar. The icons and menus in the top half of the toolbar lead to various tools and destinations, while the buttons and fields in the bottom are for navigation. The toolbar is easy for beginners, yet powerful for pros. Here are my toolbar tips:

1. As stated previously, any icon or button with a small arrow next to it reveals a menu of options when selected.

2. You can add your own icons to the toolbar. See the "Customizing Your Toolbar" tip in Chapter 2, along with other toolbar personalization tricks.

3. The buttons in the lower left corner navigate among windows on AOL and pages on the World Wide Web.

4. You can type keywords and URLs for both the Web and America Online into the white box in the middle of the toolbar. Just type them in and click **Go** or press the **Enter** key. Click the down arrow next to the box for a list of the last 20 places you've visited.

5. Best of all, the AOL logo at the right end of the toolbar "spins" when loading a page so you know when it is still busy or completed.

Contributed by George Louie
(screen name: NumbersMan)

Meet George

I met George in a People Connection Help Room over five years ago when he was a Guide. He's continued his online career and I'm proud to say he is now in a position to help tens of thousands of people get more out of America Online. His past achievements include a stint as a programmer, engineer, online publishing specialist, and a sysop on the now-defunct eWorld (which he thinks should have been called gWorld after himself). Thank you for everything, George!

Exploring AOL Today   :) :) :)   **Win & Mac**

. . . or how to get your daily dose of America Online

Have you ever gotten online, looked around idly, and wondered what the heck was going on?

Wonder no more — America Online makes it easy to get your daily dose of online news with AOL Today. Reminiscent of the front page of a newspaper, AOL Today highlights current events, news headlines, new areas online, live events, sports scores, and more. But unlike a newspaper, the face of AOL Today changes several times during the course of a day. It spotlights news and events of interest appropriate to the time of day — current events in the morning, business at midday, general interest in the evening, and entertainment in the late night. You can get to AOL Today quickly via the button at the top of the Welcome window, or by using keyword: AOL TODAY.

Today's top five tips:

1. Visit AOL Today as soon as you sign on — if nothing going on right now tempts you, you can use the list of channels at the left to go somewhere else.

2. Check back with AOL Today when you're online — the page changes frequently. Updates are apparent not only by the text and pictures but also by the colors — the backdrop is a sunny yellow during the day and a twilight blue at night.

3. The news headlines in the upper-right corner are constantly changing. If you see a headline that catches your interest, just click it. If you're a news junkie, position AOL Today at the top of your screen so these headlines are always in view wherever you are online (or try keyword: NEWSTICKER).

4. Explore the buttons at the bottom of the AOL Today window for time-sensitive information and events.

5. Feel free to add AOL Today to your Favorite Places list. You'll always return to the current day and time, not the one you saw when you added the favorite place to your list.

Contributed by Brendan Rice
(screen name: KUBrendan)

Traveling With Keywords :) :) :)   Win & Mac

... or how to use the transporter

Frustrated by how long it can take to get around? I don't blame you; noodling around with icons and buttons won't get you anywhere fast. Thankfully, the *AOL Companion* knows the secret of transportation: keywords. Okay, so you've been hearing a lot about keywords already and they aren't much of a secret. But it's no wonder — they are one of the best and fastest navigational tools around.

Simply put, keywords are words or phrases that you can use to transport yourself directly to an area online. You enter the keyword, press **Go**, and presto! How do you enter a keyword? You can either type it right into the field at the bottom of the toolbar, bring up a special keyword window by pressing **Ctrl+K** in Windows or **Command+K** on the Mac, or just click the **Keyword** button on the toolbar. Type in the keyword and press the **Go** button.

How do you know which words or phrases are keywords? There's the catch — you almost always need to know the keyword before you can use it. Sure, you can guess, and you might hit the comet on the tail, but you're better off knowing where you're going first. You wouldn't want to find yourself in the Delta quadrant with no way to get home, would you?

The first tip concerning keywords is that there is an entire list of them — just about every public one known — at keyword: KEYWORD. America Online offers this list in alphabetical order, or sorted by channel. If you don't relish the idea of browsing through over 12,000 keywords online (there is no search function), I have a book much like the one you hold in your hands with each of the keywords listed and categorized, plus hints, tips, tricks, reviews, and special keyword lists. There are even some keywords in there that don't show up in the online list. The book is called, you guessed it, *AOL Keywords, 3rd Edition* (MIS:Press, 1998). Like this book, many experienced AOL community leaders contributed keyword reviews, and I think that makes it rather special.

I couldn't possibly go into every keyword tip here — there are enough for an entire book, remember — but I can give you some highlights:

1. URLs (those long Internet and America Online addresses with all the funny characters and numbers — see "Finding URLs" later in this chapter for more information) can be entered directly into the keyword window, too. For example, `aol://4344:1588.mainkey1.12265348.578972741` takes you right to the list of keywords by channel.

2. You can't get your own keyword, but if you create a Web page (see Chapter 7 for details), you'll have your own URL, which is almost as good.

3. Watch for keywords when you visit your favorite areas and make a note of them. They'll often be written near the bottom corner of a window.

4. If you spell a keyword incorrectly, or are just a bit off, America Online will usually give you a list of alternatives (see Figure 3.1).

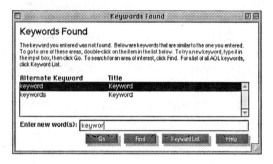

Figure 3.1 America Online gives you keyword choices when one doesn't work (view from the Mac).

5. Make your own keyword list using your shortcuts and never lose your keys again. See the following tip on creating shortcuts in your software.

6. Don't be shy about guessing. You may not get exactly where you want to go, but you can often find some interesting places!

7. If you're feeling adventurous, try keyword: RANDOM. See the last tip in this chapter, "Randomizing."

Creating AOL Shortcuts   :) :) :)   **Win & Mac**

. . . or how to soup up your software

Wouldn't it be nice if you could customize the menus in America Online? You can! Well, you can customize at least one: the *My Shortcuts* menu. Too often this feature is overlooked in favor of the flashier, glitzier navigational aids introduced recently. And it is no wonder — it is hidden pretty well. Yet this little menu packs a powerhouse of convenience and begs to be customized.

First, where do you find the My Shortcuts menu in the AOL software version 4.0? On Windows, you'll find it under the Favorites icon on the toolbar. On the Mac, you'll find it under the Window menu at the very top of your screen. If you're using AOL software version 3.0 or lower, it is more conveniently located right within the Go To menu, at the bottom.

To customize the My Shortcuts menu, locate your menu as described earlier and select **Edit Shortcuts** from the menu itself. A window with ten lines and three columns appears. In the first column, type the name as you want to appear in the menu (for example, *Book Shelf* or *Jennifer's Home Page*). In the second column enter the action, either a keyword or URL (for example, *BOOK-SHELF* or http://members.aol.com/jennifer/). The third column shows the keyboard shortcut assigned to the menu item. You may have some or all of the ten shortcuts already filled in — America Online enters recommended areas. Feel free to remove any or all of these and replace them with your own shortcuts.

My Shortcuts may seem similar to Favorite Places (discussed in the next tip), but it has a powerful advantage: the keyboard shortcut. Each of the ten slots you can add to My Shortcuts has a preassigned keyboard shortcut (keyboard shortcuts are discussed in more detail later in this chapter). That means you can go to your favorite forum or service without lifting your fingers off the keyboard. For example, I've customized My Shortcuts with the Walt Disney World area in the first slot (keyword: WDW). That means I can press the number **1** key while holding down the **Ctrl** key (or the **Command** key on the Mac) and go directly to the Big Mouse House!

Taking Keyboard Shortcuts   :) :) | Win & Mac

. . . or how to wax down your keyboard

Touch typists rejoice! Many common functions are accomplished far more swiftly with the press of a few keys! Do you want to go to a keyword, print a file, copy, cut or paste text, or open an Instant Message? You may be tempted to move your hand off the keyboard and over to the mouse, move the mouse up to the toolbar, and finally click the keyword button. (Are you really tempted now?) Instead of all this, just hold down the **Ctrl** key and press the **k** key (Mac users: hold down the **Command** key and press **k**). You'll memorize the keyboard shortcuts that mean the most to you in nothing flat!

Shortcuts to the shortcuts:

1. Most keyboard shortcuts are listed on the drop-down menus at the top of your screen, right along-side their associated commands.

2. Learn the keyboard shortcuts for your computer operating system. Shortcuts for major features such as copy and paste are common to all programs on your computer, not just the AOL software.

3. *AOL Keywords, 3rd Edition* (MIS:Press, 1998) includes a list of keyboard shortcuts in the appendix, along with lots of other useful information. The following table lists a few of the most useful short-cuts.

Shortcut	Windows	Macintosh
Keyword…	Ctrl+K	Command+K
Read Mail	Ctrl+R	Command+R
Compose Mail	Ctrl+M	Command+M
New IM	Ctrl+I	Command+I

More keyboard tips: In chat rooms and auditoriums, you can send a line of text by pressing the **Enter** key. And you can send Instant Messages with **Ctrl+Return** (or **Command+Return** on the Mac). Far fewer know that pressing **Tab+Spacebar** in Windows sends text in Instant Messages, chat rooms, and auditoriums.

Contributed by Dave Marx (screen name: Dave Marx)

Using Favorite Places :) :) | Win & Mac

. . . or how to capture their hearts

The America Online universe is vast! Once you start clicking around and exploring, you may never see the light of day again. When you find someplace you really love and want to revisit again and again, chances are you will have forgotten how you got there. Never fear — Favorite Places are here.

Have you noticed that nearly every window on America Online contains a little red heart icon in the upper right-hand corner? This heart holds the exact address of that window. Just click that heart and, on Windows, drag it to the Favorites icon in your toolbar or, if you're on a Mac, press the **OK** button in the box that pops up. Now everything you want is just a double-click away in your Favorite Places list, accessible under the Favorites icon in the toolbar. And it gets cooler than that. Favorite places work everywhere America Online can take you, whether you're visiting an America Online forum or using America Online to browse the World Wide Web.

When you open your Favorite Places list, you can double-click any item listed and go directly there. You can also organize your Favorite Places folder by dragging items into topic-related folders — make new folders by clicking the **New** button, choosing **New Folder**, typing a name, and clicking **OK**. You can change the titles of the items for greater clarity, and even edit the addresses (URLs) if, as often happens on the Web, an address changes. You can also create them from scratch if you have the URL.

But wait! The power of the favorite place has yet to be fully unleashed! You can share your finds with your friends. Let's say you're talking to a friend in an Instant Message and you find a cool new forum. You can drag the heart directly to the Instant Message! They'll get a blue "hypertext link," just like on a Web page. They can click and go! The same holds true for e-mail — drag a heart onto a Compose Mail window and send it to fellow members. (If you send it across the Internet, they'll see the URL address, but the link won't work.)

Have you had enough yet? Try this: Open your Favorite Places list while you're signed off, and double-click a favorite place. America Online will start the sign-on process (you'll need to enter your password or have your passwords stored) and take you directly to wherever you want to go. This also works if you read e-mail containing a hyperlink offline.

Favorite tips:

1. Drag items from your Favorite Places list onto an Instant Message or e-mail window, as just mentioned.

2. Build a portable Favorite Places list in e-mail and send it to your friends.

3. You can't send a hypertext link to a chat room, but you can send the URL from your Favorite Places list by dragging the favorite places heart to the text entry box on a chat window. The URL and description will be displayed in the chat room. The folks reading the URL can copy and paste it into the keyword window. (URLs, whether on the Web or on America Online, can be used as keywords.)

4. Did I mention message boards? You can drag favorite place hearts from the new-style America Online message boards, topics, and postings to your Favorite Places list and return to them without navigating the inevitable windows that precede most message boards.

I've neglected to mention AOL software version 4.0's text editor. This built-in, mini-word processor will also handle Favorite Place links. There's even a special Insert Favorite Places button (designated by a small, blue heart) at the top of the window to facilitate sharing. Make lists of all kinds, save them to floppy disk, and use them at the office. To use, click the **File** menu at the top of your screen and select **New**.

One caveat: Be cautious of indiscriminately following Favorite Place links sent to you by strangers. There are unscrupulous people out there who try to trick unsuspecting members into going places that are undesirable, or even dangerous. Your best bet is to see where it leads before you click it — details are in the next tip.

Contributed by Dave Marx (screen name: Dave Marx)

| **Finding URL Addresses** | :) | **Win & Mac** |

... or how to pinpoint an address

Just what is a URL? Well, it stands for *Universal Resource Locator*. Helpful, eh? Simply put, it is a pointer. On the World Wide Web, a URL is an address to a Web page — for example, http://www.aol.com leads to AOL's Home Page on the Web. We also have URLs on America Online, though they are generally less obvious. An America Online URL looks something like this: aol://4344:3013.main.18678151.5291 85606 (that's the URL for the Amazing Instant Novelist at keyword: NOVEL).

What good is it to know the URL? If you are using AOL software version 3.0 or higher, you don't necessarily need to know URLs in order to get to places on the AOL service. You can use your Favorite Places and hyperlinks (those blue, underlined words). On the other hand, knowing the URL is helpful when you're not sure where it leads, when you want to add it to the My Shortcuts menu, and when you are creating Web pages, among other things.

How do you find the URL? It depends on the source:

- **On the Web:** Copy it from the field near the top of your America Online window.

- **In a favorite place heart:** First add it to your list of Favorite Places (see the previous tip for help). Now, open your Favorite Places, highlight the new link, and click the **Modify** button. A window pops up with two fields: the second field shows you the URL, which you can copy if you wish.

- **In a hyperlink:** If it is a Web URL, just hold the cursor over the hyperlink (don't click it) to get the URL in Windows. If it is an AOL URL, copy the hyperlink, paste it to a new window (**Ctrl+N**), and double-click the hyperlink — a small box appears with the URL. On the Mac, just hold down the **Control** key, click the hyperlink and select **View Address**. If you're using AOL v3.0, copy and paste the hyperlink into a new window, close the file, and open the file in a text editor such as Notepad (Windows) or SimpleText (Mac). Open the file and the URL associated with the hyperlink is displayed within it.

Searching the Member Directory :) :) | Win & Mac

. . . or how to find pen pals and mouse mates

In a universe as large as America Online, how do you locate folks who share your interest in mind-meld techniques? Or find that long-lost friend you met at the Centaurian pub last shore leave? Easy! Use the Member Directory.

The Member Directory is America Online's roster. But becoming a member of America Online does not automatically create an entry for you in the Member Directory. You create your own entry by going to keyword: PROFILE and clicking **My Profile**. Most folks include their first name, city, state, and hobbies, but it is entirely up to you. This can be a great tool in networking and finding other members who share your hobbies.

To search the directory, begin at keyword: MEMBERS (see Figure 3.2). Enter as little or as much information as you like, keeping in mind that the more you specify, the more narrow your search. And see that little box titled "Return only members online" near the bottom? When it is checked, it will only show you members who are currently online. Once you've told America Online what you're looking for, click **Search**. Too many matches? Be more specific. Too few? Broaden your search.

Don't overlook the small, almost incongruous button labeled Advanced Search. Clicking this gives you much greater control over your searching. It is best used when you know exactly what you're looking for, or when a Quick Search displays too many matches. Keep in mind that you can also use *wildcards* and *Boolean phrases* in your searching. For more information on these, see Chapter 7.

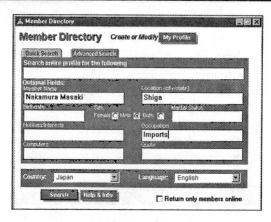

Figure 3.2 Searching the Member Directory (view from Windows).

Some helpful searching tips:

1. Search words must be at least three characters long.

2. Feel free to switch between **Quick Search** and **Advanced Search**. As long as you keep the window open, your text remains in the window until you delete or type over it.

3. When browsing your results, remember to click the **More** button at the bottom (if available).

4. America Online can find only 100 entries at a time. If you search on *Jennifer*, it will tell you there are over 100 matching entries, but that doesn't mean there are only 100 Jennifers online. Not even close. I think my friend Jennifer may have more than 100 screen names all on her own.

5. Every profile contains three buttons at the bottom: **Locate** (to check if they are online), **E-Mail** (to send them some e-mail), and **Help & Info** (if you get stuck). Use them!

6. A reminder to those under age 18 (and to their parents): Be careful how much information you put into your profile. I strongly suggest you keep your full name out. A first name is plenty. Also, don't put the year of birth when 9/5 will do the trick.

7. Remember that your profile can be seen by *anyone* on America Online (that's over 12 million members), so don't put anything there that you wouldn't be proud to hear on the evening news.

8. In the event you find something offensive in a profile, feel free to report it at keyword: I NEED HELP.

Contributed by Brian Thomason
(screen name: JBThomason)

Using the Find Feature :) :) | Win & Mac

. . . or how to fine-tune your search

Information overload. You read a lot about the problem. How do you find what you need when there's so much more of it every day? The answer? Search tools! On the World Wide Web, some of the more famous search tools are Webcrawler, Yahoo!, and Excite. Within the walls of America Online there is *AOL Find*.

AOL Find's primary purpose is to help you locate the forum or forums that you need. It won't dig deeper than that, but that's plenty! Are you interested in cars? The text search tool in AOL Find turned up 32 forums that address that interest (see Figure 3.3). Selecting any one of them from the list takes you to a page that includes links to the forum and related areas.

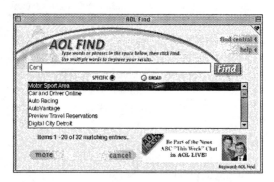

Figure 3.3 Searching AOL Find (view from the Mac).

AOL Find also provides a link to *Find Central*, an extensive collection of specialized search tools collected from America Online and the Internet — search America Online's software libraries, the Member Directory, and the Live Events listings. One useful surprise is the Channel Guide search tool (keyword: CHANNEL GUIDE). Select a channel you're interested in for links to all areas in that channel, organized alphabetically and by topic. This is much faster than the Channels window.

Where is AOL Find? Click the **Find** button on the toolbar and select **Find it on AOL**, or use keyword: FIND.

Contributed by Dave Marx (screen name: Dave Marx)

Surfing with AOL NetFind   :) :)   Win & Mac

. . . or how to find what you need on the Internet

Are you tired (or afraid) of getting tangled in the Web?

When it's time to find information on the World Wide Web, everyone can use a research assistant, and AOL NetFind is a dandy! Their slogan says it all: "Why search, when you can find!"

Enter a word or phrase, name, or topic, and AOL NetFind will use its artificial intelligence (pretty smart stuff, actually) to find the most relevant information. Its search efforts go beyond the literal phrase you've entered. It's smart enough to understand the kind of information you want. There are separate search facilities for general searches, locating people, combing newsgroups, hunting down e-mail addresses, finding businesses, and more — each optimized for the purpose at hand.

AOL NetFind is available all over America Online — linked into channels and forums under buttons, icons, and items in list boxes. AOL NetFind is also under the **Find** button on the toolbar (click **Find it on the Web**), at keyword: AOL NETFIND, within AOL Find, and at `http://netfind.aol.com`.

Here are some AOL NetFind tips:

1. This is the best tip I can give: Check out AOL NetFind's Search Tip area. The folks who offer the search tips here explain even the most technical stuff in an entertaining and easy-to-understand manner.

2. To get the most out of AOL NetFind, search for phrases, rather than individual words, and enclose those phrases in quotation marks (" ").

3. A kids-only version of AOL NetFind is available at keyword: KIDS FIND.

Contributed by Dave Marx (screen name: Dave Marx)

Recognizing Cursors :) :) :) | Win & Mac

. . . or how to give yourself a hand

These days, software can get pretty fancy. Take cursors, for example. Cursors are what you move about with your mouse on your screen — your virtual pointer. There are different cursors for different activities, like the classic arrow for just zipping about the screen and the "I" (I-beam) when you're typing text. Some software packages even let you customize your cursors. One of the cursors I use is a bottle of wine being poured into a glass. It's quite entertaining, I can assure you, but not all that useful.

Most folks take the cursor for granted (except when it can't be found). But paying attention to your cursor can give you important navigational information. Specifically, have you ever noticed the hand cursor?

Whenever your cursor glides over a button, icon, or area that can be clicked in AOL, your cursor will change to a hand. Next time you see the hand cursor, click. Watch for the hand as you move about online and you'll learn to recognize the "doors" and "windows" available everywhere. Some are obvious, but others are much more cleverly hidden. You may even find some "Easter Eggs" (entertaining surprises hidden by software designers).

Another good cursor to watch for is the empty arrow. As you've probably noticed, a run-of-the-mill arrow is all black. When you perform an operation that takes some time (say opening your list of mail), you get the hourglass (Windows) or beach ball (Mac) cursor. That is until your cursor passes over a title bar or a scroll bar, when it changes to an arrow outlined in black. The outline arrow means you can do something even though the software is otherwise busy. Experiment with it.

Two other important cursors show up on the Mac. One looks like a menu bar behind the black arrow, and appears if you hold down the **Control** key. Click in a window with the menu cursor to reveal a hidden window. The other cursor looks like a speaker, and it appears when you're pressing the modifier key to hear button labels spoken aloud (see the tip "Hearing AOL Talk" in Chapter 2).

Watch your cursor. It leads to great things!

Contributed by Brian Thomason
(screen name: JBThomason)

| Stopping Incoming Text | :) :) :) | Win & Mac |

... or how to escape, period

"Command, we have incoming!"

"Oh, no! Escape, escape, escape!"

Have you ever noticed that it can take a while for some texts and graphics to finish appearing online? I'll bet that more than once you thought, "I didn't want that!" but the hourglass (if you're on Windows) or beach ball (if you're on the Mac) just kept going and going.

While America Online is not as expensive as it used to be, your time is still precious. How do you stop that incoming text cold? What about those graphics? Take the advice of command control — press the **Escape (Esc)** key on Windows, or the **Command+.** (period) keys on the Mac. It stops incoming text and many graphics dead in their tracks! Just remember, you don't need to press **Escape** more than once. No, really. Trust me on this.

Some types of graphics can't be stopped that way, though. When America Online sends "screen artwork" for a particular window or forum — like the button graphics, icons, and some fancy backgrounds — all you can do is close the window. With Windows 95 and Mac, there's a button in the upper right-hand corner of the window that closes it outright with a single click. Windows 3.1 users can double-click the window's "control box" — the icon in the upper-left of the window.

Can you use this escape technique to stop mail you've just sent from going through? No, but you can "unsend" mail once sent so long as you do it before anyone reads it. Details on how to do this are in Chapter 4.

Follow these tips and you'll escape unscathed!

Contributed by Dave Marx (screen name: Dave Marx)

Finding New Services	:) :)	Win & Mac

. . . or how to explore strange new worlds

America Online is no longer a small community where every new area is welcomed, talked about, and critiqued. New forums and services don't always come in with a bang, and often leave with a whimper. Keeping up with the changes is challenging. Yet I don't believe in the philosophy of sitting back and waiting for something to catch my eye. I won't find what I need this way, and neither will you. There is treasure out there, but sometimes you have to dig a bit to get to the really good stuff.

I have several techniques for finding new forums and services online. Here's my top ten list:

1. The quickest way to locate specific things and interests on AOL is by using keyword: AOL FIND.

2. To expand your search to include the Internet, check out Find Central (keyword: FIND CENTRAL).

3. Use keyword: NEW to reach the list of new features. This is where you'll find about half of what arrives online, particularly the flashier stuff.

4. Visit your favorite channel and look for the What's Hot button. Subscribe to newsletters, which often announce new services (keyword: NEWSLETTER).

5. Note the announcements when you arrive and leave.

6. Pay attention to media ads. Often companies or organizations announce their intention to go online

before it is made public here. Press releases from America Online (keyword: PRESS) are good, too.

7. Use keywords. Use keyword: RANDOM (discussed later in this chapter) and explore the alternate keywords that come up when you type in the wrong one. There is a delightful element of surprise here!

8. Read the AOL Insider at keyword: INSIDER. Meg, the AOL Insider, sometimes pre-announces services.

9. Check the "Where on AOL service do I find…" folder in Members Helping Members (keyword: MHM).

10. Finally, don't neglect to browse. Some of my best finds were stumbled over while out exploring.

Contributed by Ben Foxworth (screen name: BenF7)

Using AOL Member Perks   :) :) | ‹ | Win & Mac

… or how to be a big shot in a members-only club

Members only. The phrase conjures up posh clubs and upscale services. Then again, it also brings to mind wholesale department stores and buying collectives. Both produce a good feeling — the difference is generally reflected in your wallet, with the latter leaving more money in it. Happily, America Online's Member Perks also save money for *members only*.

America Online flexes its 12-million-member muscle to get special benefits for members only. Member Perks vary from a long-distance calling plan and a travel club to a magazine outlet and the AOL Visa card, with plenty in between. To see the full range of your member perks, go to keyword: PERKS or click the **Perks** button on your toolbar. The main Member Perks window highlights the more popular or pressing offers, but be sure to click the **More AOL Member Perks** button to get the full list of perks, too.

A particularly "rewarding" perk for members only is AOL Rewards. By taking surveys and buying particular products, you can earn points towards merchandise, discounts, and free time on America Online.

Another nifty perk is the Deal of the Day (get there quick with keyword: HOT SAVINGS). Besides the main product which is usually offered at a good discount, there are other money-saving offers and information on what's up for bid today in the online auction.

My favorite perk is the free reminder service. I can create future reminders for myself and receive e-mail two weeks (or four days) before the event. It works great for birthdays. Included in that e-mail is a list of gift ideas (it is sponsored by the Shopping channel) though you're under no obligation to purchase anything.

Contributed by Kimberly Trautman
(screen name: KTrautman)

Randomizing :) :) :) | Win & Mac

. . . or how to amuse yourself when bored

Round and round and round it goes. Where you'll land, nobody knows!

The hot topics in the online universe these days include how to efficiently locate what you're looking for, and how to have your customized needs delivered to your doorstep automatically. America Online's Random feature takes a somewhat more, shall we say, roundabout and perverse route to America Online's content.

Go to keyword: RANDOM. You'll hear the sound of a marble rolling around a roulette wheel, et, voila! a roulette wheel appears. Click the wheel (it says it right there, "Click the Wheel!") and you'll be transported somewhere on America Online. If it has a keyword, it's fair game for Random. You'll be amazed at what can turn up. What a way to explore the world's largest online service!

Random notes and suggestions:

1. Click the wheel!
2. Click the wheel again!
3. Don't give up, there must be something that interests you !
4. Repeat after me, "Serendipity is bliss!"

5. Don't give up until you say, "Wow! I didn't know America Online had that!"

Remember that Random is — well, random — the chances of getting back to the same page again anytime soon are pretty slim. If you see something you like, note its keyword or add it to your list of favorite places. If you forget, try checking your history trail in your toolbar to see if it is still listed (see the tip "Using the Toolbar" for more on the history trail).

Despite its tiny size (about that of a postage stamp), Random is so popular that it carries advertisements! I think that says it all.

Contributed by Dave Marx (screen name: Dave Marx)

Companion Confessions

There was a time when I knew every forum on America Online and could give directions without pausing. These days, I'm lucky if I can still get to my favorite areas. Don't get me wrong, I continue to visit every new area and I haven't lost my sense of direction. It is just that America Online is changing so rapidly that it is hard to know if something is coming or going. But understanding how to navigate America Online has helped me make sense of it all. I know that when something isn't where I remembered last seeing it, I can find it using one of the navigational tips. Here are some examples:

1. Traveling with keywords. Oh, you've heard me talk about keywords. After collecting them for years and writing a book about them, we've gotten to know one another well. But everyone has to start somewhere. My affair with keywords began by visiting every known forum and gathering the keyword off the bottom corner of the window. And I guessed a lot. Aren't you glad you don't have to?

2. Taking keyboard shortcuts. I'm a busy person. A few years ago I felt I'd found my saturation point — but as time wore on, I realized I'd added even more activities and responsibilities to my life. These days,

I'm doing even more. I suspect next year will be even busier. I now understand that I can continue adding more because I find shortcuts. And one of those is keyboard shortcuts. The majority of the time I'm online, my fingers never leave the keyboard. I can move much faster and more fluidly. It took me a year or so to get them down to the point where I used them daily, but it made a significant difference.

3. **Searching the Member Directory**. People fascinate me. Even so, I must admit I don't spend a lot of time surfing profiles. I do use the Member Directory a lot, however: I use it to look up quotes, phrases, and sayings all the time. A little weird, but it works really well. The quotes and phrases are what real people use, not what a scholar has collected into a musty tome (or dusty CD-ROM).

CHAPTER 4

COMMUNICATING WITH OTHERS

Letter writing is not my strong suit. Take the last time I tried to write and mail a letter. My intention was to send a simple reply to Shari, my best friend from high school.

First I had to find a piece of paper — I've long since lost that pretty box of stationary and the Super Bright White copy paper just wasn't going to cut it. After securing a single sheet of parchment from a paper samples kit, I set out in search of a pen. Even when you use a pen everyday (which I do not), pens are hard to find.

Finally, armed with paper and pen, I sat down to write. I hadn't written more than a few words before I made a mistake. Drat! Not having enough paper to start over, I continued only to have my hand cramp up on me.

After several rest breaks, I finally completed the letter. It wasn't much to look at, but at least it was done. I stuffed it in one of my bill envelopes and sealed it. Whew!

I then had the huge task of addressing the envelope, as I'd mislaid her return address. And I'm totally unreliable when it comes to getting to the post office and, of course, I never have stamps on hand. Needless to say, the letter was never sent. But my story serves as a reminder of how good I have it with America Online's e-mail.

Imagine if I had opened America Online, pulled up a new mail window, typed my letter to Shari, addressed it with her screen name or Internet address, and clicked the **Send** button. No paper, pens, envelopes, stamps, or guilt. There is no waiting for the post office to deliver it; she gets it within seconds. And I can save a copy, review what I wrote, and get a quicker reply.

You, too, have the power of America Online's e-mail at your fingertips. Use the tips in this chapter to tap into this power and begin communicating like a pro.

Now, if only I could get my friend Shari online . . .

Using the Mail Center :) :) :) | **Win & Mac**

. . . or how to avoid the post office

E-mail. FlashMail. Mailing Lists. Mail Controls. Internet Mail. It's hard enough to remember what all those things are, much less how to use them! Yet when it comes to communicating, these are powerful tools. Although detailed explanations of how each works are beyond this book, it is important to have the basics down. That's where the Mail Center comes in.

The Mail Center is one-stop shopping for just about anything related to e-mail. When you first sign on, go to the Mail Center to read your new mail and write messages to others. You'll find it under the **Mail Center** icon on the toolbar, at keyword: MAIL, or in place of your mailbox if it is empty (see Figure 4.1).

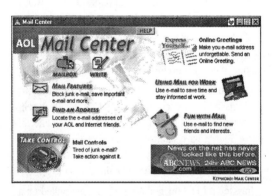

Figure 4.1 Learn the basics of e-mail at the Mail Center (as viewed from Windows).

Beyond the basics are links to the mail tools themselves, along with full descriptions and instructions on what they do and how they work. Even better, you'll find collections of tips and tricks for using your mail for work, plus ways to have fun with your mail. You can even directly contact the Mail Team for answers to all your questions. And if you want to get announcements about a specific topic, forum, or channel here on America Online, you can subscribe to a newsletter! Scattered throughout the Mail Center are nuggets of helpful information, essential to any dedicated letter writer. Make the most of it!

Contributed by Bradley Zimmer
(screen name: Bradley476)

Addressing Mail   :) :) | Win & Mac

. . . or how to drop names

I adore Jane Austen. Besides being a poignant novelist, she was a great letter-writer. Though I did not acquire this skill from reading her stories, I did learn a bit about the art of letter writing: to receive letters, you must first send them. And you need an address. As much as I am captivated by the nineteenth century, I am thankful for the simplicity of e-mail addresses — on America Online, we only need to know screen names. Even so, addressing e-mail is challenging to new members. Allow me to share the art of e-mail addressing.

1. If you are eager to try your hand at e-mail before finding an appropriate address, send *yourself* an e-mail. Just click the **Mail** button in the toolbar and type your screen name in the **Send To:** box. You must type your screen name exactly as it appears — if you aren't sure, go back to your **Welcome** window and check the name in the window's titlebar. If it feels too narcissistic to send an e-mail to yourself, you are welcome to send one to me. Address the e-mail to screen name: *Jennifer*, give it a subject like "AOL Companion E-mail," tell me what you think of the book or ask a question, and I will reply.

2. If you know your friends or family are on America Online, find out their exact screen names — remember, on America Online our screen names are our e-mail addresses. If you can't reach them, try the Member Directory to search for them (see the tip "Searching the Member Directory" in

Chapter 3). If you have no friends or family online, find a pen pal in the Member Directory or try keyword: PENPAL.

3. Remember to type in the exact and full screen name — I get a great deal of mail intended for other Jennifers whose pals and parents don't understand that screen name: *Jennifer* belongs to me and that their Jennifer has an entirely different screen name.

4. To send mail outside America Online to the Internet, you need an Internet address. See "Finding Internet Addresses" in Chapter 7.

Keeping an Address Book   :) :) :) | Win & Mac

. . . or how to have a little black book

Some online names are easy to remember (like *Jennifer*); others are weird mixtures of letters and numbers, which make little or no sense at all (such as *DaveM26011*). Still others are Internet addresses with so much punctuation that it takes longer to type out the address than to write the e-mail! America Online has a solution to all this: the *Address Book*. Much as you might imagine, the Address Book is your own place to put the names of people you like to e-mail. You can find your Address Book by clicking the **Mail Center** icon on the toolbar and selecting **Address Book**. You can also access your Address Book when you're composing e-mail — just click the button marked **Address Book**. Sound easy? It gets better.

Rather than explain step-by-step how to use the Address Book (the online and offline help guides do a good job of that already), let me share my top ten tips for using it:

1. You don't need to actually type in first and last names when setting up a new entry — "Mom" may suffice in a pinch. You do need to enter the exact and complete e-mail address, however. Most likely *Mom* is not your mother's screen name, so be careful here. If she has an Internet address, it will look

something like this: mom@sendmemoney.com (be sure to get all of it).

2. Add notes to help you remember important things such as your Mom's birthday or her favorite flower.

3. It is easy to overlook the Picture window available in individual's address entries. To find it, click the **Picture** tab at the top of the window when you are adding or editing an address. Add pictures (of your friend, their pet snake, or whatever you like) to their address entry with the **Select Picture** button, or drag and drop them into the picture window. You can also store pictures for use in e-mail — just copy them from the Picture window and paste them into your e-mail.

4. You can use the **Find in Top Window** command to search for listings within your Address Book. It is located under the **Edit** menu. Those using a Mac can also access **Find** by holding down the **Control** key when they click anywhere in the list of addresses.

5. If you frequently send e-mail to the same group of people (such as the folks at the office or an online club), you can create a single Address Book entry containing all their names instead of having to type each address in a separate mail message. Just click the **New Group** button and type in their screen names or addresses, separated by carriage returns.

6. Remember that you can enter both America Online and Internet addresses into your Address Book.

7. All entries can be edited and/or deleted. This is useful when Mom stops sending you money.

8. You can begin writing your e-mail right from your Address Book. The easiest way is to double-click the appropriate entry in the Address Book — this opens a new, pre-addressed mail window. You can also select the address and click the **Send To** button (for direct mail), the **Copy To** button (for a courtesy copy), or the **Blind Copy** button (for discretion — see the tip "Blind Carbon Copying" later in this chapter). Alternately, you can drag and drop the address from the Address Book to the mail window.

9. On Mac AOL software version 4.0 and up, you can view your Address Book entries alphabetically by **Name** or by **Address** — just click either word at the top of the Address Book to toggle between modes.

10. Mac AOL users can take their Address Books with them when they travel. First open your **System folder**, then your **Preferences** folder, then your **America Online** folder, and finally your **Data** folder — you will see your **Address Book** file. Save the file to a floppy or send it to yourself in e-mail and download it when you arrive (see the tip "Attaching Files to Mail" for help with the latter).

Using Styled Text   :) :) :)   Win & Mac

. . . or how to have a stylish background

E-mail is a fun and easy way to stay in touch with your friends, as well as an efficient way to communicate with business associates. But as with any text-based information system, it can be difficult to emphasize the really important things. It used to be that you had to use characters such as * or + (for example, *wonderful*), to substitute for **bold** or *italic* type. While this lead to plenty of creative uses for punctuation, it didn't always lead to clear communication. With AOL software version 3.0 and higher you can use *styled* text in your e-mail (see Figure 4.2), and with AOL software version 4.0, you can even choose your favorite fonts. The days of boring e-mail are over!

What is styled text? For those of you who are unfamiliar with it, you'll find an easy introduction to it in "Setting Your Style" in Chapter 2. Now you're ready for the next step — applying it to your e-mail. Here are some special tips on styled text in e-mail:

1. **Send a greeting card.** Styled text in e-mail gives you the tools to make a custom greeting card for family and friends. Get creative with colors and sizes and font — you'll find a centered alignment works wonderfully for this. ASCII Art (described in Appendix A) really comes to life when set in color.

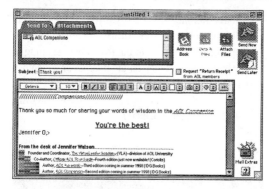

Figure 4.2 Fun with styled text in e-mail (view from the Mac).

2. **Set the background.** If you set the background color in an e-mail, it is applied to everything. That means if you add a background to a note you're forwarding, you change the background for the entire e-mail — both the forwarded note and your own comments. The exception to this is when the note you're forwarding had a background already — in this case, the last background applied flashes and changes to the initial background. You can actually do multiple forwards with different backgrounds, creating a colorful light show in your e-mail.

3. **Highlight important words.** Using styled text in e-mail, you can assure the recipient gets your point when it is typed in bold, italics, or underlining. I like to use the bright yellow background on the text I want to emphasize. Sort of a cyber-highlighter.

4. **Give them a link.** You can place hyperlinks right into e-mail, giving your readers a shortcut to an area on America Online or the World Wide Web. To get a hyperlink into your e-mail, drag it right from your Favorite Places window into the mail. It shows up as blue underlined text when properly placed. Be sure to let your less-savvy readers know that the hyperlink can take them somewhere when clicked. On AOL software version 4.0, your reader can view the URL before they click it. In Windows, the URL appears in a little yellow dialog box that pops up when the cursor is over the hyperlink. On the Mac,

hold down the **Control** key as you click the hyperlink and select the **View Address** option in the pop-up menu. Keep in mind that when sending a hyperlink to someone on the Internet or a member using a older version of the AOL software, they only see the URL. You can find more information on URLs in Chapter 3 and Chapter 7.

Contributed by Kate Tipul (screen name: KMTipul)

Checking Your Spelling :) :) | Win & Mac

. . . or how to aviod tiping badd

The age of voice mail and videoconferencing is here, but don't throw away that dictionary. Along with all those other new gizmos and doodads comes America Online's electronic mail, which is resurrecting the art of letter writing. According to a recent survey by Robert Half International, over 98 percent of executives claim that proper spelling is important to advancing your career. And if that isn't enough, there's a good chance your fourth-grade teacher is now online, and armed with an electronic dictionary of her own.

Thankfully, you now have the same resources as your spelling teacher. Specifically, online dictionaries (keyword: DICTIONARY), a virtual thesaurus (keyword: THESAURUS), and best of all, a spelling checker. The built-in spelling checker is easy to use; simply write your letter, click the spelling button at the end of the format bar in your mail window (it has the letters "ABC" and a check mark next to it), and begin checking your spelling. When it finds a word it doesn't know, the spelling checker highlights it, and a dialog box pops open that enabless you to **Skip** the word, **Skip All** words like it, **Replace** it with a suggested one, **Replace All** words like it, and teach the word to the spelling checker for future checks (**Learn** on Windows or **Add** on the Mac). This is a full-featured spelling checker, much like what you find in the big, fancy word processors.

You don't have to wait until you've completed your letter to check it, either. If you have a question about a single word or just a few words, highlight them by dragging the mouse across the words you wish to check and click the spelling button. You can use the spelling checker outside the e-mail window, also — try it on documents and message board posts on America Online.

Contributed by Brendan Rice
(screen name: KUBrendan)

Adding Pictures to Mail   :) :)   **Win & Mac**

... or how to bring your mail to life

Imagine opening an e-mail and seeing a picture of your grandchild or another relative taken just minutes ago! Imagine following the progress of your friends' trip with photos and descriptions sent in an e-mail every night.

Even a year ago this would have been impossible, but with America Online software version 4.0 it's here today! Images displayed within the e-mail, rather than simply attached, add a lot of impact and convenience for the reader. Send detailed schematics to your boss, photos of your family to relatives, or put your company logo at the top of business messages — the possibilities are endless. By using the background image feature, you can even create your own personal online stationary.

To add images to your e-mail, you can either use the e-mail toolbar or drag and drop them from another window. You can find more details on usage in your online and offline help resources. Add a few images, choose a background, and put some fun and excitement into your daily e-mails!

Here are some fun and creative ideas:

- Illustrate letters with graphs, figures, and photos.
- Create a family album and send it to your friends and relatives.
- Include your company logo at the top of e-mail to create personalized letterhead.
- Use the background feature to add a photo behind the text of your letter. This is a great way to simulate fancy stationary.

Be considerate of the time it will take your recipient to download the photo. Also, keep in mind that if your recipient isn't using AOL software version 4.0 or higher, they will not see any of the imbedded images (but they will see any text that you typed).

Contributed by Bradley Zimmer
(screen name: Bradley476)

Attaching Files to Mail   :) :)   Win & Mac

. . . or how to send an encyclopedia

Just as you can't fit an encyclopedia into a letter-sized envelope, you can't fit an encyclopedia into the body text of an e-mail. You need a carton when the envelope won't do, and you need to attach a file to e-mail when the body of an e-mail won't do. An attached file is simply that — it's a file that goes along for the ride with a piece of e-mail, but it can hold far more information than the body of an e-mail (up to 16 megabytes [MB] of data). When you send the e-mail, the attached file is uploaded from your hard drive and is stored on America Online's computers. The recipient of the e-mail can then choose to download the file. Here are some tips to use attached files more effectively:

1. If you need to attach a number of files and send them to the same person, combine or archive them into one file, then attach the archived file to the e-mail. With Windows AOL software version 4.0 and all Mac AOL versions, you can select several files and the AOL software archives them automatically.

2. Be sure that the person you send the attached file to knows what type of file it is. You don't know how many times I've received files from my friends and had to try a number of programs to open them.

3. Speaking of mystery files, if a stranger ever sends you one, don't download it. Instead, forward it to screen name: *TOS Files* (or check keyword: NOTIFY AOL for the latest address). Files from strangers can be full of mischief even if they claim to be something else. You can even set your preferences to automati-

cally refuse e-mail with attached files — see the "Blocking Mail" tip later in this chapter.

4. For those files you send out often, remember that forwarded e-mail retains its attached files. This means that you can send an attached file to yourself, keep that mail in your in-box, and forward it when necessary. Just remember that unread mail or mail "kept as new" only stays around for about 30 days.

Contributed by George Louie
(screen name: NumbersMan)

| Creating a Signature | :) :) | Win & Mac |

. . . or how to be the next John Hancock

Signatures are like snowflakes — no two are exactly alike. And though there are many benefits to being online, you can't exactly grab a pen and sign your John Hancock at the bottom of e-mails or message board posts. But you can have a text-and-graphic-based signature that is as unique and creative as the one you put down on paper.

A signature can be anything as simple as your screen name, or as creative as you can imagine! And with styled text (see "Using Styled Text" in this chapter) and the introduction of embedded images (see "Adding Pictures to Mail," also in this chapter), you can add a logo or photo.

Signature tips:

1. Include your name or nickname. You may be surprised at how much more interesting you seem when folks can put a name to the person, especially if your screen name is a complicated one. Don't share personal information you want kept private.

2. Let folks know about your interests, whether online or off. Do you have a favorite forum you hang out in? Take pride in it and let folks know in your signature.

3. Favorite quotes are commonly found in signatures. Some folks change theirs daily or weekly.

4. ASCII Art, when tasteful, can add personality to a signature. There's more on ASCII Art in Appendix A.

5. Signatures are generally used for e-mail, but also work great in message board posts.

Do keep in mind, however, that a signature can be overdone. A good rule is to keep them within four lines in length. A useful feature in the message boards is the ability to save your signature, so you don't need to re-create it each time you make a post (available under the **Preferences** button in the message board window). There isn't yet a place to save an e-mail signature — until America Online adds it, just save your signature as a text file and then copy and paste it at the bottom of your e-mail.

Contributed by Bradley Zimmer
(screen name: Bradley476)

Using Mail Extras   :) :)   Win & Mac

. . . or how to make the little extras count

Do you want to put more pizzazz in your e-mail, but can't figure out how? Click the **Mail Extras** button on a new mail form and see a whole world of exciting possibilities. Mail Extras is really just a "getting started" tool, but it's a bit more fun than most. Not only does it tell you how to liven up your mail, but it gives you a painless head start by supplying samples you can use in your own e-mail.

The **Colors & Style**, **Smileys**, and **Stationery** features are all examples of something called *ASCII Art* — illustrations made with the characters from your keyboard, like these: :-) and [_]P (coffee mug). With America Online e-mail you can change the color and size of those characters, center the text, add bold and italics, and add a colored background behind fonts (see the "Using Styled Text" tip elsewhere in this chapter). **Photos** and **Hyperlinks** both train you in the same technique — using Favorite Place "hearts" to create those blue hypertext links you see in text around America Online and the Internet. Finally, there are links to the American Greetings Online Greetings store.

Let's concentrate on my two favorites: **Colors & Style** and **Stationery**. The rest is so self-explanatory that I'd be wasting ink to describe them here.

The neatest feature of **Colors & Style** is that you can preview a piece of "mail art" and then add it to a new piece of e-mail with one click. Pretty nice. In fact, give it a try now if you're online. Click the **Mail Center** icon on the toolbar at the top of your screen, click **Mail Extras**, **Colors & Style**, **Hello**, and then finally click **Add to a New Mail**.

Now let's have some fun! With your mouse, click and drag to highlight the red brick wall. Notice that the centered text button is depressed on the styled text format bar? We're really just using a word processor! Click the Flush Left or Flush Right buttons. See how the wall moved? Now recenter it. Let's make it a yellow brick wall — highlight the wall again, click the background color button (an "A" on a blue background), click the bright yellow rectangle, and click **OK**. One last exercise: Make the wall larger. Again, use your mouse to select the wall, click the little down arrow next to the number **10**, and select the number **18** with your mouse. This takes your wall from 10-point text to 18-point text. As you can imagine, you can modify the art in many ways!

Stationery provides a collection of letterheads that America Online personalizes just for you (Windows only). If you select a piece of stationery from their collection and click **Create**, you are asked for information that is used to personalize the stationery. Neat! You can use this feature every time you write a letter. If, however, you create a piece of stationary (and maybe modify it the way you did with the brick wall), why not save it as a template and never have to fill in your name again? Here's how: create and modify your stationery to taste. Then **Save** the e-mail as a file called `stationery` (Windows 95 users may want to save that to their **My Documents** directory). The next time you want to use it in e-mail, open a new mail window, click the **Insert a Picture** (camera) icon on the styled format bar, select **Insert Text File**, and **Open** the stationery file. Your stationery is automatically copied into the e-mail!

Contributed by Dave Marx (screen name: Dave Marx)

Meet Gen

Genevieve Kazdin (screen name: *GenK*) and I were being mistaken for one another long before we met. Besides the similarities of our name — "Gen" sounds like "Jen" — we also share another passion: helping both members and fellow community leaders (volunteers). Gen is now the Assistant Program Manager for the AOL Families Channel. While I haven't met the majority of my online companions in person (isn't modern technology amazing?), Gen is an exception. We've met several times "face-to-face" at conferences. I am happy to report she is as delightful offline as she is online. And we have yet another thing in common: Gen and I both joined America Online in 1992!

Thank you, Gen!

Blind Carbon Copying   :) :) :)   Win & Mac

. . . or how to conspire in secret

Gee, I sure wish there were a way to send Susie a copy of the love letter I'm writing to Johnny without him knowing. But wait — a *blind carbon copy* would be just the thing! The blind carbon copy (or BCC) feature enabless you to simultaneously send the same e-mail to a third party without the original recipient's knowledge. Johnny has no idea he's not the only one reading those amorous words.

To BCC someone on America Online's e-mail system, you simply type or place the address(es) — a screen name or Internet e-mail address — in parentheses in the **Send To** or **Copy To** fields of a new mail window. The BCC designation tells America Online to deliver the mail to all parties, but to keep anyone in parentheses a secret (shhhhhhh!). On the Mac AOL software, you can also use the small drop-down menu to the left of an address to set a BCC.

The primary recipient (in this case Johnny, whose screen name was not in parentheses) only sees his screen name at the top of the e-mail. On the other hand, the blind carbon copied recipient (Susie, whose screen name *was* in parentheses) sees the e-mail addressed to Johnny *and* herself, indicating that she was BCCed. Now, let's say you're living a *Melrose Place* life and want to BCC yet another interested party — say, Max the gossip columnist — on this well-read love letter without Johnny *or* Susie knowing. Easy! Just BCC Max too (put his screen name in parentheses) and Max receives the e-mail addressed to Johnny and himself, but he doesn't know about Susie, Susie doesn't know about Max, and Johnny is totally in the dark.

This feature has many uses aside from the love triangle. Send a memo to your boss and BCC all your co-workers. Send e-mail to the target of a surprise party and BCC all the invitees. Or BCC yourself to keep an extra copy or so you can monitor when it is read from another name.

Blind carbon copying is an easy and valuable America Online e-mail feature — and no one need be the wiser!

Contributed by Adrienne Quinn (screen name: AAQuinn)

Sending Mail to a Group   :) :)   Win & Mac

. . . or how to carpet bomb your friends and family

Have you ever wanted to send one piece of mail to more than one person without having to address it to each person individually? Maybe you are the lucky one in charge of setting up your family reunion, or you came across a timely news article and felt it would be of interest to your co-workers. In both of these cases, and many more, you can accomplish your goal by sending just one piece of mail instead of several separate pieces.

One way to do this is to simply type everyone's e-mail address into the **Send To** box of a new mail window. Separate each address with a comma (on the Mac commas work to move the addresses to separate lines, too). You can include America Online screen names and Internet addresses all in the same box — just make sure you separate each address with that all-important comma. You may also do this in the **Copy To** box in the

Windows AOL software. Now everyone you listed receives a copy when you send it.

Do you send e-mail to these same people on a regular basis? Is it getting hard to remember all those names? You certainly don't want to forget anyone (well, maybe you do, but this can't be your excuse). To make things even easier, you can create an entry in your Address Book that includes all these addresses. Open your Address Book and click the **New Group** button. In the window that pops up, type in a word or phrase in the **Group Name** box that will identify this group of people (be nice, now). You might use *Family Reunion* or *Newshounds*. In the bottom box, type the screen names and/or Internet addresses of all those on your mailing list — remember to separate each one with a comma. If you already typed the names in an e-mail window, you can just drag and drop them into your Address Book's New Group window. When you're finished, click the **OK** button to save your list. Your new group is now in your Address Book and ready for you whenever you like. Just double-click the entry to bring up a new e-mail, pre-addressed with the entire group of addresses.

Consider the benefits of blind carbon copying (BCC) the members of your group, particularly if it is large. Blind carbon copies can protect the privacy of the members, since each recipient sees only his/her name. They can also save a considerable amount of time when the reader opens the e-mail — the more screen names that need to be displayed, the longer the e-mail takes to display. To blind carbon copy a group, highlight the group entry in your Address Book and click **Blind Copy**. If you want to blind carbon copy only a portion of your group, you can either edit the group entry itself (put parentheses around the entire list of those who should be BCCed), or separate those who need to be blind carbon copied into their own group.

Contributed by Kate Tipul (screen name: KMTipul)

Meet Kate

A self employed graphic artist, Kate Tipul (screen name: *KMTipul*) has been online since 1993 and has been helping members most of that time. If you've ever seen the MCI commercial where the woman gets her kids on the bus, e-mails over oatmeal, and attends meetings in her PJs, that's Kate (sans bunny slippers). She's been a guide, a volunteer at keyword: HOT, the person behind "Ask the Staff" at Parental Controls, and helped launch Digital City. Now Kate is the Program Manager for the new Influence Channel — quite a stretch when she lives in the middle of a blueberry farm in Ohio. She sincerely hopes her deep, dark secret is safe with you.

Kate has met many wonderful people online who have changed her life in countless ways. She has a large family — all of whom are online — and especially enjoys e-mailing her father even though her parents live 15 miles away. She's a wife and mother of two teenage boys who are responsible for her wicked sense of humor (I know you were wondering).

Thank you, Kate!

Taking Mail Shortcuts :) :) | Win & Mac

. . . or how to avoid the dogs

If you're anything like me, you've come to rely on e-mail. It doesn't matter how much or how little e-mail you send — there's always something to be said for doing something faster and better. And as a power-mailer, I have some shortcuts to make your daily mail run go quicker.

First, learn the shortcuts to reading mail: To pull up your new mail list, press **Ctrl** and **R** on Windows, or **Command** and **R** on the Mac. Now use your arrows to scroll through your mail. The up and down arrows on your keyboard will take you through the list (use the **Return** or **Enter** key to open a highlighted piece of mail), and the left and right arrows will help you move from one piece of mail to the next when mail is open.

Next, learn the shortcuts to composing mail: To open a new window and write a letter, press **Ctrl** and **M** on Windows, or **Command** and **M** on the Mac. To move from field to field without resorting to your mouse, use the **Tab** key. On Mac AOL software version 3.0 and above, CC (carbon copy)and BCC (blind carbon copy) address-es can be indicated by typing either a **[** or a **(** before the screen name, respectively. Note that the **Return** key or a comma will move your cursor down to the next line so that you can add a new address. To send your mail, press the **Ctrl+Enter** keys on Windows, or **Enter** on the Mac. On Windows AOL software, you can also use the **Tab** key to move among the buttons within the compose mail window.

Remember also the hidden menus trick mentioned in Chapter 3. On Windows, right-click in any of the boxes to bring up a variety of menus — the menu in the main body of the e-mail is particularly rich with **Font**, **Text**, **Justification**, **Text Color**, **Background Color**, **Insert a Picture**, **Background Picture**, **Insert Text File**, **Insert a Hyperlink**, and **Spell Check**, among other options. Remember you can use your up and down arrow keys to navigate here, too. On the Mac, press the **Control** key while clicking in a box.

Learn just one shortcut at a time, or pick them up as you need them. You'll be amazed by how they can speed up your e-mail, without resorting to buying a new computer.

Reading Mail Offline :) :) :)   Win & Mac

. . . or how to flash 'em

We have flash cards, flash memory, flash floods, even Flash Gordon.Why not *FlashSessions*?

What is a FlashSession? Like the others, it's quick. Unlike them, however, a FlashSession happens when you use the Automatic AOL feature to sign on, send and/or receive all of your waiting e-mail and newsgroup mes-sages, and sign off . . . all in a flash!

You can schedule Automatic AOL to FlashSession at any time, even while you're asleep! What's more, your mail and newsgroup messages are stored in your Personal Filing Cabinet on your hard disk, effectively "solidifying" these otherwise fragile and fleeting electronic entities, enablinging you to read, write, and respond to them — offline and at your leisure.

Setting up Automatic AOL to perform FlashSessions is remarkably easy (hey, it'll even walk you through the whole setup!), but it does vary on the platform (Windows or Mac) and the AOL software version you are using. Consult the online and offline help in the **Mail** menu, under **Setup Automatic AOL Now (Flashsessions)**.

If you find the idea of enabling your computer to act autonomously on your behalf a bit unsettling, you're not alone. For those who'd rather be in complete control, you may also run a FlashSession at any time while you are already online. As before, these messages may be read and responded to offline, but you also have the option of doing so while you're still online, retaining the benefit of automatically saving them in your Personal Filing Cabinet for future reference.

Though Automatic AOL does provide you the option to automatically download files attached to e-mail, this can be risky with all of the computer viruses and Trojan Horses out there (see the tip "Understanding Trojans" later in this chapter). Strongly consider disabling the automatic downloading option in the initial setup.

Here are some time- and money-saving ideas for using Automatic AOL and FlashSessions:

1. Set up your AOL software to collect your e-mail on a regular basis, such as in the mornings before you wake up. You can set times and days for pick-ups in your **Preferences** (under the **My AOL** button).

2. If you are away from your computer for a while and regularly get a lot of mail, be sure to FlashSession so the mail doesn't pile up. It is even a good practice for those serious about online security. Unread mail or, worse yet, a full mailbox can be dead giveaways that no one is minding the shop.

3. Remember that you can reply to mail offline, too. Write your mail and click **Send Later** to have it sent out when you sign on or flash session.

4. If you're sending out a lot of e-mail, like a bunch of family reunion invitations, write it all ahead of time, mark it to **Send Later** and FlashSession it while you're busy doing something else away from the computer.

Contributed by Bob Trautman (screen name: PhotogBT)

Meet Bob

Bob Trautman (screen name: *PhotogBT*) is an electronics engineer by profession, as well as an author and a photographer (I'll bet you never would have guessed). He writes articles for photography, electronics, and other types of publications, plus poetry, and I hear he is even working on a novel. His photographs have been exhibited and published in various places and are often used to illustrate his articles. Bob also contributes to the Kodak Photography Forum (keyword: PHOTOGRAPHY), and he has been a member of America Online for over four years. His old stomping ground is AOL Live (keyword: AOL LIVE). For fun and fitness, Bob is also a helicopter pilot and an active gymnast. He lives in northern Virginia with his two sons. Thank you, Bob!

Using the Personal Filing Cabinet :) :) | Win & Mac

. . . or how to get a secretary-in-a-box

Oy! So much to keep track of! Mail I've read, mail I've sent, mail I plan to send, files, newsgroups, and postings. Where do I keep it all? In my Personal Filing Cabinet!

The Personal Filing Cabinet automatically saves all this information in a single, orderly place. Do you use Automatic AOL (FlashSessions) to collect and read your e-mail, newsgroups, and message boards offline? This is the place to find it all! You can also set your mail preferences to save all the mail you read and send.

You can create and organize folders in the cabinet for any topic or category that makes sense to you, and drag the individual letters and posts into those folders. Your **Download Manager** list is duplicated here, too. It even comes with a search tool, so you can find that long-lost love letter! Your Personal Filing Cabinet is easy to find, too — just look under the **My Files** icon on the toolbar.

AOL 4.0 users, your Personal Filing Cabinet can now be password-protected. In previous versions anyone with access to your computer could read the mail saved in your Personal Filing Cabinet. Now you can padlock your Personal Filing Cabinet at: **My AOL** ⇨ **Preferences** ⇨ **Passwords** (you need to be signed on to use this preference). I do not recommend using the Sign-On password feature, though. That reduces your security.

Tips for personal filing:

1. Keep your Personal Filing Cabinet neat. Drag the mail you've read into appropriate folders as quickly as possible, and delete the junk!

2. Check your **Mail**, **Newsgroup**, and **Message Board** preferences and set them accordingly.

3. Back up your Personal Filing Cabinet often — it is a single file kept in the **Organize** directory (Windows) or the **Data** folder in your **America Online** preferences folder in the **System Folder** (on the Mac), and bad things can happen to it. Back up the entire Organize directory regularly.

4. Windows users: If you save your e-mail as individual files rather than use your Personal Filing Cabinet, you're wasting lots of disk space. The larger your hard disk, the more space each file takes. The Personal Filing Cabinet is much more space efficient.

As your Personal Filing Cabinet grows, it will take longer and longer to do everything. Dragging mail from the top to the bottom of a long list of e-mail is a killer, and waiting for the Personal Filing Cabinet to open or close is a drag. There are a number of strategies that can help:

1. Toss out the trash often (delete).

2. Compact your Personal Filing Cabinet periodically to make it run faster (there's a button for this).

3. Put everything inside folders, and put folders inside of folders if necessary so it doesn't take long to travel from top to bottom.

4. Keep the Personal Filing Cabinet open or minimize it (see "Organizing Your Desktop" in Chapter 2).

5. Reorganizing a long row of folders can be difficult — if you drag a folder and drop it between two other folders, it will end up inside one of those folders. Here's what you do: drag a bunch of e-mails to the beginning (or end) of that row of folders (be sure to not drop them into the folders). You can then drag and drop folders in-between those messages. After the folders are in the order you desire, you can drag those e-mails out of the way. Sometimes when you reread old e-mail, that mail will be duplicated at the top of your e-mail section (this is a bug, not a feature). Delete the duplicates.

6. Windows users can move or delete a group of folders or documents all at once. Try this: Click a document, then hold down the **Shift** key and click another document somewhere further down the row. The first and last e-mail, and every message in-between, will be highlighted. Now, hold down the **Ctrl** key and start clicking individual files — if they were highlighted, they'll revert to normal. If they weren't highlighted, they will be. Now you can drag or delete the e-mails as a group. This works for folders, too. Mac users have it simpler: just press **Command** and **A** to select all, and hold the **Shift** key while clicking to deselect.

Contributed by Dave Marx (screen name: Dave Marx)

Checking Mail You've Sent   :) :) :) | Win & Mac

... or how to track letters

Have you ever sent e-mail and wondered if you accidentally sent it to *Mom* instead of *Mom37962*? Do you wonder if everyone in the office has read your mail about the meeting time change? Did you misspell the boss's name in that same e-mail? If so, you're a likely to benefit from this useful mail feature: the ability to check sent mail.

Checking mail you've sent is easy! If you're using AOL software version 4.0, just click **Read** on the toolbar and then click the **Sent Mail** tab at the top of the resulting window. If you're using Windows AOL software version 3.0, Mac AOL software version 2.7 or anything below either of them, select the **Mail** menu and choose **Check Mail You've Sent**. You can now manage your previously sent mail. Just highlight the e-mail you want to work with and click any of these buttons:

- **Read** — You can read mail up to approximately three days after you sent it. This is an excellent tool for finding out when someone replies to your mail with "yes" and you haven't a clue what you asked. Do note that on Windows AOL 4.0, you can change the number of days (from one to seven) sent mail is retained in your **Mail** preferences (accessible under the **My AOL** icon on the toolbar).

- **Show Status** — Lets you check if mail has been read (and the time it was read), deleted, ignored, or simply unread.

- **Unsend** — I find nothing is a better motivator for spell checking than that **Send** button! If the recipient(s) has not read the mail yet, you can **Unsend** your mail. Be sure to save a copy if you need the information as no copy will remain in your mailbox after you unsend it.

- **Delete** — The highlighted mail is deleted from your mailbox with this option. Don't confuse this with **Unsend**, as once an e-mail is deleted, there's no way to unsend it or get it back into your mailbox.

Contributed by Kimberly Trautman
(screen name: Ktrautman)

Getting Return Receipts   :) :) :)   Win & Mac

... or how to increase your e-mail return

Do you sometimes wonder when or if your friends and business contacts read the e-mail you send? Sure, you can check the mail you've sent and click **Status**, but there's an easier way: return receipts. What's the difference? As soon as your recipient(s) read your mail, a piece of e-mail is sent to you right then and there announcing who read the mail and at what time.

How do you request a return receipt? Open a new mail window and take a close look at it. Do you see the little check box labeled **Request "Return Receipt" from AOL members**? Click inside the box to "check" it. That's all there is to it. Now when your recipient reads his or her e-mail, a receipt is e-mailed to you instantaneously. It arrives in your mailbox from the screen name of the mail recipient and the subject line reads "Receipt for (the subject of your original e-mail)." Open it and you see something like this:

```
Message subject: Return Receipt Test
When sent:  98-04-17 14:57:57 EDT
Read by:    SueBD
When Read:  98-04-17 14:58:08 EDT
```

If you sent your e-mail to several people, you get a separate receipt each time one of your recipients reads your letter. If someone clicks the **Delete** button on your e-mail, you won't get a receipt because it wasn't read.

Return receipt notes and tips:

- Return receipts only work with America Online addresses, not Internet addresses.
- Be careful not to request a return receipt on that e-mail to the 613 members of the Good Samaritans' Club. You'll live to regret it.
- If you want to know when someone is online and you can't use the Buddy List, try sending them a mail with a return receipt requested.

Contributed by Sue Boettcher (screen name: SueBD)

. . . or how to lock your mailbox

E-mail is a great way to communicate, but sometimes it can be too much of a good thing. Like most folks, there will probably be times when you want to block some incoming e-mail. It could be harassing mail (which should first be reported by forwarding to *TOSMail1*); it could be Internet junk e-mail (which you should always forward to screen name: *TOSSpam*); it could be that you just can't get off someone's mailing list; or it could be that you're going on a two-week vacation and don't want to come home to an overflowing e-mailbox.

Thankfully, AOL has created powerful controls to block e-mail. With those, you can block or permit all e-mail, block or permit e-mail from only specific addresses, permit all e-mail from AOL members and a select group of Internet addresses or domains (the part of an Internet address that follows the @ symbol), block e-mail from certain domains, and block file attachments to e-mail.

To use these mail controls, sign on under your master screen name (this is required) and then use keyword: MAIL CONTROLS. Now click the **Go to Mail Controls** button. The next window will be a list of the screen names under your account. You can set the mail controls for each individual screen name, and each can be different. This is helpful in tightening control on a child's screen name, for example. Simply follow the clearly written instructions. You just click check boxes and circles to select or unselect your options and, in the case of blocking/permitting specific addresses or entire domains, you will have to type those in the appropriate box.

If junk e-mail is a particular problem, check out keyword: JUNK MAIL for everything you need to know about taking care of that particular problem that plagues all of us. Unless you conduct a large volume of Internet correspondence, you can use Mail Controls to eliminate almost all junk mail originating on the Internet. Try accepting mail from America Online members and select Internet addresses only to eliminate Internet mail you don't want.

Contributed by Kate Tipul (screen name: KMTipul)

Verifying Screen Names :) :) | Win & Mac

. . . or how to check up on someone

It's a sad fact of online life: people change names on America Online about as often as you get junk mail. Okay, perhaps that's an exaggeration — everyone knows there's more junk mail than there are people to receive it — but it's darn close. How do you know if your Instant Message buddy is gone for good or is just spending more time offline? You could search the Member Directory, but that only helps if they have a profile. The solution is simple: send them e-mail.

When you send mail to an invalid screen name (not an Internet address), America Online tells you they are ". . . not a known AOL member." This is a nuisance when you send a piece of e-mail to multiple recipients, since none of them receive the letter, but can work for you, too!

To see if particular screen names are in active use, just send mail to those names. If you want to keep your investigation confidential, add one known invalid screen name to the mailing list (the number *1* will do). By including one known invalid name, you will get a report telling you the status of every name you test, without letting the people know you're checking up on them.

Another reason to verify screen names is to learn if someone claiming to be an employee or volunteer really is one. Unfortunately, con artists abound. No staffer will ever ask you for your account information online.

Here are some tips to help you verify staff screen names:

- Check with the forum: If someone claims to be a staff member, visit the forum and look for a staff list.
- Don't trust everything you read in a Member Profile. If they faked the name, they can fake the profile, too.
- Check for "lookalike names" — an uppercase *i* looks like a lowercase *L*, or a *1*(one). *Zero* (0) and *O* (oh) are also easy to confuse. *JenniLynn0* looks a lot like *JennilynnO*, doesn't it? If you are unsure, type out the name yourself, the way you think it is

spelled, and send an Instant Message or e-mail to that name to see if they are one and the same.

Contributed by Dave Marx (screen name: Dave Marx)

Understanding Trojans :) :) | c | Win & Mac

. . . or how to look a gift horse in the mouth

Perhaps the best place to start understanding Trojan Horse files is to think about the origin of the name. Remember the epic story of the 100 Greek warriors hiding in the huge, wooden horse sent to the city of Troy as a peace offering? When the horse was safely inside the city and while the unsuspecting citizens slept, the warriors emerged from their hiding place and opened the gates to their troops waiting secretly outside. By morning the city was in ruins and nearly all its inhabitants slain. Gasp.

The moral of this story applies in today's world as well, with a little alteration: Beware of attached files bearing gifts. Trojan Horse files may promise to do one wonderful thing, when in fact they do something completely different, and almost always malicious in nature. They do their nasty work entirely in the background, recording your keystrokes, secretly sending your password to their masters, and possibly even preventing you from changing your password at all — and all done without your knowledge because Trojans hide deep in your system, much like those Greek warriors. A Trojan Horse may also copy everything you type over and over or cause your screen to look as if it's melting. More severe Trojan Horses can and will completely wipe out your hard disk drive. They could even compromise your account and then wipe out your hard drive, so you might not know about it for a while.

Keep in mind that you must actually download the file to your hard disk either from an attached file in e-mail or from a link on an Internet Web site, decompress the file (if compressed), and run the file in order for a Trojan Horse to do its deed. You cannot get a Trojan Horse by reading e-mail, responding to an Instant Message, or reading/posting in a newsgroup.

So what can you do to protect yourself and your computer from a Trojan Horse file? Simple. Do not download files from strangers, or people claiming to be America Online staff, or from Internet Web sites — especially if these files promise free games, free time, faster modem connections, beta software, pictures of "friends," or anything else that might tempt you into giving it a try.

If you receive a suspicious file in e-mail, don't mess around with it — forward it to screen name: *TOSFiles* right away. Do note that any files found in America Online's software libraries have already been scanned and are safe for downloading.

In the interest of preventative measures, you should also get yourself a good anti-virus software program and scan any suspicious files before you run them. There is more information, expert help, and software demos available at keyword: VIRUS INFO. See also the tip "Preventing Viruses" in Chapter 6.

Protect your America Online account and your computer — don't fall for these scams. Remember, if it sounds too good to be true, it probably is.

Contributed by Kate Tipul (screen name: KMTipul)

Resetting the Mail Flag   :) :) :) | Win & Mac

. . . or how to find your mail again

What, no mail *again*? Do your friends swear they sent you mail but nothing appears? Or does that disembodied voice keep insisting "you've got mail," yet your mailbox remains empty? Before you decide your friends are liars and your computer is mocking you, would you believe your America Online "mail flag" can get a little rusty? It's entirely possible that your mail flag needs to be reset!

Why does this happen? One reason is that if you leave mail unread in your mailbox for more than 30 days, America Online software automatically deletes it — and sometimes forgets to reset your mail flag. Maybe one day this bug will be fixed . . .

In the meantime, resetting your mail flag — or anyone else's for that matter — is an easy task. Just send yourself e-mail with the words *set mail flag* (all lowercase letters and no quotes) in the **Subject** field. Voila! Your hidden mail should appear immediately. If this trick doesn't solve your mail problem, contact Member Services for additional assistance.

Contributed by Adrienne Quinn (screen name: AAQuinn)

Companion Confessions

Since the advent of e-mail, communication has become significantly easier for me. I can now do business, gab with friends, and stay in touch with my family, all with e-mail. It is easy, quick, convenient, and relatively painless. I will admit it — I would make an ideal poster child for electronic mail. Here are a few of the ways I make the most of e-mail on America Online:

1. **Attaching files to e-mail**. I don't know what I'd do without this feature. Well, I'd certainly waste a lot more time, that's for sure. For example, I wrote an entire book last year without once speaking on the phone to the editor. Everything was done through e-mail messages and attached files. No hitches, either. Isn't modern technology wonderful?

2. **Taking mail shortcuts**. I write a lot of mail. Probably between 100 and 150 pieces, and that's on a slow day. If I didn't use shortcuts, I'd either have to spend considerably more time on e-mail or I'd end up not communicating well. I particularly like using (and [for CCs and BCCs on the Mac, rather than the drop-down menu, which takes a lot of time.

3. **Reading mail offline**. I get a lot of mail. And even though I do read it all, I cannot answer it all. So I often keep it in my mailbox with grand hopes I will eventually find the time to reply. This results in a full mailbox, with mail all the way back through the past 30 days or so. So once a month, I collect all my mail using Automatic AOL so it doesn't scroll off. The Personal Filing Cabinet is my friend.

4. **Checking mail you've sent**. Not only do I often refer back to mail I've sent, but I really find it helpful to check on the status of a piece of mail. If I see

that my mother hasn't yet read the mail I sent three weeks ago, I'll know that she's more likely to be having computer problems than just ignoring me.

P.S. — Here's a hot tip for you — read the tip in Chapter 7 about AOL NetMail. You can access your America Online e-mail from anywhere on the Internet!

CHAPTER 5

MAKING AND MEETING FRIENDS

I have a secret. Although I originally became a member of America Online to help with my blossoming desktop publishing business, I stayed for another, less-professional reason. It wasn't the friendly, easy-to-use interface, though that was a plus. And it certainly wasn't the price, because back then the service was not cheap. No, it was the ability to meet people and make friends in chat rooms and Instant Messages that really held me. The truth is, the scope and simplicity of it all intoxicated me to the point where I was interested in little else. I was crocked, pickled, plastered, smashed, under-the-table, stewed-to-the-gills, and three-sheets-to-the-wind drunk with chat.

Oh, I tried moderation. I figured out how much I could afford each month, and then budgeted my time accordingly. But a few extra minutes here engrossed in a chat on time travel and a couple hours there talking to my best online friend quickly added up. Supporting my habit became difficult, but I was still hooked. I knew a good thing when I saw it. Not only was I meeting some of the most interesting people in my life, I was learning to open up and be more outgoing, too. It was more than just social chatting; it was a rewarding growth experience.

Eventually, like the college student who gets tired of hangovers, and no pocket cash, I settled down. Rather than trying to meet every member, I concentrated on maintaining the friendships I'd made. All that time I'd spent chatting meant I really knew my way around — a fair price for a lifetime of friends. Thankfully, with unlimited pricing and the *AOL Companion*, you can have the same thing for a lot less money in a lot less time. And I get the satisfaction of sharing my knowledge and experiences. Please return the favor by sharing it with the folks you're bound to meet — they may become your best friends.

| Chatting Online :) :) | Win & Mac |

. . . or how to type out loud

Imagine you're at a crowded party. You know no one. You're feeling a little uncomfortable, and you begin pretending that you're terribly interested in the plants. Just then the hostess comes up to you, introduces herself, and makes polite conversation. Others overhear your conversation and jump in. Suddenly, the party isn't so dull. In fact, you're having a great time, meeting lots of new people, and the night is still young.

Now translate this experience to an online chat room on America Online. It's really not that different! A chat room is much like a party where few people know one another. And all it takes is some simple, polite conversation to get the "party" going.

Chatting for the first time can certainly bring on bouts of anxiety. You may find yourself thinking "What if they don't like me?" "What if I say the wrong thing?" "What if, what if, what if. . ." I know. I asked myself the same questions my first few times in chat rooms. There is an important distinction between a real-life party and an online chat conversation that comforts new chatters: you have the power to leave an uncomfortable situation — instantaneously and unobtrusively — at your fingertips. Every window can be closed. But usually you won't want or need to do this. Chat rooms really are wonderful places to meet others with similar interests and to make some new friends. All you have to do is relax, chat, and enjoy yourself!

The first thing to do is get yourself to the People Connection, America Online's chat center at keyword: CHAT. Before you jump into a chat room, take a look around. If chatting is all new to you, click **Show Me How** for help and information or click **The Community Center** for a fascinating glimpse at hosts, fellow members, and the world of chatting. Once you have your bearings, join a chat! The next tip, "Finding Chats," details how to do just that. If you're eager to start, you can go directly to a chat room by clicking the **Chat Now** button on the People Connection window. Within a matter of seconds, a chat window appears on your screen with other members like yourself (see Figure 5.1).

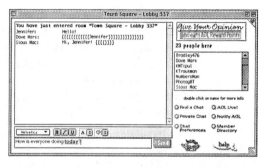

Figure 5.1 A chat in the Lobby — America Online style (view from the Mac).

The best way to start any chat is to pay attention to what others are saying and jump in only when you have something to contribute. See the "Chatting Fluently" tip later in this chapter. Many chat rooms have a host who is much like the hostess I describe earlier in this chapter. The host often greets you as you enter, makes sure you feel welcome, updates you on what's going on, and encourages conversations. Feel free to ask the host any questions you may have — they have a wealth of information and can help you understand America Online. If you are unsure how to spot these helpful folks, see the tip "Recognizing Hosts" at the end of this chapter.

Once you get the hang of chatting, a good understanding of AOL's community standards becomes important. The details are found online at keyword: TOS, but let me give you a crash course here. No profanity, harassment, solicitation, or disruption is allowed online — mostly common-sense stuff. America Online tries hard to provide a family service all can enjoy. If you observe someone violating these community standards, you can make a report with the **Notify AOL** button in chat rooms (or use keyword: NOTIFY AOL).

If there is one essential tip I can give you that will improve your chat experience, it is the Golden Rule:

Do unto others as you'd have them do unto you.

Finding Chats :) :) | Win & Mac

. . . or how to look in the right places

With thousands of chats going on at any one time on America Online, it's certainly not going to be hard to find chats with people who share your interests, laugh at your silliest jokes, or commiserate about your overbearing boss. Finding chats is one of the easiest things to do online — you just have to know where to look.

The People Connection at keyword: CHAT is chat central. Use the **Find a Chat** button to display the list of existing chat rooms and their respective topics — double-click it, or highlight and click **Go**. If the room is full, you have the option of moving to another one like it (see the next tip, "Getting Into Full Chat Rooms"). Don't be shy about moving from room to room.

Once you're comfortable with chat and ready to seek out new opportunities, visit keyword: INTERESTS. The Interests channel has a virtual smorgasbord of different leisure time activities and hobbies such as pets, gardening, collecting, and cooking. Check out the forums that interest you by reading and posting on their message boards, taking note of their chat schedules, and visiting their conference room. Soon you'll be getting and giving advice to other members of the forum and marveling about how this medium brings people together.

Since birds of a feather do seem to flock together, another channel to try is keyword: LIFESTYLES. Men, women, kids, and teens can explore their beliefs, their heritage, and their lifestyle choices with others who know and understand. Pick a forum and jump in!

Beyond this, every channel, and almost every forum, has it own chat room (or two). Some are obvious, others take a bit of scouting. You can often spot them in lists by the small icon of two heads facing one another (see the tip "Understanding Buttons" in Chapter 3).

Bottom line: America Online is full of great places to start lifelong friendships, cultivate intriguing relationships, discover soulmates, and even fall in love. Yes, it can even happen to you — with a little help from your friends.

Contributed by Kate Tipul (screen name: KMTipul)

Getting Into Full Chat Rooms :) :)   Win & Mac

... or how to open sesame

It happens to everyone sooner or later. The chat room you really, really want to enter is packed to the gills and you cannot enter. You can sense the laughter and the fun going on inside, but you're stuck outside. You discover yourself whining back to the monitor in frustration, saying "No... I don't want to create another room like it ... I want to get into this room!"

You have a few options. You can do the laundry. Or take out the garbage. Or even rearrange your Personal Filing Cabinet while you wait and your frustration mounts. No? Then try one of these handy tricks to squeeze in:

- **Be negative.** If it rarely happens that you cannot enter a room, or you're patient by nature, you might just keep clicking the **No** button until you either get into the room or get tired. It will help if you line up your windows so your mouse doesn't have to travel too far each time. Just move your window with the list of rooms so the room name is positioned just about where the **No** button pops up.

- **Add to your arsenal.** If you find you're frequently denied entrance, download one of the AOL software add-on programs designed specifically for this purpose. You'll find several of these for Mac or Windows at keyword: FILESEARCH. RoomBust, MacWedge, and RoomPlease are just a few examples of these utilities. Each allows you to specify a room to target and continues to try to gain entrance until it is successful, or until you stop it.

If you choose to try one of these alternatives, be aware that they are most effective when you are not already in a busy chat environment (like a Lobby), as the constant updating of your screen slows your computer. Try creating a quiet private room for yourself as a temporary headquarters while waiting to get into the target room.

Bypassing the Lobby   :) :) :)   Win & Mac

. . . or how to slip in the back

The chat room you frequent is warm, friendly, and comfortable. All of the regulars know your name. But to get there during prime evening hours takes all the skill you can muster to negotiate the Lobby and arrive, breathless and panting. There are easier ways to join your friends! Next time try one of these methods:

1. **Use Find a Chat.** Select the **People** button on the toolbar and choose **Find a Chat**. Locate and select your favorite room and then press **Go Chat**.

2. **Join a friend.** Select the **People** button on the toolbar and choose **Locate**. Type in your friend's screen name and — if they are online and in a public or member chat room — click **Go**. You are taken to their chat room automatically!

3. **Invite yourself.** Use the Buddy Chat feature in your Buddy Lists to go to a private room. Stay there, or jump to any chat in the People Connection. See "Using Buddy Lists" in this chapter.

4. **Use a Favorite Place.** Every chat room has a favorite place heart you can snag and add to your list. Capture one from favorite chats for future use. Or spend some time exploring chats and create an entire collection of places that you can jump right in to (see "Using Favorite Places" in Chapter 3).

5. **Create a URL.** If you haven't picked some favorite places from the chat garden yet, you can create one for a private room of your own with URLs. Just open your Favorite Place list (click the **Favorites** button on the toolbar and select **Favorite Places**), click **New**, type an appropriate chat name, and type the

following letters and numbers just as they appear: **aol://2719:2-2-**. Now type the name of the chat room, without spaces, immediately after the dash. For example, *aol://2719:2-2-KatesPlace*. Now click **Save** and try it. A private room window with your chosen chat name should appear on your screen.

Contributed by Kate Tipul (screen name: KMTipul)

| **Creating Chat Rooms** :) :) :) | Win & Mac |

. . . or how to open your own lounge

There are those in life who want to direct their fates and are not content to be bystanders. I am one of those persons, and if you're reading this book, I'll bet you are too. So what do folks like us do when the usual assortment of chats fall below our high standards and even higher expectations? We make our own!

The easiest way to open your own chat room is with a *member room* — a chat room that can be created by a member. You can create one from inside another chat room (click **Find a Chat** and then **Start Your Own Chat**) or just click the **People** menu on the toolbar and select **Start Your Own Chat**. Regardless of the path you take, click **Member Chat** in the window that pops up. Now choose a category for your chat (double-click it) and type in a name for your chat room. Choose a name that is clear and concise — one that will tempt others to join you. Click **Go Chat** and your new chat room opens for you. At the same time, your chat room is automatically listed in the member room chat category you selected — other members will also enter if your topic interests them. Greet them and get the ball rolling! You can invite friends to your chat personally rather than have them wade through all those lists. Just drag the heart on the chat room window to an e-mail or Instant Message (see "Using Favorite Places" in Chapter 3).

If you'd prefer that your chat be "by invitation only," select **Start Your Own Chat** and this time click **Private Chat**. Give your chat a distinct name that isn't likely to be in use by others — you neither want to disrupt their private conversation or have them interrupt yours. Once created, a private chat is just that — private. It is not listed anywhere. However, anyone who knows the name can join you by creating a private chat by the same name. Invite them with a favorite place heart, or use the Buddy Chat feature (described later in this chapter).

And if you are interested in hosting one of the *featured chats* in the People Connection, apply to become a community leader (see the last tip in this chapter).

Meeting People Online   :) :)   Win & Mac

... or how to get their attention

I am shy. Naturally, at first I was apprehensive to enter a chat room with 22 strangers. In time I overcame this fear and was pleasantly surprised to discover how many new people I was able to meet online — with just a bit of effort. Anyone can meet people and make friends, regardless of their prevailing interests, orientations, or persuasions. Use these tips to catch their attention in subtle and obvious ways. Someone is waiting to meet you!

My tips for standing out in the crowd:

1. **Choose an intriguing screen name.** Your screen name is the first glimpse others have of your personality. Create one that captures the true you. Unless you're an accountant, a name with lots of numbers probably isn't it. Good screen names draw people to you. For instructions, see "Creating More Screen Names" in Chapter 2.

2. **Create an interesting profile.** Entice them with unique details about yourself or a tantalizing glimpse of your personality. Include that unusual hobby, bizarre interest, or pithy saying. Can't think of anything? Be forthright and genuine, generously sharing part of yourself. If someone is looking at your profile, they want information. If you are uncomfortable including personal information like a last name or hometown, leave it out but offer another "byte" to satisfy their hunger to know more about you, like your World Wide Web page address.

3. **Say hello.** When people enter a chat room, greet them by name. Newcomers to chats often feel a bit overwhelmed and may be tempted to sit back and observe the room for a bit. Remember how you felt? Make them feel welcome and at ease by initiating a conversation and including them in the discussion. You may also Instant Message them once the "public" introductions have been made — let them know that if they need help learning about the chat, you are more than happy to help.

4. **Start your own chat.** Catch their attention with a special topic member chat room in the People Connection. Not only does this draw people to you, but it attracts those with similar interests. See the previous tip for help and instructions.

5. **Send them e-mail.** Did you meet someone in a chat recently that you'd like to know better? Send them e-mail to let them know you enjoyed meeting them and you hope to see them online again soon. Many people love this special attention and appreciate the fact that you remembered them. Chapter 4 is full of e-mail tips!

6. **Wish them well.** Is someone's birthday coming up soon? Send them an online greeting card — you'll find them on America Online at keyword: POST-CARDS or on the World Wide Web at http://www.bluemountain.com/index.html. Or send a virtual ice cream sundae at http://www.icecreamusa.com/cgi-bin/icusa/vrsundae/vrsundae.

7. **Create a Web page.** All members can create a Web page courtesy of America Online and have it accessible to other members. You can include much more information about yourself or your interests in a Web page, attracting other like-minded members. See "Creating Your Own Web Page" in Chapter 7.

Contributed by Maria Therese Lehan
(screen name: Sioux Mac)

Meet Maria

Maria Lehan (screen name: *Sioux Mac*) is one of the warmest and most caring people I know. And she has to be to succeed as a day care teacher, as she has been for almost ten years now in Massachusetts. She joined America Online over four years ago and loves to help fellow members and community leaders. Maria also has a great love of writing (she's still working on that novel) and photography. To learn more about her, visit her World Wide Web home page at `http://members.aol.com/sioux-mac/SiouxMacIndex.html`. Thank you, Maria!

| Chatting Fluently | :) | Win & Mac |

. . . or how to make chatter matter

Chat is a language unto itself. And like any new language, it takes some practice to become fluent. So the next time you find yourself with something to say in a busy chat room, remember these tips and you'll fit right in:

1. **Understand AOL's community standards**. Be sure to read America Online's Terms Of Service at keyword: TOS These are the general rules we are expected to follow while online. Note that some areas enforce the rules more strictly than others — find those that reflect your own level of comfort.

2. **Keep up**. Some rooms are fast. That is, the text scrolls by at speed-reader pace, and you wonder how anyone keeps up! Here's a tip: pay special attention to the last few lines of text and target your responses to them. As you get more comfortable, you can "scroll up" to catch what you missed.

3. **Use names**. When addressing a specific member in the room, do just that! Use their screen name in your answer, comment, or question. This helps them see it in a busy room, and helps the flow of the room as others can figure what the heck you meant

when you said "Jennifer, I had to take off my clothes." (I'll let you ponder that one.)

4. **Get personal**. When you speak to someone in a chat room and use their name as suggested here, remove any "nonpersonal" elements of the screen name. This may be numbers (like *JaneDoe47*) or a *uniform* (like *HOST Hiva*). A question for *JaneDoe47* is addressed to *JaneDoe* or simply *Jane*, and a reply to *HOST Hiva* is addressed to *Hiva*.

5. **Be continuous**. If you need more than a single line in a chat room, add an ellipsis (. . .) at the end of a line so others know you are not finished "talking."

6. **Speak up**. Don't be afraid to speak to anyone in the room, including the host. That's why they are here.

7. **Learn the lingo.** Read the appendixes in the back of the book for a crash course in emoticons, short-hands, and phrases.

Playing Sounds in Chat Rooms :) :) | **Win & Mac**

. . . or how to pump up the volume

An America Online chat room can be quieter than a library. Everyone is talking, but you can't hear a word! It rarely stays that quiet when you know how to "play" sounds in the chat room. (The sounds don't actually play in the room — you're telling the AOL software to play sounds that already exist on the other folks' computers.)

If you're in a chat room and you hear the familiar "Welcome!" somebody in the room typed *{S Welcome*. That command told the AOL software to play that sound, which resides on your hard disk. It's simple — *{S* (with a space after it) plus the filename of the sound. Windows users, you can leave off the `.wav` — it will still play!

There are a few catches:

- To hear the sounds, your computer and AOL software must be set up for sound. All Macs are equipped to play sounds, but that is not true of all PCs.

- The only sounds you'll hear are files that already exist on your hard disk in the main AOL directory (on Windows) or in your system (on the Mac).

- This only works with Windows WAV files and Mac SND files. There are thousands of these available online, however, as well as converters if needed.

Sound advice:

- If you can hear "Welcome!" when you sign on, then you know you can hear chat sounds. Keep in mind that you may also need to adjust your chat preferences to **Enable chat room sounds**.

- You don't need a sound card to play sounds for others. You can still "send" a sound to a room, and even though you may not hear it, anyone else with that sound on their computer will hear it.

- When a sound is "playing," all other activity in the chat room may come to a halt (for those who can hear the sound). It's inconsiderate to play lots of sounds (especially long ones) in the room.

Contributed by Dave Marx (screen name: Dave Marx)

| Sending Special Characters | :) :) | Win & Mac |

. . . or how to speak a new language

Have you ever entered a chat room and seen folks typing funny and strange characters? They may have looked like Õ¿Õ or ¥¿¥ , or even been much more elaborate and taken up several lines. You may also have noticed them in an Instant Message or e-mail signature. These are known as extended characters and can be used to create more intricate smileys, emoticons, and ASCII Art (see Appendix A for more details). They are also used in foreign-language chat. You can get creative with them and make designs and signatures, or simply use them to communicate more effectively.

Members using the Windows AOL software can make these characters by holding down the **Alt** key on your keyboard while typing a three- or four-digit number using the numeric keypad (usually located on the far right).

The following table offers a list of special characters to get you started. Experiment and see if you can find some more!

135 ç	146 Æ	147 â	153 Ö
156 £	157 ¥	159 ƒ	162
166 ª	167 º	168 ¿	181 |
0131 ƒ	0134 †	0135 ‡	0137 ‰
0153 ™	0162 ¢	0163 £	0167 §
0169 ©	0171 «	0172 ¬	0174 ®
0176 °	0177 ±	0182 ¶	0191 ¿
0199 Ç	0208 Ð	0210 Ò	0212 Ô
0213 Õ	0216 Ø	0223 ß	0231 ç

Members using Mac AOL software version 4.0 can use these special characters too. Most of them are available if you hold down the **Option** key (or **Option+Shift**) while typing another character. For example, ç is created with **Option+C**, and Ô is created with **Option+Shift+J**. Use your **Key Caps** options under the **Apple** menu to see what characters are available.

Not all members can see all your special characters; those using older versions of Mac AOL software often do not receive them, and they cannot send them at all. Use them sparingly, when a normal character is incorrect or just doesn't fit your design, as well.

Ignoring Chatters :):):) | Win & Mac

... or how to make a pest disappear

Have you ever wished you had the power to make obnoxious people disappear, leaving nothing but a mushroom cloud where they had been standing? America Online chat rooms are full of friends and fun, but let's face it: every party has its crashers. And while there may be nothing you can do to escape that pest sitting next to you on an airplane or waiting in line at the supermarket, you can "ignore" people in America Online chat rooms with the click of a button. Isn't technology grand?

Ignoring another member's dialogue in a chat room is simple. Double-click the offender's screen name in the People List in your chat room and then click the **Ignore** check box. From that point on, that member's chat does not appear on your screen; it is as if you had indeed vaporized them. And they won't even know it! An ignore lasts until you or the member leave that particular chat room. If you decide you would like to start viewing the member's text again, just reverse the procedure. Other check boxes available when you double-click their screen name are **Send Message** and **Get Profile**, should you want to get to try to reach them rather than ignore them.

Etiquette tips:

- There is no need to announce that you are ignoring someone. This only serves to aggravate them further. Just click **Ignore** and continue with your conversation. Don't let them get under your skin.

- Windows members should check out Gritty Snert, a program that gives you much more control over who you ignore and how long you ignore him (for more details, see "Chatting with Gritty Snert" in Chapter 8).

- If a member is offending or harassing you, or if they send line after line of text into the room so that your conversations roll out of sight (this is called "scrolling"), ignore the member immediately, advise others to do the same, and use keyword: NOTIFY AOL to report the offender.

Contributed by Adrienne Quinn (screen name: AAQuinn)

Using Buddy Lists :):):) | Win & Mac

... or how to read buddy tags

Once you use Buddy Lists, you won't know how you survived without it! Buddy Lists tell you who's online, who just signed on (or off), and makes it even easier to send an Instant Message. Invite all your buddies to a private room, keyword, or favorite place. Control your privacy by withholding your name from other Buddy Lists, and if your friends use AOL Instant Messenger, your Buddy List will show you if they're online anywhere in the Internet (yes, you can Instant Message them there, too!) It's the online socializing tool of the decade.

First, set up your Buddy List by going to keyword: BUDDY. You'll find excellent help instructions here for your reference. The default setup displays your Buddy List when you sign on, opening an unobtrusive window in the upper right of your screen (Figure 5.2). Everyone on your list(s) who is online will be shown. New arrivals will have an asterisk (*)beside his or her name, and if they've just signed off, their name will be in parentheses.

Click a buddy's name, click **Locate,** and you are told where your friend is. Double-click a name to start an Instant Message. And double-click the title of a list to open or hide the list (they always start out opened).

Setup is where you add or subtract names from your lists, or create new lists. You'll also find **Buddy List Preferences** to control whether your Buddy List appears automatically when you sign on, play sounds when buddies come and go, and control who may or may not include you in their Buddy List.

Buddy Chat is a powerful feature that lets you set up a private room or "send" your friends to any keyword, Internet address, or favorite place. Buddy Chat is polite — it sends an invitation, which the recipients can accept or ignore. To use, click one of your lists, and click **Buddy Chat**. A Buddy Chat window opens, listing everyone on that list who is currently online. Add to or delete names from the list. Add a message to be included in the invitation. Select **Private Chat Room** or **Keyword/Favorite Place**. If you don't like the private room name America

Online creates for you, change it. To share cool stuff you've found, type in a keyword or an Internet URL address, or drag and drop a favorite place heart. When you click **Send**, the invitation goes out, and all recipients have the choice to accept or reject it — they can also reply to your invitation with an Instant Message.

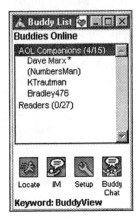

Figure 5.2 Your Buddy List lets you keep tabs on all your friends (view from Windows).

Buddy tips:

1. You can set up America Online to play sounds when buddies arrive and depart, but if you have a lot of buddies it can get pretty annoying. It's your call!

2. Even if you don't use Buddy Lists to find your friends, you can use it for protection. Click **Buddy Setup** then **Privacy Preferences** to block others. See the tip "Retaining Your Privacy" coming up.

3. If you block someone from your Buddy List, they can't use **Locate a Member Online** to find you.

4. If you hold regular online chats or meetings, put everyone in that group on a separate list, then use the **Buddy Chat** feature to gather them together.

5. A person can be on more than one list. This works well if you use **Buddy Chat** on a regular basis.

6. Don't have too many buddies. There is a limit to the total number of buddies on an account. The current limit is around 50 names per screen name (or about 200 names per account).

7. Look for the **Save** buttons in **Buddy Setup**. If you don't click **Save**, your changes are lost.

8. Go to a private room without entering the People Connection: click **Buddy Chat** and invite yourself.

Contributed by Dave Marx (screen name: Dave Marx)

| Locating Members | :) :) :) | Win & Mac |

. . . or how to see through walls

Are my friends online? How can I tell? Buddy Lists are a great way to see who's online and who's offline at a glance (see the previous tip), but there are other ways too. Here's the deal:

1. **Locate a member online**. Click the **People** button on your toolbar and select **Locate** — or press the **L** key while holding down either the **Ctrl** key (on Windows) or the **Command** key (on the Mac). Now type your friend's screen name in the window, and click the **OK** button. A window pops up telling you whether or not your friend is online. If they are online, you have the option of sending an Instant Message or going to the chat room.

2. **See if they are available.** Click the **People** button on the toolbar and select **Send an Instant Message** — or just press the **I** key while holding down either the **Control** key (on Windows) or the **Command** key (on the Mac). Now enter their screen name and click the **Available?** button at the bottom of the window. America Online tells you if your friend is online and able to accept Instant Messages.

3. **Use the Member Directory**. Use keyword: MEMBERS, enter search criteria (let's say "Macintosh" and "Redmond, WA" for Mac users living near

Microsoft headquarters), and click the **Return only members online** button. Bingo!

4. **Request a return receipt.** In a bind, you can send them e-mail and request a return receipt. You'll get e-mail as soon as they've read it (see the tip "Getting Return Receipts" in Chapter 4). This tends to work when all other methods fail, it's also clear the person *wants* to be left alone. Use it respectfully.

It's not always enough to know your friend is online, but remember that she may think it inconsiderate of you to interrupt her in a private room. Locate her first to check.

Contributed by Dave Marx (screen name: Dave Marx)

Retaining Your Privacy   :) :)   Win & Mac

. . . or how to wear sunglasses at night

Let's face it: like Greta Garbo, sometimes you just "vant to be alone." There's certainly nothing wrong with that, and as human beings we all need and deserve our privacy no matter where we are or what we are doing — online or off. But maybe you're like me and have a difficult time telling well-meaning friends and co-workers that you're a little too busy to chitchat at that very moment. Luckily, AOL includes some built-in features that let me have that space without hurting anyone's feelings or bruising egos.

The first thing you can do is to turn off your Instant Messages. See the tip "Blocking Instant Messages" later in this chapter. Some AOL add-on programs also offer an automatic Instant Message answering machine — it lets folks know that you are online, but that you can't talk right now. (Read more on AOL Add-Ons in Chapter 8.)

Sometimes blocking Instant Messages doesn't do the trick. Your chatty Aunt Edna may see you online and try to send you an Instant Message, only to discover she cannot because you blocked them. She may start sending you e-mail after e-mail wondering why on earth you don't want to chat with her. If this sounds familiar, use the **Privacy Preferences** in your Buddy List. Just bring up your Buddy List (use keyword: BV if it isn't already on your screen), click the **Setup** button, and click the **Privacy Preferences** button.

To block yourself entirely from both Buddy Lists, Instant Messages, and prying eyes trying to locate you, click **Block all AOL members and AOL Instant Messenger users**, plus **Buddy List and Instant Messages**. These two settings make you virtually invisible to others online, so long as you don't go into a chat room or attract attention to yourself. If you aren't quite so reclusive, try adding screen names of friends and family you *do* want to be able to locate you while still keeping out others you do not. Be sure to click **Save** when done to keep your changes.

Unlike Greta Garbo, privacy is much easier to obtain when you're online. Don't be shy to take time alone.

Contributed by Kate Tipul (screen name: KMTipul)

| Sending Instant Messages   :) :) :) | Win & Mac |

. . . or how to pass notes

You can chat one-on-one in total privacy using Instant Messages! Click the **People** icon on the toolbar, select **Instant Message** from the drop-down menu, type in a screen name and a message, and click **Send** (or press the **Enter** key). That's all it takes to get the conversation rolling. Of course, it helps to know if your friend is online. Use the **Available?** button at the bottom of the Instant Message (IM) window, or use your Buddy Lists.

Instant tips:

1. Use this shortcut to start an Instant Message: press **Ctrl+i** (Windows) or **Command+i** (Mac).
2. Prevent your children from using or receiving Instant Messages by using Parental Controls (see "Using Parental Controls" in Chapter 2).
3. Sending an Instant Message can be an intrusion. Be sensitive to your friend's needs.
4. When you have many active Instant Messages, keeping track of incoming text can be tough. If you have sound, you'll hear a "ding," but who rang? The title

bar of each Instant Message window has the hint: If new text has arrived, there will be a bracket ">" next to **Instant Message From: (screen name)** at the top of the window, like this: **>Instant Message from: Dave Marx.** Arrange the windows onscreen so that all the title bars are visible.

5. You can use Instant Messages while you're in a chat room. Nobody in the room will hear your whispers.

6. Harassed? Turn off Instant Messages. See the tip "Blocking Instant Messages" later in this chapter.

7. You can have many Instant Messages open simultaneously, if you can manage all the conversations.

8. No America Online employee or staffer will ask for your password or credit card information online, especially in an Instant Message. If someone does, report them at keyword: NOTIFY AOL. *Never* reveal your password.

Contributed by Dave Marx (screen name: Dave Marx)

Using Instant Images   :) :) | Win only

. . . or how to be in pictures

Who ever thought you'd have to get dressed up to use your computer? The latest feature promised by America Online is called *Instant Images*: live video or images transmitted over Instant Messages. If it isn't available by the time you read this, keep your eyes open for it.

Instant Images are started by clicking the similarly named icon in an existing Instant Message window. Once done, your Instant Message window expands to include two additional views: the top image is a preview of you, and the bottom image is from your friend.

If someone sends you an Instant Image, you must accept it before you see it. Also, the only way anyone sees the image in your preview window is if you specifically click the **Send Instant Image** button — that way you can share images with friends, but stick to text with people you don't know so well. Nobody's going to see you if you don't want to be seen! You can block Instant Images for your children with AOL's Parental Controls, and there is a **Notify AOL** button on the window to use if anyone sends you an offensive image. For a list of options you can set, just right-click with your mouse over either of the two image windows.

Installing a video camera isn't that complicated anymore either. Sure, you can opt for the fancy video capture board and TV camera, but these days it's easiest (and cheapest!) to buy a specialized computer video camera such as the QuickCam, which you just plug into your printer port, and it's ready to go. The AOL Store has several selections like this for around $100.

It's not quite like in the sci-fi movies yet — you only get a few frames per second of rather jerky motion, there's a bit of a time lag, and the video window is just a few square inches. But it's definitely a step in the right direction! So men, comb your hair, and ladies, get rid of those curlers: the days of going to your computer in a bathrobe are over! Let's sign on for a whole new way to communicate online — face to face!

Contributed by Bradley Zimmer
(screen name: Bradley476)

Blocking Instant Messages   :) :)   Win & Mac

. . . or how to hang up the do not disturb sign

Instant Messages are a wonderful tool; they allow you to communicate instantly and in real time with multiple people. Just like an open front door, they provide friends and acquaintances a way to pop in and chat with you. Yet an open-door policy can be too much of a good thing. If you find yourself wishing you had a "do not disturb" sign to hang up on your computer, you can do the virtual equivalent by turning off your Instant Messages.

The simplest way to block Instant Messages is to bring up a new Instant Message window (press **Ctrl+i** on Windows, or **Command+i** on a Mac) and type the following into the top box:

$IM_off

Now just click the **Available?** button in the lower right-hand corner of the window. If all went well, a small box pops up to let you know that you are now ignoring

Instant Messages. Anyone who attempts to send you an Instant Message is told that you are "unable to receive Instant Messages." Keep in mind that you are blocking all incoming Instant Messages. If you want to block specific individuals, type their screen name after *$IM_off* like this:

$IM_off BugU4ever2

Your Instant Messages remain blocked until you re-enable them or sign off. When you are ready to re-enable your Instant Messages, simply open another Instant Message window, type **$IM_on**, and click the **Available?** button again. Confirmation that your Instant Messages are back on pops up. Note that *$IM_on* turns all Instant Messages back on; include the screen name if you want to turn them back on for an individual. You can also use your Privacy Preferences to selectively block or allow Instant Messages. See the tip "Retaining Your Privacy."

Contributed by Adrienne Quinn (screen name: AAQuinn)

Minimizing Instant Messages :) :) | Win & Mac

... or how to clear your screen

Instant Messages can plaster over your computer screen. Get control of the clutter and minimize your problem!

Did I say, "minimize"? That's exactly what I mean! Although Windows and Mac users have slightly different solutions, where there's a mouse, there's a way! Windows users can "minimize" any window down to a small box (Windows 95) or icon (Windows 3.1) on the screen, which reduces clutter immensely. How? Click the minus sign (or down arrow) in the upper right-hand corner of the Instant Message window. You'll find the minimized window at the bottom of the screen (possibly buried beneath other windows.) Mac users can "shade" their windows, which leaves only the title bar of the window visible — just double- or triple-click the title bar. The title bar stays put (although you can drag it around).

"How," you may ask, "will I know when my friends have replied to my last comment?" When you receive new text in an IM, the title will start with a bracket, like this: **>Instant Message From: Jennifer**. Double-click the minimized window (or shaded title bar) to restore it to its full size, and reply. Once you respond, the bracket disappears until the next reply. Another hint: If you have sound, each time you receive new text in an IM you'll hear a "ding" sound.

Minimal tips:

1. Arrange the open windows on your screen so the minimized windows (icons or title bars) aren't hidden.

2. Find and straighten out your icons. On Windows, select **Arrange Icons** from the Window menu at the top of your screen.

3. On the Mac, be careful not to stack your shaded title bars like bricks. If you restore the top-most window, you won't see that you received replies to your other Instant Messages.

Contributed by Dave Marx (screen name: Dave Marx)

Using Auditoriums   :) :) :) | Win & Mac

. . . or how to get box seats

Lights! Camera! Action! Enter America Online's virtual auditoriums. Online auditoriums are pretty much like you'd expect. They hold lots of people, everyone sits in rows (and the front rows always fill up first), there is a stage, and you often get to see celebrities and experts. Auditoriums are most commonly used to hold question-and-answer sessions with famous personalities, but are also used for game shows, auctions, and even some training. You'll find doors to auditoriums all around AOL service, but the real "theater district" is at keyword: AOL LIVE, along with schedules, transcripts, and help on using auditoriums.

Here are some tips to help you make the most of auditoriums:

1. **Find your place**. When you enter an auditorium, you are placed in the next available row. If this doesn't suit your needs, feel free to row-hop! It

won't disturb anyone, and you will continue to get an unobstructed view of what happens on-stage.

2. **Create a peanut gallery**. If you and your friends would like to sit together, feel free to create your own row with a high number. There will be room for just about everyone, and it is unlikely anyone will be placed in your row automatically.

3. **Get involved**. Send a question or comment to the stage, and watch to see if it gets answered. Just use the **Interact** button. Do keep in mind that not all questions or comments can be taken.

4. **Find a friend**. If you're in the auditorium, you can use the **Find Member** button to give you the exact row location of someone you know. And consider using your Buddy Lists — if you see one of your friends online but not in the auditorium, ask them to join you in your row!

| Finding Chat Schedules | :) :) :) | Win & Mac |

. . . or how to time your talks

Are you looking for more than small talk? The People Connection is a great place to go for virtual coffee and a quick chat, but generally has no structure in its rooms. That's where forums come in: these online areas have conference rooms for more in-depth discussion about a specific topic with an expert host to lead the talk. Most forums have conference schedules listing the weekly times and topics of every organized chat held in its conference rooms, usually located on the front screen of the forum or somewhere along the path to the room. If you can't find it, just ask one of the hosts in the area!

Another great place to turn for event schedules is AOL Live where the big shots appear on America Online. Their auditoriums seat tens of thousands of members each, and daily events are featured on the main screen at keyword: AOL LIVE. **Coming Attractions**, also featured on the AOL Live screen, offers schedules of upcoming chats with the stars. See the previous tip for more details!

Finally, People Connection has put together a schedule of various hosted chats from all over the service, ranging from "Fiber and Needle Art" to "Home-Based Web Design." You can browse the **Featured Chats Schedule** or **Search Featured Chats**, both available under the **Find a Chat** button at keyword: CHAT.

Take some time to plan which chats, conferences, and events you want to attend this week or even later this month — just don't forget the popcorn!

Contributed by Bradley Zimmer
(screen name: Bradley476)

Recognizing Hosts	:) :)	Win & Mac

. . . or how to spot a suit

In many ways, America Online and hospitals are alike. Besides helping people, both have volunteers. America Online's volunteers are called *community leaders*.

Community leaders perform a variety of functions depending on their expertise and desires. They virus test those hundreds of thousands of files available online, monitor message boards, design those beautiful and ever-changing windows, host chats and conferences, and provide community assistance. These last two — hosting and helping — are the most visible of all the community leader roles. If you spend a lot of time in chat and conference rooms, you're bound to meet them. Allow me to offer a gentle introduction here.

Hosts come in all varieties. You may recognize some forum's hosts by their screen name, such as *DigC Brian* (a Digital City host), or *Host Angel* (a People Connection host). You may also see Guides and Rangers in the People Connection, also recognizable by the **Guide** or **Rnger** in their screen names. There are also volunteers in Member Services (spotted by the **MHMS** or **Upgrde** in their names). We call these screen names *uniforms*, and they are one of the best ways to spot a helpful volunteer.

Hosts exist to improve your America Online experience. They can help make your adventures and your children's adventures on AOL service safe and pleasant. They provide a plethora of information and can direct you to most anything you're looking for. Sometimes they are nothing more than a friendly face in a chat room, welcoming newcomers and making the room pleasant.

Now, a word to the wise: You've heard the horror stories of police impersonations, no doubt. And while community leaders should not be considered America Online's police force, AOL service is not immune to real-world issues. There are times when community leaders are impersonated in the hopes that you'll fall for some trick. As you've seen and heard before, no America Online staffer will ever request your password or billing information. Should someone request these of you, report them immediately at keyword: NOTIFY AOL.

Becoming a Community Leader   :) | ‹ | Win & Mac

. . . or how to give something back

People volunteer for different reasons — some want to give back to their community, others want to help plan their community's future, and even others just want to have fun by being a part of a volunteer group. The same is true for online volunteering!

Certainly one of the most rewarding activities an America Online member can participate in, volunteering online is a source of fun, challenge, and excitement. Members who volunteer online are called *community leaders*. You've probably even met a few yourself — guides, hosts, message board leaders, and many other forum personnel are generally online volunteers.

There are many different positions one could volunteer for online, but no matter what it is, the key is to find something you would find interesting and exciting to do. Just a few possibilities include hosting a chat on your favorite topic, leading a message board whose subject you particularly like, assisting other members with technical problems, or helping verify that uploaded library files work as they're supposed to. There is an application process for potential community leaders, and each area has different requirements for volunteering. All areas do provide training in order to fully prepare their volunteers for the position they'll be assuming.

The America Online Community Leader Program (keyword: LEADERS) lists online areas currently looking for additional volunteers. If you want to be a part of your favorite online area, give back to your community, and have a great time while doing it, then volunteering online is for you!

Contributed by Bradley Zimmer
(screen name: Bradley476)

Companion Confessions

Having revealed a secret at the start of this chapter, I feel compelled to throw open my closet and let out all the skeletons. Thankfully, this is a book and not a chat room, or I probably would *really* get carried away. Perhaps you'll just have to catch me online in a chat someday . . . if you can. If you don't, here are some confessions that won't embarrass me too badly:

1. **Meeting people.** I don't think I'll ever grow tired of meeting new people. Everyone has something to teach me, no matter how young or inexperienced, and I do love to find out their secrets, too. I've met plenty of people in chat rooms, of course, but also in e-mail (often sent to me accidentally), Instant Messages, and message boards. I met my best friend George in an America Online Help Room, and I met my good friend Tracy when she joined an organization (The VirtuaLeader Academy) I founded. It is hard to look in the wrong places online.

2. **Bypassing the Lobby.** I used to be a regular Lobby denizen, never venturing out to the big, bad world. These days I'd just as soon bypass it, however, so it is rare to find me in a Lobby. I generally go straight to a private room by using the **Buddy Chat** feature and inviting myself. Friends are also kind enough to send me links to rooms they want me to visit.

3. **Using Buddy Lists.** Rather than say I have a lot of buddies, let me just say my lists are long. I don't know where I'd be without them today. Besides the obvious advantages of knowing who is and who isn't online, I can watch *when* they come online and then give them a few minutes before sending a message.

4. **Sending Instant Messages.** Most of my online conversations take place in Instant Messages, rather than chat rooms. I've become skilled at using keyboard shortcuts and organizing them. When I don't have too many going on at once, I often open up the window larger so I can see more of the conversation. I do turn them off when absolutely necessary.

CHAPTER 6

SEARCHING FOR SOFTWARE

The race to get online isn't so different from the infamous Gold Rush of 1849. Like San Francisco in those wild days, America Online is being flooded with prospectors seeking fortune and fun. Though prosperity is the result for many, America Online has also had its share of pioneer problems: not enough "housing" or "protection" for citizens, gangs of "hoodlums" roaming the city, too few "steamships" to transport people, and insufficient "stages" to deliver mail. In time, America Online will be well settled and no doubt become a thriving megametropolis, serving the needs of millions effortlessly. But now? If you can brave this new frontier, you're still in time for the bonanza: there's gold out here!

Thankfully, discovering gold on America Online doesn't require a trek across country, or even across town. It is available everywhere online, with just a little digging and a little patience. This "gold" can enhance your computer, enrich your mind, and even pad your pockets. I'm talking about software, of course. And when it comes to software treasure, America Online is a virtual Eldorado. You'll find everything from free utilities that make your computer run better, to free trials of the latest and greatest commercial programs. It is all here, just waiting for you, at no additional cost. And best of all, it isn't running out anytime soon.

So grab that modem and clear some room on your hard drive — we're going prospecting!

. . . or how to get the goods

Today, software is everywhere! It comes on CD-ROMs and diskettes (for you young folks, those are the little 3.5-inch squares of plastic), which are distributed in magazines, consumer electronic stores, and mail order supply houses. But better than that, America Online has libraries of software you can download right away at no additional cost. Everything from games to utilities, applications to graphics are available. The trick is finding it, but even that is not difficult these days.

One of the easiest ways to find files is by going to keyword: FILE SEARCH. Here you can search all of the more than 100,000 files in the AOL Computing Channel's libraries. The search is quite powerful, allowing you to narrow it down by selecting categories and using wildcards and BOOLEAN expressions (see the next tip, "Searching with Skill," for more details). Your computer type is determined as you enter, and only the files intended for your computer are displayed (though there is a button to go to the other platform's search window).

Still haven't found the file you're looking for? America Online's file searches currently only search the libraries associated with the AOL Computing Channel forums and a few computer magazines. There are thousands of other libraries on the service. I estimate there are over 25,000 individual file libraries online. Now, not all of them are full — some wait for members like you to contribute new files — but there are still many that are not included at keyword: FILE SEARCH. You'll find these libraries scattered among your favorite forums. So if you're looking for Genealogy software, don't forget to try keyword: GENEALOGY. Perhaps you're looking for crossword puzzles? Try keyword: CROSSWORDS to take you to the New York Time's Crosswords Puzzles page. There are as many topical libraries as there are forums on America Online, just look around. To find these hidden gems, seek out your favorite forum and search for the libraries. If you get stuck, look for the **Index** or **Table of Contents**, often near the bottom of the window. Or try the forum's **Search** feature if available.

Of the libraries that exist outside of America Online, you can download from many of them as well. These libraries are often reached via keyword: FTP or you may find them at your favorite World Wide Web site (see "Downloading Files Through FTP" in Chapter 7 for more information on FTP). When downloading files outside of America Online libraries, always be cautious of viruses. You can be pretty sure that the files you download at a reputable company's Web or FTP site are clean (though it's a good idea to check them anyway). I would, however, be worried about downloading the latest AOL software "utility" from any site that sports an "aol-sucks" address. If you're interested in finding shareware on the Web, try these sites: `http://www.shareware.com` or `http://www.windows95.com`. America Online also has mirror sites of the Internet's most popular shareware FTP sites. (A mirror site is one that is an exact copy of the original FTP site, created to alleviate a heavy load on the original site.) Accessing one of these mirrors is often easier than accessing the actual FTP site, and it's a more responsible thing to do, too. Many FTP sites have limits on the number of anonymous users that can be signed on to them.

When you find a treasure trove of a library, click the Favorite Place heart in the upper right-hand corner. Now you can zip back to them in the future without wading through screens first. Don't rely solely upon favorite places, however; new libraries are appearing everyday!

More file tips:

1. Not all files reside in libraries; some may be linked to articles or collections of information. Leave no stone unturned in your quest.

2. Beware of accepting files from strangers. It is more likely that the program is a Trojan Horse than the latest and greatest word processor.

3. Read the rest of the tips in this chapter, plus "Understanding Trojans" and "Attaching Files to Mail" in Chapter 4 and "Downloading Files Through FTP" in Chapter 7.

Contributed by George Louie
(screen name: NumbersMan)

... or how to pan for gold

Searching for files, much like prospecting for gold, is an art. Once you've picked a location, it all hinges on your technique. Opening a file library and browsing down the list is about as effective as standing in a stream with your hand in the water, hoping some gold comes your way. Sure, you'll probably find something, but it's going to take you a while. Thankfully, searching for files is significantly less grueling than panning for gold. The only tools you need are America Online and a few tips.

First, you'll find your virtual stream at keyword: FILE SEARCH (see Figure 6.1. Note that the search window is named Software Search in Windows, but the keyword is FILE SEARCH in both Mac and Windows.)

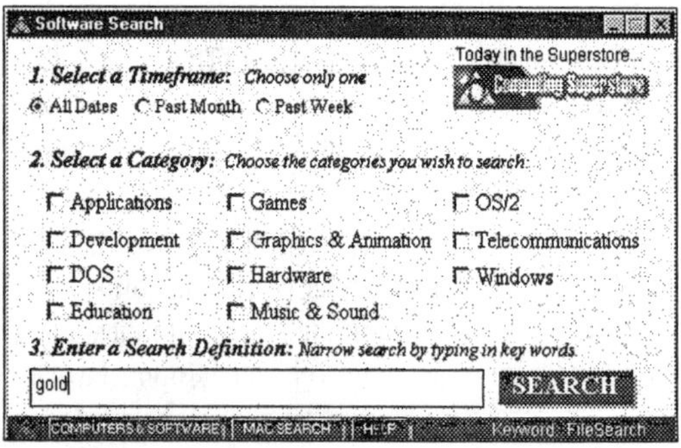

Figure 6.1 Striking gold on a search for software (view from Windows).

Here you can search for files from a huge database of files. Like most intelligent databases, you can do more than simply enter words to search on: you can specify timeframes and categories, too. There are three timeframes: files from **All Dates**, only the **Past Month** (within 30 days or so), only the **Past Week** (within 7 days). Categories differ based on whether you're using a Mac or a PC, but all correspond to the major forums within the AOL Computing Channel.

Want to really find things? Use *searchwords*. These special words help you narrow your search and avoid the "fool's gold" files that appear in a wider search. For example, let's say I want to search on the word *gold*. I can use the searchwords *AND*, *OR*, and *NOT* in my search criteria to streamline my file search. If I enter *gold AND rush*, I find all files related to the Gold Rush. I can also use the searchword *OR* to broaden my search. Searching on *gold OR money* reaps files related either to gold or money (and not necessarily both). Finally, I can use the searchword *NOT* to further narrow my search. For example, entering **gold NOT money** finds files on gold that are unrelated to money. I can mix and match searchwords to tailor my finds. For a reliable search, all searchwords separated by the searchword *OR* should be enclosed in parenthesis: for example (*gold OR money*) *NOT rush* find all files related to gold and money but not gold or money rushes.

If you're not sure how to spell a word in your search, try using the wildcard symbol: *. Let's say I want to find more information on prospecting but I can't remember if it is spelled with an *e* or an *a*. A search on *prosp** gives me all sorts of things like *PROSPELL* (a spell checker) or *Prospero* (a classic Roman font), in addition to information on prospecting. Because I know my word ends in a *g*, I can search on *prosp*g* too. I can also use the wildcard at the beginning of the word (such as **old*). Use this technique with caution as it tends to find many more files than wanted (like files with *bold* in the title*).

Search tips:

1. **America Online's search engine will return thousands of hits if your search is too broad, but like other AOL searches, it'll only display 250 of those matches. If this happens, narrow your search!**

2. **If a search is too complicated, America Online will let you know. Using searchwords can take some trial and error, and a bit of patience, but it is rewarding.**

3. Be careful: Many times the same file is found in multiple libraries, but not every library may have the latest version. Carefully check the version information and the read the file descriptions (see the tip "Reading File Descriptions" later in this chapter) to make sure you're downloading the file you need.

| Listing Library Files | :) :) :) | Win & Mac |

. . . or how to get Dave's Top Ten list

Have you ever trudged through the stacks at your local public library, wishing that somehow the shelves could be instantly reorganized for your convenience? Perhaps the classic Dewey Decimal System works for you, but what if all the newest acquisitions could be found in one place? As an author, wouldn't you love to know how popular your work is? Such awesome power awaits you in America Online's download libraries.

Lurking at the bottom of every download library window is a **Sort Order** drop-down menu. Click the down arrow to select your sort order options: **Upload Date**, **Subject**, **Download Count**, and **Download Date**. How can we use these choices to push the library around?

Upload Date is the default. The newest files contributed to the library are listed at the top, the oldest at the bottom. This is the "So, what's new?" setting. Click the **List More Files** button to display successively older files — some may go back to ancient times (the mid-1990s)!

Subject Order puts the alphabet in charge — if you know the file name or topic, and the librarians have been consistent as they name the files, you should have an easy time finding your goal.

Download Count is the true measure of popularity, both short-term and long. What interests people the most? Click **Download Count** and see the library's Top 10 list. As you continue to click **List More Files** you'll know what fails to tempt the inveterate downloader. How does your upload rate?

Download Date shows you where the action is. Did somebody download it today? Gauge the popularity of the library — a hot library will have many downloaded files for the current date. If the content is appealing, a large proportion of the library sports recent download dates.

The only real inconvenience about **Sort Order** is that every time you change the sort order you'll need to click the **List More Files** button all over again. But isn't that a small price to pay for all that power?

Contributed by Dave Marx (screen name: Dave Marx)

| **Reading File Descriptions**   :) :) :) | **Win & Mac** |

. . . or how to follow the recipe

Have you ever bought one of those so-called ready-to-prepare foods (such as macaroni and cheese) without first checking the ingredient list and reading the cooking instructions? If so, you know what a disaster it can be. You end up trying to substitute CoffeeMate and water for skim milk, or microwaving the whole mess. Ick! It just doesn't work. And the same holds true for files you download online. It pays to read before you download.

Where do you find the "ingredients" for a download? Easy! Every file you can download comes with a "recipe" of sorts — ingredients, directions, and even yields. It is usually right there on the window that has the **Download** buttons. This text — known as the *file description* — is rich with important information. The best tip: read it first and thoroughly. Here are some more descriptive tips:

1. Always check the "Needs" line to ensure that you have everything it takes to use the file. Don't waste your time downloading it if you don't have what it takes.

2. Check the estimated download time before you actually begin. Details on how to locate and use the download time are in the next tip.

3. If you have a question about downloading the file, click the **Ask The Staff** button at the bottom of the window to reach the **Download Info Center**. If your question isn't answered there, click the **Ask**

About This File button in the lower right-hand corner of the **Download Info Center** to send a specific question to the library staff. If you have a question about the file itself, send an e-mail to the author or uploader using the screen name near the top of the file description.

4. Consider saving the file description to your hard drive for later reference. It may be difficult to locate again if you are yet unfamiliar with America Online.

Determining Download Times :) :) :) | ‹ | Win & Mac

... or how to budget your bytes

Gee, how long is this going to take? Did you happen to notice that America Online estimates how long a given file will take to download? Every file description conveniently displays the estimated download time (see Figure 6.2).

Figure 6.2 Checking the download time (view from the Mac).

The time given for a download is based on the size of the file and the speed of your connection to America Online (note the baud rate in parentheses in Figure 6.2). Though this is only an estimate, the quoted time is usually pretty close to the actual download time.

However, as with anything in this online medium, variations are to be expected. If you have a bad connection, everything may move slower than molasses in January. If you're online during the evening prime-time hours, America Online may respond slower than usual as it tries to keep up with demand. And, of course, if you are doing something else online during the download, America Online has more to do and is bound to get a little bogged down. If all that isn't enough, actual download times for two files of the same size sometimes vary, based on the density of the files and their file format.

If you're finding that your actual download times are significantly longer, try saving file downloads for the early morning hours, or for times when you don't need to be exploring America Online or the Internet at the same time. I also heartily recommend the Download Manager for avoiding busy times and automating the entire download process (more details later in this chapter).

Downloading Files   :) :) :) | ¢ | Win & Mac

. . . or how to mine the ore

Files. They live on our hard drives and floppies, and quite a few of them reside on America Online's computers. America Online has files that are used to operate the service; those are the ones we never see. Then there are other files meant to be downloaded by members; these are the files we're going to concern ourselves with.

As an America Online member, you encounter files in four basic areas online: file libraries, file searches, pages, and e-mail. There are other places where you'll find files, like World Wide Web pages and FTP sites, but for now we're going to concentrate on the files you'll see on the America Online service-proper.

It's easy to download files you come across. No matter where you find a file on America Online, it'll almost always have a **Download Now** button. Click that button and the file begins transferring to your computer. Almost as often, the file has a **Download Later** button. Click this button and the file is marked by your AOL software for later download (see the next tip for more details on how this works). Pretty easy, eh? Here are a few things you can do to make downloading even easier:

1. Practice, practice, practice. If you're worried about downloading, or just want a bit more information,

visit keyword: DOWNLOAD 101 for help. There's a practice library there so you can experiment!

2. Keep an eye on your progress. The window that appears on your screen while downloading is a progress thermometer and tells you how long the download should take. Use it as a gauge and check it once in a while.

3. Do something else. You don't have to continuously watch your file download — that's about as exciting as watching paint dry. You can do just about anything else online (except download another file) while the download is in progress.

4. Use the Download Manager (see the next tip).

Contributed by George Louie
(screen name: NumbersMan)

Using the Download Manager   :) :) | ‹ | Win & Mac

. . . or how to distribute the load

Getting files while online is much like shopping. You browse a bit, pick up something here or there, and generally spend too much time. Can you imagine how much worse shopping would be if you had to check out after selecting every item? Fortunately, there's a download shopping cart — the Download Manager. You don't even have to wait to check out, but can have the files delivered at your convenience.

As you find files you like, place them in your "cart" by clicking the **Download Later** button rather than "checking out" right away with the **Download Now** button. The files you've selected are added to your Download Manager, and you can continue exploring the service for even more files to download. When you're finished, open the Download Manager (under the **My Files** button on the toolbar) and download all the files you collected on your shopping spree through America Online. You can also schedule the downloads to take place later, when nobody is using the phone or after prime-time online hours when the traffic is lighter — just FlashSession with Automatic AOL (as described in Chapter 4).

One day you may start your downloads, walk away, and come back to find the 10MB *Warcraft II Demo* download never finished. Do you need to start over? No, the file will show up as partially finished in the Download Manager. Just sign on, if you haven't already, select the file in the Download Manager, and tell America Online to finish downloading it; the file resumes downloading where it left off. Smart! Even if you didn't tell America Online to download the file later, but selected the **Download Now** button, the partially finished file still appears in the Download Manager.

One caveat: If you're signed on as a Guest, you won't be able to finish interrupted downloads or use the **Download Later** button. You must sign off, select the screen name that originally marked them for download on your **Sign On** screen and sign on again.

Contributed by George Louie
(screen name: NumbersMan)

Preventing Viruses :) :) ¢ Win & Mac

. . . or how to get your shots

Viruses aren't just for bodies anymore. We now have files that can "infect" a computer, causing simple mischief or total disaster. But like real viruses, you can do a lot to prevent them. Your first stop is the virtual clinic at keyword: VIRUS, America Online's Virus Information Center. There's one for the Mac and one for the PC. If you're new to downloading, take time to read the text in these areas and to download a virus checking utility. Install and use it. It can make a difference in your computer's life, as well as the lives of those you come into contact with. Remember, when you download a file, you're not just downloading a file which might have been exposed to a virus on the uploader's computer; you're downloading a file which could have picked up a virus from every other computer the uploader's computer came in contact with (and when you get online, we can be talking millions here).

Fortunately, most America Online forums have staff responsible for checking files for viruses before they are released to the public, but I have seen some areas that aren't as careful. When you read a file description, check the very bottom — there should be a note indicating the file was scanned for and found free of viruses. You'll see this in every AOL Computing Channel library and most others online. If you're still skittish about viruses, scan your downloads with a virus checker.

And another thing about viruses: don't download files attached to e-mail from people you don't know. Especially those files claiming to be AOL-sanctioned utilities (America Online will never send you a file through e-mail), pornography (control those hormones), or utilities to get America Online for free (the only one who gets it for free is the creep who sent you the file). Most of these files are Trojan Horse programs (see the tip "Understanding Trojans" in Chapter 4). If you suspect you've downloaded a Trojan Horse, contact AOL's Member Services immediately. They'll be able to help you secure your account and remove the Trojan program.

Contributed by George Louie
(screen name: NumbersMan)

Decompressing and Installing Files :) :)　Win & Mac

... or how to get it out of the box

Decompressing — that's something a deep sea diver does, right? With luck, it's something you get to do after a hard day at work. It's also something a downloader will do fairly often.

Many downloadable files are "compressed," which can accomplish several things — it speeds the download by removing empty space from the files, and/or (as an "archive") allows a group of files to be received as a single download (important for Windows programs, which normally consist of a number of files).

When an America Online member sends you multiple files attached to a single e-mail, his/her AOL software automatically "zips" or "stuffs" (compresses) the files into an archive and then uploads it as a single file. When it's downloaded by the recipient the attachment is treated like all other compressed, zipped, and stuffed files you will learn about in this tip. Read on.

Your AOL software can be set to automatically decompress the most popular compressed file formats: ZIP (Windows) and SIT (Mac). Set that up in your Download Preferences. The files will be decompressed when you sign off America Online. The AOL software even creates a new directory/folder in your `Download` directory/folder for each decompressed file.

You can also use your AOL software to manually decompress, if you'd prefer — even while you're online. Windows users can decompress by opening their Download Manager, clicking the **Show Files Downloaded** button, selecting the file in question, and clicking the **Decompress** button. Mac users have it easier: simply select **Open** from the **File** menu, find the archive, click the **Open** button, and click **Decompress** when asked if you want to decompress the file.

Certain kinds of archives are automatically decompressed by your AOL software — ZIP archives (Windows and Mac) and SIT (Mac only). Reading the file description is a must, though. Windows users won't know whether a ZIP file contains one or many files unless they read the description, and this can be important if you hope to find them all after decompression.

There are also self-extracting compressed files, which decompress without the help of any other program, including America Online. On the Mac, look for the `.sea` file extension. Windows users can't tell if a file is a self-extracting archive until they try to **Open** (or **Run**) it. Always read the file description!

In Windows/DOS the `.exe` file extension signifies an executable program. After you download an EXE file you must **Run** the file in order to use it. When you run it (double-click the file in Windows Program Manager [Windows 3.1], My Computer [Windows 95], or Windows Explorer [Windows 95]), chances are either (a) an installation program will start or (b) the file was a self-executing archive, and the archive will expand into a group of individual files. Again, be sure to read the file description before you download. Sometimes there are special instructions to follow before running a program.

Some older Windows programs are installed in a two-step process. First, AOL software automatically decompresses the ZIP archive into a directory/folder of its own. Then you need to run the installation program. You should find a `Readme.txt` file and a `Setup.exe` (or `Install.exe`) file in that directory/folder. Open the `Readme` file to get important information (see the tip "Reading the About Files" later in this chapter) and then run the `Setup/Install` file to proceed with the installation. Once decompressed, you generally don't need the original compressed file. You can delete the original manually, or have AOL software do it for you. See your **Download Preferences** to configure automatic deletion after decompression.

AOL software can't deal with all the compressed file formats out there. If you go beyond the basic ZIP (PC) and SIT (Mac) files (and you will, if you download from the Internet), you'll need at least one decompression program. Search for a decompression program at keyword: FILE SEARCH, and be sure it handles the right types of files.

Contributed by Dave Marx (screen name: Dave Marx)

| **Reading the About Files**   :) :) :) | **Win & Mac** |

. . . or how to believe what you read

When Alice discovered the bottle labeled "Drink Me," she obligingly emptied the bottle — with alarming results. During your own adventures on America Online, you will undoubtedly download many files. If, upon opening or installing them you find a file labeled `Read Me`, don't worry. These helpful little files — more commonly known as *About files* — only make you grow wiser (not taller).

About files are nothing more than text files, included with applications, fonts, utilities, and so forth. They provide valuable clues on how to install and use the file you just downloaded. Don't confuse these with the file description, which is online; About files are specific to a program or file and are only readable after it is down-loaded. They are your key to unlocking the secrets of your download.

The first step is finding them. They come in a variety of names, like About, About.txt, Readme.txt, Read Me, Read.Me, Read Me 1st, and Important. Usually they will be in the same directory or folder as the file. Remember, too, that not all files have these, and some that do may incorporate them into the program itself.

If you do find one, you need to read it. Usually they are opened with the AOL software, as they are simply text files. Just use the **Open** command under the **File** menu. If that is unsuccessful, try Notepad in Windows or SimpleText on the Mac. You may need to fiddle with the file a bit. For example, in Windows I've found that adding a .txt at the end of the file will make it easier to open with the AOL software or Windows Notepad. Also on Windows, keep in mind that some About files may have been created on a different platform — if so, you just need to let your computer know what "type" of file it is. I've actually associated the extension .me (for those files named Read.Me, which tend to be Mac Read Me files) with text files so I can open them right up in Notepad.

So next time a tiny file looks balefully out at you from the monitor and whispers "Read Me," take it up on its offer. Save valuable time and effort, and don't get caught saying, "I'm late, I'm late, for a very important date."

Getting Credit for Bad Downloads :) :) | ¢ | Win & Mac

. . . or how to recover a loss

Not every download goes as smooth as silk. Downloads can get interrupted, files can get corrupted, or America Online may crawl to a stop. Back when I was a Tech Live Advisor the most reassuring things I could tell a member frustrated by download woes was, "You can apply for credit for the time you lost downloading, at keyword: CREDIT." Of course, back then it cost $2.95 an hour to use America Online, so a bad download could amount to real bucks! These days the vast majority of members use the Unlimited Pricing Plan. If you're on Unlimited Pricing you can't get credit.

If you do pay for hourly use, America Online still grants credit in the form of additional online time. The credit only covers the time spent downloading. Your personal time and other costs (like telephone company charges) are not reimbursed.

The easiest way to apply for credit is at keyword: CREDIT. Supply the time and date of the occurrence, the amount of online time lost, and select the nature of the problem from a short list. You'll be notified of America Online's decision regarding your credit request via e-mail. If granted, the credit appears in your current bill at keyword: BILLING.

The second way to receive credit is to speak directly to one of America Online's Online billing representatives at Billing Help Interactive. It's open between 8:00 a.m. and 12:00 midnight, Eastern Time. Finding Billing Help Interactive can be a challenge — it doesn't have a keyword. Go to keyword: BILLING, select **Frequently Asked Questions**, and then **Talk With a Billing Representative**.

Here's the bad news: America Online does not grant credit for access costs. If you pay a surcharge for accessing America Online (like $6.00 per hour for the 800 or 888 access number), those charges will not be credited.

Luckily, bad downloads are much less of a problem these days. But if it happens, you've got a place to turn.

Contributed by Dave Marx (screen name: Dave Marx)

Uploading Files :) :) | Win & Mac

. . . or how to show off your stuff

If we compare downloading to "panning for gold," uploading is the equivalent of "sharing the loot." Whether you're sharing a photo, drawing, sound, story, or software isn't that important. What's more important is that you're contributing to the online community and putting a bit of yourself online for everyone to see and share.

Uploading, logically enough, is the reverse of downloading — you're sending something to an America Online forum, which others can then download. Your uploaded file is reviewed by a file librarian who scans it for viruses, checks it for proper function, and evaluates it for compliance with America Online's Terms of Service (TOS). Most libraries have posted policies regarding the type of files they will accept. Please pay attention to them and save the volunteer file librarian needless trouble.

You upload to America Online when you're in a file ("download") library. Do you know which library is appropriate for the file you want to upload? Decide, and go there! Do you need a suggestion? Try keyword: GALLERY. If the library accepts uploads, the **Upload** button will be available at the bottom. Start by clicking **Upload** and filling in the form that appears. As an experienced downloader you'll have a good idea of what information is needed and should appreciate the importance of giving complete information. Next click the **Select File** button, locate the file on your hard disk, and start uploading. Allow the librarians a day or so to review your file, and voila! Your file will be up in lights!

There's one big difference between downloading and uploading besides the direction of travel — when you upload, the rest of America Online gets "locked out" — you can't chat, reply to Instant Messages, read message boards or cruise the service during the upload. This may make you seem rude to your friends. You may want to warn them before you start a long upload. On the upside, regardless of your pricing plan you don't need to pay to upload; uploading to libraries is always free.

Contributed by Dave Marx (screen name: Dave Marx)

Saving and Printing Windows :) :) :) | Win & Mac

. . . or how to record your travels

Every window you open on America Online is a gold mine of information, which you undoubtedly want to record forever. What? Is that a murmur of disbelief I hear? Well, perhaps I exaggerate. There are, however, a number of windows that you may want to share with friends who

aren't online. (Was that another gasp? I know, I know —
I can't believe that there are folks not online yet either!)
Or you may simply want to keep text to use or read later.

Most windows within America Online can be saved to
disk and/or printed out. Some even come with **Save**
and/or **Print** buttons. Windows without these convenient
little buttons may be a little trickier to save or print, but
they are not difficult. Directions for each are as follows:

- **To Save**: Verify that the window you want to save is
  forefront on your screen, and then select **Save** or
  Save As... from the **File** menu. Those who prefer
  to use the keyboard can accomplish this by pressing
  Ctrl+S (on Windows) or **Command+S** (on the
  Mac). A standard file-saving dialog box appears and
  asks you to give the file you're creating a name. You
  can also choose a specific place to save it at this
  point (be sure to remember where you put it).

- **To Print**: Verify that the window you want to print is
  forefront on your screen, and then select **Print...**
  from the **File** menu, click the **Print** button on the
  toolbar, or press **Ctrl+P** (on Windows) or
  Command+P (on the Mac). A standard Print dialog box appears — verify that your settings are correct and print! Occasionally you'll find materials that
  you can't print or save. Forums have the power to
  prevent printing and saving to protect their
  copyright.

If you prefer to gather and save large quantities of
information from windows, I suggest you investigate the
Log Manager feature (under the **My Files** button on the
toolbar). Logs can be printed out within America Online
also, assuming they are too large to be displayed. See the
tip "Using the Log Manager" in Chapter 2).

Finding Text in a Window   :) :) :) | Win & Mac

... or how to avoid speed reading

I have another confession to make. I can't always remember where I've seen something I've read. I know, I
know — it's a big burden to live with. There are also

times when I'm looking for a specific piece of information in a long text file, and searching for it would be tedious and time-consuming. What to do? Use the **Find in Top Window** command built into your AOL software.

To find text, simply make sure the window you want to search is forefront on your screen and then select the **Find in Top Window** command from your **Edit** menu. You are prompted to enter the word or phrase you want to find. Once you click **Find**, your AOL software searches through the text in the topmost window, stopping and highlighting the first occurrence of the word or phrase.

Usage tips:

1. You can use the **Find in Top Window** feature in several kinds of windows, including e-mail (as well as your list of e-mail), message boards, libraries, World Wide Web pages, chat rooms, and Instant Messages. In the case of the latter two, click the text itself to make sure you're searching in the right part of the window.

2. If you want to narrow your search, click the **Match Case** (or **Case Sensitive Search**) check box.

Meet Kimberly

Kimberly Trautman (screen name: *KTrautman*) is one of my original Companions and contributors. A true leader, Kimberly is the Promotions Coordinator for AOL Live and an expert on all things America Online. On top of that, she's warm, friendly, and generous. She introduced two of our newer Companions — Adrienne Quinn and Bob Trautman — to the joys of contributing to this book, in fact. Her quote in her profile says it all! Thanks, Kimberly!

Becoming a Beta Tester   :)   Win & Mac

... or how to be a virtual spy

Imagine you're James Bond. You're walking through Q's secret lab. New gadgets and gizmos are in development all around you, and you get to play with them months ahead of the rest of the world. Sound fun? If you love to get a sneak peak at the latest and greatest, you can become a virtual spy in your own right as a software beta tester. Sure, things "blow up" every now and then, but half the fun is trying to figure out what went wrong!

Beta testing on America Online involves using pre-release copies of AOL software to report problems and suggest solutions. Developers need members like you to put the software through its paces — it helps them test functionality and find problems. As a beta tester, you also get the chance to see and contribute to the progression of software and features from their early stages to "Golden Master" release version. It's not quite a BMW with missiles and ejection seats, but you'd be amazed by all of the features that are being tested right now by America Online's team of beta testers.

Along with the privileges of being a beta tester come responsibilities. You must maintain confidentiality — no sending copies of beta software to your friends! And you must report the problems you find — if they aren't reported, they cannot be fixed. One thing you don't need to worry about, however, is being a computer expert. The AOL software is designed for all levels of expertise, so it only makes sense to have all levels of beta testers! Would you believe America Online now has over 70,000 beta testers? That's higher than the total America Online membership figures back when I originally volunteered to beta test! (Hmm, how about *Agent 0070000*?)

If you're interested in beta testing, go to keyword: BETA APPLY. You might have to keep applying if America Online isn't currently looking for testers, but eventually you'll get a chance.

Until next time, the name's Zimmer. Bradley Zimmer. This book will now self-destruct in five seconds.

Contributed by Bradley Zimmer
(screen name: Bradley476)

... or how to click your pictures

Do you love downloading pictures? Does your hard disk groan under the load? Do you want an easy way to share your favorite pictures with your friends? The Picture Gallery in your AOL 4.0 software will help you peer into those files with a minimum of fuss, make it easy to edit and modify the file(s), and make incorporating the image into e-mail a breeze.

Let's get started! Select the **File** menu at the top of your screen and choose **Open Picture Gallery**. Now you need to select a folder/directory on your hard disk that contains image files. Why not start with your **AOL Download** folder? Simply choose it from the standard file selection box that pops up. Once selected, the Picture Gallery window opens, displaying every compatible graphic in that directory/folder. The Picture Gallery displays several "thumbnails" — postage stamp-sized images — to give you an idea of what your images look like (see Figure 6.3). On Windows, you can stroll through the Gallery by clicking the **Next** and **Prev** buttons. On the Mac, just scroll down to see more.

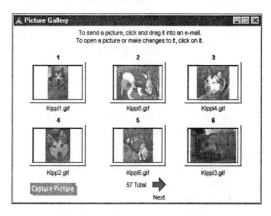

Figure 6.3 A visit to the Picture Gallery (view from Windows).

Only compatible graphics are displayed — GIF, JPG, BMP (Windows and Mac), PICT (Mac only), Kodak

PictureDisk images, and America Online's proprietary ART formats. Other types of graphics won't be displayed, but this list covers a lot of territory.

Picture Gallery tips:

1. Drop a preview image from Picture Gallery into e-mail. Click and drag a thumbnail image into an e-mail as you write it. It remains thumbnail sized. This has limited value for most images. However, if you plan to attach that file to the e-mail, it's a neat way to give folks a preview of their download.

2. Insert a full-sized version of the image into e-mail. On Windows, just double-click the image (it opens full-sized for viewing) and click the **Insert in E-mail** button. On the Mac, just click the image once, click the **Insert** button, and select **Picture**. If you select **Background**, your picture will be "tiled" in the background of your mail (at full size) and your text is layered on top of it.

3. Windows: Edit the image before uploading or attaching. Double-click the image. If the image is in an editable format (GIF, JPG, BMP) America Online provides simple tools for modifying the image. See the next tip, "Editing Graphics Files," for the details.

4. Edit the image before uploading or attaching (Mac). The Picture Gallery window includes a **Set Editor/Viewer** button. Click this to select an image editing program to use along with the Picture Gallery. Then, if you double-click an image in the Gallery, it opens the image editing software automatically. You need to have an image editing program installed on your computer to use this feature.

5. Use Picture Gallery as a hard disk housekeeping tool. When it's time to do some spring cleaning on your hard disk, use Picture Gallery to peer into the graphics files on your disk. It's a quick way to see what you want to keep, delete, or reorganize. Open America Online and, at the same time, your computer's file management utility — such as My Computer, Windows Explorer, File Manager, or Finder. Arrange the windows so you can see both

programs simultaneously. Use Picture Gallery to view the files, and use your file management utility to do the rest.

Contributed by Dave Marx (screen name: Dave Marx)

Editing Graphics Files	:) :)	Win only

... or how to spiff it up

Cousin Marc just e-mailed you a fabulous GIF from the family reunion — you and grand-aunt Sylvia, chatting over coffee. Well, to be honest, your aunt looks a bit cross, but you look great! This would be just the photo to upload to the AOL Portrait Gallery (keyword: GALLERY). You think, "Well, maybe I can cut Aunt Sylvia and the kitchen table out of the shot and make myself bigger. And the lighting could be a bit better." You could buy a $500 image editing program and spend the next month learning how to use it, but why not use the image editing tools built right into AOL for Windows 4.0? They're not the most sophisticated image editing tools you'll find, but that makes them simple to learn.

First, pull down the **File** menu, select **Open**, and find the graphic you want to edit. If it can be edited, a row of icons appears above the image. They're not labeled, but if you let your mouse pointer hover for a moment, balloon help comes to the rescue. Here's what you can do:

- **Rotate picture** in 90 degree increments and lay on your side.
- **Flip Picture Horizontally** to face left instead of right. It pays to look ahead!
- **Flip Picture Vertically** and stand on your head.
- **Zoom In/Out** to shrink or grow at whim.
- **Select and Crop Picture** to keep the best, and toss the rest.
- **Increase and Decrease Picture Contrast** and sharpen things up.
- **Brighten and Dim Picture** to add some sparkle.

- **Invert Picture** to make your negatives positive and your positives negative.

- **Convert Picture to Grey Scale** to turn the Blue Boy into Dorian Gray.

At the bottom of the window are **Save** and **Revert** buttons, as accidents will happen.

My main tip is, play around to your heart's content! The tools are simple versions of the ones the big kids use, so they're a great introduction to basic digital image editing. Be sure you saved a copy of the original image in another folder/directory, in case you get carried away.

Here are a couple of tips to get you over the trickier parts:

- The **Select** and **Crop** Picture button is a bit finicky. Your first step is to draw a frame around the part of the image that you want to keep. Click the **Select/Crop** button once and then click and drag the mouse pointer diagonally across the image. This creates the frame. There's no way to reposition or resize the frame once you've drawn it, so you need to get the hang of it. To undo the frame click **Revert** and then click once in the image to reset the **Crop** tool. Once the frame is where you want it, click the **Select** and **Crop** button again. (Did you notice its icon changed to a scissors after you drew the frame?) The unwanted parts disappear.

- Now that you've cropped, you may want to enlarge the image. You'll quickly learn the limitations of enlargement — I don't have to describe them here. The thing to look for with the **Zoom In/Out** tool is the **Other. . .** feature. When you click the Zoom In/Out button you can select a range of amounts to enlarge or shrink the image. The limits are enlarge 200 percent and shrink to 25 percent; however, if you click **Other. . .** you can type in almost any amount you desire, from 1 percent to 999 percent.

Contributed by Dave Marx (screen name: Dave Marx)

Meet Adrienne

Adrienne Quinn (screen name: *AAQuinn*) is one of my newest Companions. She's a graduate student in psychology and a whiz at using America Online (they go hand-in-hand, you know). In her spare time she sings and bowls, and has a passion for both contemporary gospel music and NBA basketball (particularly her beloved, yet hapless, L.A. Clippers). Most of all, she's charming and friendly! Thank you, Adrienne!

Companion Confessions

I must admit I'm not much of a gold-digger, much to the chagrin of those who'd benefit by my riches. And though I don't download files as much as I did when I first arrived on America Online, I still gather a few nuggets here and there. I find myself doing a lot of searching for files, oddly enough; sometimes I'm just looking for information (who *was* that author of that program?) or to see if a file still exists (how *did* I find that file before so I can tell my friends about it?).

1. **Finding files**. Finding a library full of fascinating or helpful files can be exciting. At one point I was so intrigued I began compiling a list of all the libraries I found. Needless to say, I gave up when I realized the scope of my undertaking.

2. **Uploading files**. The first file I ever uploaded was a graphic border for Easter. Once it appeared online, I went back and visited it every day for the next two weeks to watch the download count rise. I got a big kick out of the fact that other people found my simple work useful. You can still find it online in the Mac Graphic Arts Forum — try searching on *Jennilynn*. (*Jennilynn* was the first screen name I used with any regularity on America Online.)

3. **Finding text in a window**. I often find myself lost in windows, blindly searching for a word or phrase. Though I'm still stubborn enough to try to find something on my own first, I know when to get smart and use **Find in Top Window. . .** under the **Edit** menu. It is fast and accurate, and much more reliable than my infamous skimming techniques.

4. **Browsing graphics in the Picture Gallery**. One of my best friends, George (yes, the same one who contributed to this book), gave me a digital camera last year. I love it! And the Picture Gallery is ideal for browsing and selecting all 56 (oops, make that 57) shots of my dog, Kippi. Well, can I help it if she's adorable?

CHAPTER 7

EXPLORING THE INTERNET

If using America Online is comparable to living on the western frontier, then getting to the Internet is much like discovering the New World. It is a vast, uncharted wilderness, full of as many dangers as there are discoveries. Unfamiliar natives, untapped resources, and breathtaking wonders await you around every bend. Like the Americas themselves, there is incredible potential in the Internet for those colonists willing to brave the unknown. And this book is your ticket on a chartered ship sailing west — the *SS Companion*.

Luckily, we don't have to sail far. The Internet is not only easily accessible through America Online, it is seamlessly integrated in many places. America Online doesn't call itself the "World's Largest Internet Online Service" for nothing. With America Online you can explore the Internet in a safe environment, or you can go deep into the wilds and stake your own claim. Practically every Internet resource — from e-mail to newsgroups, World Wide Web pages, and *File Transfer Protocol* (FTP) sites — is available to you as an America Online member. This is a brave new world, but not one in which you have to get lost.

Exploration of the Internet begins at home with e-mail — chances are you've already received some, and perhaps even sent some as well. From there we move on to finding treasures with *Gopher*, *Wide Area Information Servers* (WAIS), and the infamous World Wide Web. Then we sail on to the lesser-explored territories of FTP, *MUDs*, *MOOs*, *Telnet*, *IRC*, and *AOL Instant Messenger* (AIM) (exotic-sounding places, aren't they?). Finally, outfitted with some supplies and a bit of advice, you can head off on your own to explore the many wondrous and strange spectacles to behold on the Internet.

So climb aboard. . . it's time to hoist our phone-line anchors and ride the carrier waves to the Internet.

Mailing on the Internet :) :) :) | Win & Mac

. . . or how to send net.air mail

Electronic mail, or e-mail, is a simple but powerful tool. Every member on America Online can send and receive e-mail to and from the Internet, unless restricted by Parental Controls (see details in Chapter 2). So not only can you send private text messages and files to other America Online members, you can send them to other Internet users as well, including folks on other online services. No more messages in bottles!

How does it work? Not much different than regular e-mail. First bring up a new mail window (**Ctrl+M** on Windows, or **Command+M** on the Mac). Next type your letter as you normally would, leaving out any different colors, text, or sizes (they won't translate across the Internet). Now enter the address of the Internet user you want to mail — an address is usually longer than a typical AOL software screen name, and it almost always contains the @ symbol somewhere in there. For example, `watson@horiba.com`. Your own Internet address is your screen name plus `@aol.com`. For example, my Internet address is `jennifer@aol.com`. Internet addresses are usually shown in all lowercase, unless uppercase letters are required. You can find Internet addresses on e-mail, business cards, Web sites, word-of-mouth (if you have a good head for lots of characters and numbers or a handy napkin to write on), or even from a directory of addresses (see the following tip).

Sending attached files to other Internet users can be a bit tricky, as the Internet only sends plain text through the system. Non-text files are converted into pure text using special software and then retranslated once it reaches the recipient, provided he or she has the correct program to translate the file. Your best bet is to attach a file, send it, and then check with the recipient to see if it worked. If you receive such a file from someone on the Internet (usually in MIME format), you can download a decoder program by searching for one at keyword: FILE SEARCH. Or try keyword: MIME for more information and links to various types of decoder software. For more information, see keyword: MAIL and INTERNET.

Finding Internet Addresses :) :)   Win & Mac

. . . or how to discover long lost friends

Just like street and city addresses in America, Internet addresses are essential on America Online. The power of Internet e-mail is lost without a way to get it to the right person. Luckily, there are several ways to look up Internet addresses. Their address sources are diverse, from mailing lists and newsgroups to Internet service providers and self-registrations.

Here are a few tips on finding Internet addresses:

1. Keyword: WHITE PAGES helps you search for names and addresses in its large database. You may also add your own e-mail address to this listing for friends and relatives who may be looking for you. Your listing is password-protected so no one else can add to or modify your information. You can look up the publicly available names, phone number, street addresses, and e-mail addresses of friends and colleagues in less than a second. Businesses can be found using a similar search engine at keyword: YELLOW PAGES.

2. The AOL Research & Learn channel has an entire area dedicated to finding addresses at keyword: PHONE BOOK. Check out the list of helpful links and references here, like the Association Directory, the Chamber of Commerce Directory, and Congressperson Directory (which gives a whole new meaning to "mail your congressperson!").

3. Still can't find your old flame's e-mail address? Try these other Internet address directories:

   • http://www.four11.com

- http://www.whowhere.com
- http://www.bigfoot.com
- http://www.infospace.com
- http://www.worldpages.com

Finally, there's the comprehensive IAF (Internet Address Finder) at: http://guide.netscape.com/guide/people.html, which conveniently combines all five search engines above into one page.

Subscribing to Mailing Lists   :) :) | Win & Mac

... or how to get lots of e-mail

Mailing lists are a way of distributing information and exchanging ideas by way of e-mail. They can bring together like-minded individuals to discuss and exchange information on one or more topics. It is one of the oldest and most popular resources the Internet has to offer. It differs from newsgroups in that anyone with e-mail can participate. There are no special tools other than a way to read e-mail. Mailing list topics cover just about everything you can imagine, plus a few you probably can't. There's something for everyone.

Subscribing to mailing lists is easy. First, you find one you'd like — there is a searchable database at keyword: MAILING LIST. For mailing lists maintained on America Online, you bring up a new mail window and address it to: listserv@listserv.aol.com. The contents of the subject line are unimportant, but you can use *Subscribe* if you like. In the body of the e-mail, you'll want to type: **SUBSCRIBE <listname> <firstname> <lastname>**, where *<listname>* is the exact name of the list and your first and last names immediately follow. For example, if I wanted to subscribe to a mailing list titled TOURBUS (for Internet site reviews), I would type the following:

```
To: listserv@listserv.aol.com
Subject: Subscribe
Body of Mail: Subscribe TOURBUS
Jennifer Watson
```

Because this subscription e-mail is read by machine and not humans, it's important that you format it correctly. Check the mailing list's subscription information for formatting instructions. Don't include *please* or *thank you*, as these are not commands the software understands and your subscription request may not go through. If there is a problem, you'll get e-mail. If your subscription is successful, you'll get e-mail too, this time explaining how the mailing list works. Save this e-mail for later reference.

More information, help, and tips can be found at keyword: MAILING LISTS.

Digging with Gophers :) :) :)   Win & Mac

. . . or how to dig the Internet

The Internet is a strange world where commonplace words suddenly take on new meanings. *Mouse* is a perfect example, as is *web* and *page*. (Not sure what I mean? Check Appendix C.) True to form, *Gopher* is not a small, furry creature that burrows. Nor is it a small, furry character on a well-known sitcom from the '80s. Rather, Gopher on the Internet is a place where information is stored so you can *go for* it. Think of it as the Filing Cabinet of the Internet — it is fast, simple, and crammed full of useful stuff.

To get to Gopher, use keyword: GOPHER. From there you have several options. If you've never used Gopher before, I recommend exploring the **What is Gopher?** and **Help** areas. After that, you can start digging in the **Directory**, root about for something specific in **Search**, or, if you know where you're going, take a direct tunnel with **Quick Go**.

Gopher uses the same window as your World Wide Web sessions (see the next tip), so you can jump between Gopher and Web sites without a problem. In fact, you don't even need to use keyword: GOPHER — many Gopher directories are linked right into Web sites, and you can go to those you already know by typing their URL address right into the keyword window (more details on URLs are in Chapter 3).

Go-For-It tips:

1. Gopher menu items have plain, simple names. Pay attention to them and it is hard to get lost.

2. Gopher links you all over the world. Take advantage of this power. You'll be surprised at the information you can find.

3. To "download" information from a Gopher site, all you have to do is click a menu item, wait for it to display in the window, and save it.

Although Gopher has been on the scene for a while now, the sites usually lack the flash and glitz of better-known Web pages. It is substantially faster, however, and easier to navigate. Give it a try.

Browsing the World Wide Web :) :) :)   Win & Mac

. . . or how to surf the Web

World Wide Web may be a mouthful, but is also an eyeful, and earful, and a mindful. If you're new to this hot online phenomenon, you're in for a treat. It is immensely large, wholly untamed, and a lot of fun. When they say "surf the Web," they're not too far off the mark.

You start your adventure with a *Web browser*. The AOL software has a built-in Web browser, though you can use others if you prefer (see the tip "Using Alternate Web Browsers" later). America Online's Web browser, which is actually a customized version of Microsoft's Internet Explorer, is constantly being revised and refined to fit seamlessly into AOL's software. In fact, if you weren't familiar with browsers before reading this tip, you may never have known you were using one — in AOL software version 4.0, Web sites and America Online pages are well-integrated and accessed in much the same way.

You open America Online's Web browser just by going to a Web site. You can do that in a number of ways. If you know the URL address (see Chapter 3 for more details on understanding URLs), type it right into the toolbar or the keyword window. Alternatively, you can go to a *jumping-off point* at keyword: INTERNET. You can even go to some keywords that lead directly to Web pages, like keyword: DILBERT or WIRED (these are all listed in my book, *AOL Keywords*, also published by MIS:Press). Finally, there are *links* to Web sites in America Online forums — look for a small globe icon in front of the title, or the word *Web* somewhere near it.

The biggest difference in functionality between a Web site displayed with your browser and a regular page on America Online is navigation between subsequent sites. Regular America Online pages stack up on your screen, each in its own window, while Web sites generally share just one window (your browser window). Use the forward and back arrows in your toolbar to navigate. There is also a stop, reload, and home button, like standalone browsers. If you're using an earlier version of the AOL software without the fully integrated browser, buttons much like this appear at the top of the browser window.

Searching the World Wide Web :) :) | Win & Mac

. . . or how to scan for life

The World Wide Web contains millions and millions of sites. As you can imagine, it's practically impossible to locate even a few of the resources available for your topic much less a good assortment of them, without some kind of help. Books with lists of Web sites sorted by subject help somewhat, but they can't list everything and they quickly become outdated. An online *search engine* (database search program) doesn't have these problems; it can include as much data as its databases allow and information can be updated as pages are created, changed, or removed. Another advantage is that it's much easier to simply type in a phrase and press the **Enter** key than it is to search through book after book.

There are several large search engines on the Internet with the sole purpose of keeping track of every Web page in existence, indexing them, and enabling people to search for information by matching a word or phrase. A list of the top Web search engines would begin with America Online's own NetFind at keyword: NETFIND (for more detail, see Chapter 3). In addition, there is infamous Yahoo!, at `http://www.yahoo.com;`

WebCrawler, at `http://www.webcrawler.com`; and HotBot, at `http://www.hotbot.com`. And if you want to search Web pages (individual "windows"), not just sites (the overall area), use `http://www.lycos.com`. Each has its own features, and though I don't have the space here to describe them all, I'd certainly recommend that you try them yourself to find the one that works the best for you. Also, while you might fail to find any useful information with a search on one, searching another quite possibly could yield what you're looking for.

These general-purpose search engines don't charge for their services (though there are specialized ones that do), and there's usually no limit to your use of them. Most are fast, easy-to-use, and accurate.

My best Web searching tip? Leave no stone unturned nor Web site unwoven.

Contributed by Bradley Zimmer
(screen name: Bradley476)

Understanding Cookies :) :) | Win & Mac

. . . or how to avoid the cookie jar

The growing popularity of the World Wide Web has resulted in delectable additions to our online vocabulary. One need scarcely begin Web surfing to encounter terms like *Java* or *cookies*. And cookies, as tasty as they sound, are our topic of the moment.

An Internet cookie is a small amount of information sent from a Web site to your computer. Contrary to cyber-legend, a cookie does not sneak a peek at your hard drive and send back confidential data to the Web hosts. Rather, a cookie simply stores information about your visit to a particular Web site. This is generally done to provide you with better service upon future visits to that site, by greeting you by name, storing a user password, or recording your preferences. A large Web site receives too many "hits," or visits, to archive such information itself.

As cookies don't do anything other than store information, they do not pose a great security risk. Unless, of course, you give out sensitive information when visiting a

Web site, like credit card information. This information could then be stored in a cookie, and someone with access to your hard drive might be able to retrieve it. Fortunately, a Web site can only access cookies that *it* created.

If you wish, you can set your Web browser preferences to notify you before accepting cookies. The precise method for setting preferences varies depending on the browser used — check your **Help** if you get stuck. Do note that if you refuse cookies, sites may limit your access to their pages.

If you wish to examine the contents of cookies stored on your computer, search your hard drive for files named *cookie*. A word processor or text editor (like Notepad or SimpleText) should be able to open the file and let you see exactly what your cookies might contain!

Contributed by Ben Foxworth (screen name: BenF7)

Watching the World Wide Web   :) :)   Win & Mac

. . . or how to turn your computer into a TV

It's time to boot up your computer and watch some television! Courtesy of RealNetworks, the RealPlayer software brings sound and video to the online experience. It is available either live or on demand, and it is here today. Now granted, the video isn't up to standard television quality, but it's good enough considering all it takes is a normal modem connection to get the video and sound. And it is all viewed in real time so there's no wait for a lengthy transfer. The quality of the feed is dependent upon your speed, so a faster modem delivers more.

For AOL software version 4.0 and above, the RealPlayer software is either pre-installed or set up to download when needed. If you're not yet using version 4.0, you can download the RealPlayer software at http://www.realplayer.com. Directions on installation and usage are also available here. RealPlayer will generally appear as a small video window in a corner of the screen (see Figure 7.1), or may be integrated right into your America Online windows.

Figure 7.1 A prime-time broadcast shown in RealPlayer (view from Windows).

So what can you watch? The RealPlayer Web site has links to all of the major RealAudio and RealVideo servers. From music and live broadcasts, to video clips on demand and even live video from C-Span or Fox News.

Contributed by Bradley Zimmer
(screen name: Bradley476)

Purging Your Web Cache   :) :)   Win & Mac

. . . or how to keep it fast and fresh

Is your Web browsing slowing down? Are more and more sites getting harder and harder to access? Well, you could blame it on the Web's popularity, or America Online's legendary system overloads, but maybe the problem is right there on your computer's hard disk, in the *browser cache*. The what? The browser cache is a folder in your hard disk filled with "Temporary Internet Files" — the Web pages you've visited recently, and the Web graphics that decorate those pages.

The browser cache is an ingenious invention, based on the premise that it takes a long time to download a Web page, so why not save it to the hard disk where it won't have to be downloaded a second time. That's great in theory and generally works very well, but eventually your cache folder will get clogged by thousands of files. It's at that point that the clutter can become too much for your browser to handle, and a spring cleaning is in order.

To clean house on America Online's integrated browser, first click the **My AOL** button on the toolbar, select **Preferences**, and open your **WWW** preferences. After this, the precise method for emptying your browser cache varies depending on the browser used — check your **Help** if you get stuck. Once set, your browsing should breeze along (relatively speaking.)

Here are some extra browser preference tips:

1. **Pages stored on your hard drive can go stale.** Your browser can be configured to search out newer versions of the stored pages.

2. **Cached Web pages can take over your hard disk.** Set limits on how much disk space the cache can take.

3. **It's a little-known fact, but America Online uses graphic compression to accelerate your browsing.** The problem is, compressed graphics don't always look so good. Fortunately, you can turn them off — just be prepared for slower browsing.

Contributed by Dave Marx (screen name: Dave Marx)

Creating Your Own Web Page :) :) ¢ Win & Mac

. . . or how to publish your stuff

Everyone who's anyone has done it. You know you want to. Well, America Online makes it easy for you to fulfill your fantasy. Yes, that's right . . . you, too, can have your very own Web page! And at no extra cost. Each screen name is automatically allocated 2MB of disk space on America Online's computers (that's a full 10MB for the entire account) for posting personal Web pages.

Not sure what to do? America Online goes one step further and provides a myriad of options to help you create your own page — for the novice, as well as for the expert HTML writer. What is HTML? Not to worry; visit keyword: MY PLACE for all the tools you need to create your Web page on America Online without having to learn the technical stuff. America Online even offers its members a program called *Personal Publisher* that helps you build a Web page quickly and easily (see keyword: PERSONAL PUBLISHER). There's also *AOLPress* for design and creation of more complicated pages (see keyword: AOLPRESS). All are free!

Web-weaving tips:

1. **Count your hits**. Put a *counter* on your Web page and watch it increase as folks visit it. A counter keeps track of how many people open your Web page — it often looks like your car's odometer. Details on how to add one are available at keyword: MY PLACE.

2. **Spread the word**. Let other folks on the Internet know about your page by getting it linked into some of the Web page directories out there. A good place to start is at `http://www.ep.com/faq/webannounce.html`.

3. **Show it off**. Once your Web page is complete, enter it in America Online's Home Page Contest at keyword: MHP CONTEST.

Using Alternate Web Browsers :) :) :) | Win & Mac

... or how to find greener grass

Did you ever hear the story about the cow that was convinced grass was greener on the other side of the fence? I think of that every time I see a Web site proudly displaying an "Optimized for Netscape" sign. Netscape refers to Netscape Navigator, an alternate to the standard Web browser that comes with the AOL software (Microsoft's Internet Explorer). If you're wondering what all the browser hullabaloo is about, you're free to play in their yards through your AOL software!

Using an alternate browser is usually very simple. You just sign on to America Online as normal, open your alternate browser, and start surfing. The connections are generally made automatically in the background. It is really quite amazing if you stop to think about how complicated the process of not only connecting to the Internet but communicating between two programs must be.

But I'm getting ahead of myself. Let me back up a bit to *finding* alternate browsers. If you don't have one yet, they are easy to get. The usual choice is *Netscape Navigator*, a sophisticated Web browser popular with the Net-savvy crowd (see Figure 7.2).

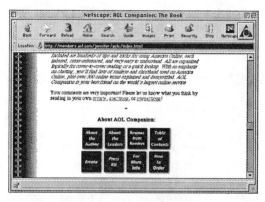

Figure 7.2 Netscape navigates on America Online (view from the Mac).

You can download Netscape Navigator online at keyword: NETSCAPE. Other possibilities include Opera (an international browser), NCSA Mosaic, HotJava, PowerBrowser, and Ariadna. There are links to all these free programs and more at `http://cws.internet.com`.

Once you've downloaded and installed your browser of choice, you may find that it doesn't connect as easily as I claimed. If this happens, you're probably missing an important component necessary for communications between the AOL software and your browser: a *winsock*. This is only necessary if you're using AOL software version 2.5 or 3.0 for Windows, but they are easy to find and install. Download one, along with complete instructions on its use, at keyword: WINSOCK. If you connect to America Online using your own Internet service provider, forego the winsock and even starting the AOL software. You simply run your browser and connect directly to the Web through your provider.

An Internet service provider can make a great deal of sense for other reasons! If you connect to America Online using your Internet service provider exclusively, you can save more than half of your monthly AOL membership fees! Just go to keyword: BILLING, select **Bring Your Own Access**, and sign up for the $9.95 per month rate for unlimited access to America Online. This is also an excellent way to avoid busy signals and that dreaded AOL timer, which sounds like very green grass indeed!

Contributed by Ben Foxworth (screen name: BenF7)

Meet Ben

Ben Foxworth (screen name: *BenF7*) is one of my oldest and dearest Companions on America Online. I met him in early 1993 in a chat room, where he gently introduced me to many of the chat and communication tips in this book. Ben was one of the first to encourage me to become a community leader, becoming one himself at much the same time. He's dedicated to excellence, fascinated by the online experience, and brilliant in his insights into this world. I'm lucky to work with him in the VirtuaLeader Academy now. Thank you, Ben, for everything!

Downloading Files Through FTP :) :) | ¢ | Win & Mac

... or how to find diamonds in the rough

It's time to leave the cozy nest at America Online to explore the world of downloading from the Internet, via File Transfer Protocol (FTP). FTP is a method of transferring files to and from a computer that is connected to the Internet (such as your own when you are on AOL service). There's a lot to discover out there, but it's also quite an adventure. Many things you take for granted on

America Online — informative file descriptions, automatic unzipping/unstuffing of downloads, the Download Manager, files pretested and scanned for viruses — don't work the same way, or may not exist at all. Still, with a little patience, a little knowledge, and a good virus scanning program you'll find a world of riches out there.

America Online gives you two ways to enter FTP space. Keyword: FTP takes you to an America Online page where you can learn about FTP, select popular FTP sites, search for other sites, or enter the address of the site you want. Here you explore FTP space with support from America Online — the "style" is familiar and the windows include **Open, View File Now**, and **Download Now** buttons. You navigate through a world of folders — just open a folder, and see the files and/or additional folders within. You can view short text files without downloading. **Download Now** works in conjunction with your Download Manager — you can interrupt a download by clicking the **Finish Later** button and manually decompress the files before you sign off (see the tip "Using the Download Manager" in Chapter 6). What doesn't work is **Download Later**, and you can't use the Download Manager to keep track of FTP files.

You can also go to FTP space with your Web browser. Just enter the URL in your toolbar (or the keyword window) like any Web address. An FTP URL (address) looks like this: `FTP://ftp.cic.net/pub/hunt/questions/`. The FTP display is actually a Web page — click the hyperlinks to read brief text files, or go another level deeper into a site. When you download through your browser, you bypass Download Manager — you lose its unzipping features, and you can't resume an interrupted download — you have to start from scratch.

FTP tips:

1. FTP, upon first glance, is a bleak world of filenames and file sizes. It can be hard to find what you're looking for, or determine if a file is worth the download. Search through the text files provided by the site to find guidance and help on using the site.

2. Not every FTP site is open to the public; some require a login name and password, which are dif-

ferent from your America Online screen name and password. The sites that are freely available to you use the "Anonymous FTP" protocol; they accept *anonymous* as your login name, which the AOL software automatically applies when requested.

3. You can also upload to FTP sites under some circumstances. When available, the site describes the rules for uploading, and America Online provides the uploading tools.

4. All America Online members have 10MB of FTP space — 2MB per screen name. While the space is most commonly used for Web pages, you can supply downloads and permit uploads, too! Imagine . . . a download library of your very own! Learn about member FTP space at keyword: FTP and keyword: MY PLACE.

5. Get a good unzipping program — one that can handle many different file compression formats.

6. Download and install Adobe Acrobat Reader (a free download at many sites). Acrobat PDF (portable document format) is an increasingly popular file format that enables a complex document to be viewed on almost any type of computer. The download is easier to get using Adobe's Web site at `http://www.adobe.com/prodindex/acrobat/` than it is via FTP. Go figure!

Contributed by Dave Marx (screen name: Dave Marx)

Traveling with Telnet   :) :)   Win & Mac

. . . or how to get your modem to multitask

Oracles have pondered the riddle of how to do more than one thing at a time . . . and do them well. While I don't know the answer as it applies to life, I do know how to do it on the Internet: Telnet! One of the pillars of the Internet, Telnet is a communication method that lets you connect with other computers over your existing connection (in this case, your connection to America Online).

To use Telnet, you first need a Telnet program installed on your computer. Many computers come with

Telnet software pre-installed. In Windows 95, for example, it's as simple as going to an MS-DOS prompt, typing **telnet**, and pressing the **Enter** key. If you aren't sure if your computer's operating system includes Telnet software, check the manual. If it does not, you can download a program online at keyword: TELNET, such as the popular shareware program CommNet (Windows) or NCSA Telnet (Mac).

Once you have a Telnet program installed and running, the next step is to tell it where you want to go. You do this by entering an address, and possibly a port number, for example: `kore.colo.neosoft.com` (the address) and `5000` (the port number). There is usually a separate field in which to enter the port number; be careful not to include it with the address if this is the case.

But where to go? Sites that allow public Telnet connections include *bulletin board systems* (BBS) and public agencies such as weather bureaus. Visit the Ultimate Telnet Directory at `http://www.internet-database.com/telnet.htm` for a listing of more than 1,800 Telnet sites (at the time of writing). Probably the most popular use of Telnet: *Multi-User Dungeons* (MUDs). MUDs are online gaming systems that offer real-time play with others (more information on this in the next tip). Additional lists of Telnet sites you can connect to are found at keyword: TELNET.

Contributed by Bradley Zimmer
(screen name: Bradley476)

Meet Bradley

Bradley Zimmer (screen name: *Bradley476*) is one of those computer whiz kids. He started online when he was quite young and soon began volunteering in The Grandstand forum as a host of the American Saddlebred Horse chat. From there his involvement grew to the AOL Sports channel. He is now a member of The VirtuaLeader Academy, and the founder of his own online services studio. In addition to all this, he's pursuing a degree in law and business. Thanks, Brad!

Playing in the MUDs   :)   Win & Mac

. . . or how to play dirty

Playing in the MUD has a whole new meaning online! Multi-User Dungeons (MUDs) are virtual worlds whose community members interact through an electronic persona in a Telnet interface. Through them, you can chase dragons, hunt for treasure, play a friendly game, or hang out at a bar. They are a cross between chat rooms and text-based adventure games, but infinitely more fun because real people play with you.

Like the mud puddles of our youth, no two MUDs are the same. Each multi-user game type can have an entirely different culture and style. MUDs are mainly combat-oriented games involving role-playing. There are also *MUSHes* — community-oriented games with an emphasis on socializing. Rules and atmospheres differ depending on the environment, so it's always best to do your homework and spend some time observing before jumping in with both swords swinging.

As MUDs require Telnet, use the preceding tip to get it set up with America Online first. Next find yourself a MUD or two to jump in. You'll find hundreds of links to MUDs in the MUD Connector Web site at http://www.mudconnect.com. If you need more help or information, use keyword: TELNET for more tips and links. This is one time that nobody will mind if you play in MUD!

Contributed by Bradley Zimmer
(screen name: Bradley476)

Chatting with Internet Relay Chat   :)   Win & Mac

. . . or how to chat with the world

If you've only experienced the salons and saloons of America Online, you're in for a surprise. The vast wilderness of the Internet is replete with hordes of chatters roaming wildly and freely, congregating at innumerable watering holes known as *Internet Relay Chat* (IRC). Don't worry, it isn't as bad as it sounds; there are pockets of civilized chat (if that is indeed what you want). Internet users use IRC to hold online, real-time conversations with one another, much as America Online members do in their chat rooms.

To access IRC through America Online, first download and install an IRC program. There are several good ones — I recommend mIRC (for Windows) and IRCle (for the Mac) — both are shareware and are available online at keyword: FILE SEARCH. Once installed, link your program. If you aren't sure how, sign on and go to keyword: IRC for step-by-step directions.

Your next step is to find an IRC channel. You can often find lists of channels and their addresses by searching for IRC at keyword: FILE SEARCH. There are also plenty of links throughout the Web; keep an eye out!

Inter(esting)Net chat tips:

1. To enter an IRC channel, you use a *nickname*. Your nickname can be your real name, though if it is common it is probably taken: You'll need something unique (your screen name may do in a pinch). When prompted to enter a password for your nickname, *don't* use your America Online password.

2. You can call for help anytime you're logged into an IRC channel by typing /help.

3. You can send a private message (think Instant Message, but much simpler) by typing /query and their full nickname.

4. If someone bothers you, you can ignore their chat just as you can on America Online. Type /ignore plus their nickname, followed by the @ sign, and then their hostname.

Using AOL Instant Messenger :) :) | Win & Mac

. . . or how to communicate cross-culturally

The more you use the Internet, the more friends you're apt to make. And not all will be members of America Online. That means communication will be essentially limited to Internet e-mail or things like IRC. Or will it?

With the introduction of America Online's new Internet tool — *AOL Instant Messenger* — your friends from the Internet can send you Instant Messages while you're on America Online! (See Figure 7.3.)

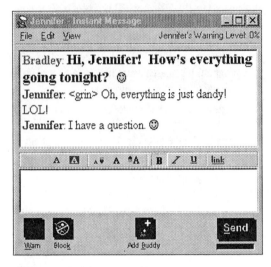

Figure 7.3 AOL Instant Messenger opens up new worlds of communication (view from Windows).

How does it work? Your friend downloads and installs the tool, gets on the Internet, and after a bit of setup, can send and exchange Instant Messages with anyone else currently using the tool, or regular AOL software. They even get Buddy Lists, so that they can see when you're online (and you can see them). Send your Internet friends a link to AOL Instant Messenger at keyword: AIM. The software is available for Windows, Mac, and Java.

There is even a "neighborhood watch program" built in to AOL Instant Messenger, empowering the community with the ability to regulate itself. It relies upon the users of AOL Instant Messenger to report offensive and harassing messages. Warnings are issued for misuse of the features, and users are barred after repeated warnings.

If you connect to the Internet yourself (and not through America Online) but want to stay connected at all times, be sure to get AOL Instant Messenger. You can use your current America Online screen names, if you wish, or choose a new name.

Using AOL NetMail   :) :)   Win 95 only

... or how to calm your mail cravings

If you're like me, one of the first things you do in the morning is check your mail. Reading the belly-busting jokes from my friends and the career-making news from my colleagues really gets my day started in the right direction (I can do without the money-saving offers though). But what do you do when you're visiting a relative who only has the Internet? Or when you're at work and they don't want the AOL software on their network? Use AOL NetMail!

AOL NetMail is a new service from America Online that gives you the ability to send and receive your AOL mail directly from the Web (see Figure 7.4).

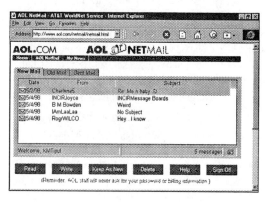

Figure 7.4 AOL NetMail delivers mail on the Web (view from Windows).

No AOL software is required. All you need is Windows 95, Microsoft's Internet Explorer version 3.0 or higher (you probably already have it), an Internet connection (such as an ISP or an office network — yes, it works through firewalls), and the free AOL NetMail software.

To get started, connect to the Internet and go to America Online's Web site at http://www.aol.com with Internet Explorer. Click the **AOL NetMail** button and follow the directions. Once installed, you are asked for your screen name and password. Enter them and voila: your new and old mail are all accessible.

Please keep in mind that you cannot use NetMail while you are signed on to America Online, even if you just want to check your mail on a different screen name. AOL NetMail only works with a separate Internet connection.

Contributed by Kate Tipul (screen name: KMTipul)

| Getting Internet Help | :) :) :) | Win & Mac |

. . . or how to find net.help

Venturing beyond the gates of America Online can be a bit scary, but it's almost always rewarding. If you've already tried it, you'll probably have noticed the big difference between the easy-to-use interface of the AOL software and that of the Internet. It can be a jungle out there! And like any good expedition, it helps to have a guide.

Before you set out on your adventure, make a side trip to America Online's net.help area (keyword: NET HELP). Read up on the Internet and outfit yourself with the basic knowledge essential when you're out there on your own. If you've ever wondered just what that `http://` thing means, or which civilization speaks the *Hypertext Markup Language*, you'll find the answers here.

If you're looking for more help, try these resources — all available through America Online:

- **Learn a lesson!** Keyword: INTERNET HELP is AOL Member Services' step-by-step introduction to the Internet and the World Wide Web.

- **Take a class!** Keyword: ONLINE CLASSROOM offers several free courses on how to use the Internet, such as "Web Searching — How It Works."

- **Network!** Keyword: ON THE NET offers Internet information and resources to America Online members. The message boards are excellent!

- **Connect!** Keyword: IC leads to the Internet Connection, labeled as your "gateway to the Internet." Click **Internet Extras** for the information and links to goodies.

- **Exchange!** Keyword: NET EXCHANGE is an Internet traveler's crossroads, where you can swap sites with other America Online members and get help.

- **Go home!** Keyword: AOL NET HELP is the America Online home page's list of helpful links on understanding and using the Internet.

Don't neglect the wealth of information on the Web, too!

Contributed by Bradley Zimmer
(screen name: Bradley476)

Companion Confessions

When I first arrived on America Online, the Internet was still a scraggly band of networks of little interest to folks outside universities or the military. I had the dubious pleasure of watching it as it struggled to its feet and into the public consciousness. These days it is hard to go anywhere without hearing Internet this, Web that, or hot-potato-triple-dub-dot-com (that's `http://www.com`). Here are some of my own experiences with the Internet:

1. **Mailing on the Internet**. Like most, e-mail was my first brush with the Internet. These days I'd be lost without the ability to send and receive Internet mail. Almost all the plans for this book were made in mail, for example, and there is one friend in particular who I've been getting to know better almost solely through the exchange of mail. Internet e-mail is my lifeline, as neither my editors nor my friend are on America Online.

2. **Creating your own Web page**. As you might imagine, I was on the scene when personal Web pages became all the rage. I spent many late nights putting up the obligatory who-am-I-and-what-do-I-like pages, and having a blast learning along the way. Those pages are still on the Web at `http://members.aol.com/jennifer/`. Since then I've put up pages for my books, reaching folks who aren't yet on America Online. The *AOL Companion* has a home page at `http://members.aol.com/jennifer/aolc/index.html`.

3. **Using AOL Instant Messenger**. Although I don't use it myself yet, my friends Tracy, Shelley, Varian, Paul, and Amy, plus my Grandma Darla, all use AOL Instant Messenger, and it works great for us. Some of these folks are America Online members and others are not. I get their Instant Messages just as I would any others, with the sole exception of the one-time message informing me they are trying to reach me from the Internet. I can even see them on my Buddy List when they are using it.

CHAPTER 8

ENHANCING WITH ADD-ONS

Do you remember your first car? Mine was as big as a boat and quite spartan. Oh, don't get me wrong — I was overjoyed to have it. But once I got over the initial ecstasy of having my own transportation, I began to notice it was lacking some things I needed. I started enhancing my car. I added a drink holder, a nice stereo, cruise control — I even had it painted silver. Those personal touches made all the difference to me. I could go further and do more. You can do the same with America Online!

The AOL software "off-the-disk" does answer the majority of member needs, but not everything. And rightly so. If America Online implemented every request, they would be too busy to do much of anything else and the software would be unwieldy. Instead, America Online makes it easy for other software developers to create *add-ons*, separate programs intended to work hand-in-hand with AOL's software. What can they do? Probably everything except wash your car.

Success with add-ons does require an understanding of their nature. First, like the cruise control I installed on that old car, add-ons are separate and distinct from your AOL software; that means I can't contact America Online when I have a problem with an add-on. Most of the add-on developers provide good technical support, and are happy to help. Second, because add-ons are separate, there may be a separate fee for their use — though you can often try them out for free. Third, add-ons are always designed specifically for your kind of computer and software. Not all add-ons are available for all computers.

With that said, let's take a drive through the world of add-ons for America Online. Oh, and, I'm sure you knew this, but . . . that convenient "drink holder" that pulls out from your computer is actually for CD-ROMs. Really.

Finding Add-On Software   :) :) :)   Win & Mac

. . . or how to soup up your software

Have you ever been to one of those auto parts superstores? If so, you probably felt a little overwhelmed, knowing there was something in there you could really use but just not sure where the heck to find it. This is a lot like trying to find America Online add-ons. Add-ons are all over the place, but finding the one you need can be like searching for a quarter to pay the toll. So let me give you a map to the major add-on destinations:

1. **Use File Search.** Search for all add-ons in AOL Computing Channel libraries by using keyword: FILE SEARCH, clicking the **Shareware** button, and entering **AOL Add-On**.

2. **Browse libraries.** Several good libraries are dedicated exclusively to add-ons. For starters, go to keyword: DOWNLOAD SOFTWARE and open **Utilities & Tools**. At this point, Windows users open **Miscellaneous Tools**, and open the **Windows AOL Add-On** library. Mac users open **Telecom and Internet Tools** and then the **America Online Add-Ons** library. Keep in mind that these libraries may move around a bit, but should always be somewhere in their home forums.

3. **Accessorize.** Keyword: ACCESSORIES is an America Online-sponsored area with links to several third-party and offline add-on applications. New add-ons may appear here, so check back regularly.

4. **Go to the source.** Several add-ons have special areas of their own. Here is a mini keyword directory for America Online add-ons:

Add-On	Keyword
AOL AutoDialer	Keyword: AUTODIALER
Gritty Snert	Keyword: GRITTY NEWS
PowerTools and PowerKids	Keyword: BPS
AOL Instant Messenger	Keyword: AIM
AOL NetMail	Keyword: NETMAIL
AOL PowerPac	Keyword: POWERPAC

We'll go into more detail on several of these important add-ons in this chapter!

Getting Online with AutoDialer :) :) :) | Win 3.0 only

. . . or how to ram the gate

America Online has had growing pains. If you've been around the block online, you know what I'm talking about. If you're new, let's hope you never do. Realistically, however, it is likely that we'll feel more pain in the future. America Online continues to grow, and with growth will come more busy signals, particularly during peak times. If you encounter busy signals using version 3.0 of the Windows software, you'll soon wish you had a way to redial the number more than just once. And you're in luck: America Online created the AutoDialer, which does just that.

AOL AutoDialer can help you get online easier and faster by redialing those same numbers up to nine times in a row. Installation is simple and the program is free of charge. You'll find it at keyword: AUTODIALER. Just read the directions and click **Continue**. Be aware that the installation process requires that your AOL software be restarted; save your work and finish your conversations before you begin it. Once installed, you can set the number of times you'd like a number dialed in your normal setup (see Figure 8.1)! No extra programs or weird steps.

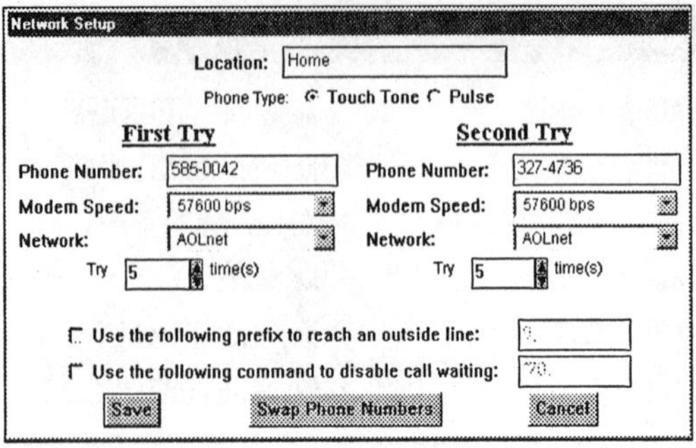

Figure 8.1 The AutoDialer integrates seamlessly (view from Windows AOL software version 3.0).

Using AOL software version 4.0? There's no need to download this add-on — a built-in autodialer is in your software already!

Powering Up with PowerTools :) :)   Win only

. . . or how to get a jolt

America Online's interface has improved greatly over the years, yet I still don't have every feature I'd like to see in the software. Enter *PowerTools*, a wonderfully powerful set of software tools that lets me manage everything from chat to e-mail to keywords.

Created by BPS Software, this Windows-based program can only be appreciated by using and testing it out for yourself. I am a PowerTools addict because of its ease of use and the functionality it's brought me both as a member and as a community leader. You can download it at keyword: BPS and try it out. If you like it, just send in your registration fee and continue using it. If you don't, just throw it away. Sorry, Mac users — at this time there are no plans to create a Mac version.

PowerTips:

1. **Customize the toolbar.** PowerTools lets you change the standard toolbar to meet your needs. Get rid of the stuff you never use, or just redecorate.

2. **Record your actions.** There's an Action Recorder that keeps track of all your movements and saves

them, enabling you to repeat them with the click of a button.

3. **Make hotlists.** Beef up your list of Favorite Places, which include FTP sites, action files, and chat rooms, as well as the standard Favorite Places.

4. **Find your keys.** Import and access the latest list of keywords and search them all.

5. **Bang down the door.** You can use their Get In! feature to get into full chat rooms of all kinds.

6. **Chatter up.** You can assign colors to specific chatters, type longer sentences, and keep better track of who recently entered and left the room. There's also a review function, which lets you view and copy all available chat from other members in the room. Oh, logging is easier and more reliable, too!

7. **Phrase it right.** A PhraseEditor function enables you to store often-used phrases, letter templates, ASCII Art, and much more. These are megamacros!

8. **Keep tabs on IMs.** Use the PowerIM window and receive all Instant Messages in a single window. Screen names are displayed on tabs at the top of the window so you can toggle back and forth. New messages show up as red tabs to avoid confusion. Better yet, you can set auto-answers for incoming messages when you're busy or away from the keyboard.

9. **Make waves.** A Wav Manager function organizes all your sound files (WAV) for use anywhere at anytime. You can even give your sounds more descriptive names.

10. **Time yourself.** A Timer & Alarm function keeps track of the time you've spent online, whether you need to budget your money, your time, or your sanity.

In addition to these features, PowerTools incorporates some of the most popular features of PowerMail, another add-on by BPS Software. Included are style sheets to let you preconfigure styles and formats, form letters for frequently sent mail, and its own spelling checker.

These are just a few of the useful things PowerTools offers. I highly recommend you try it out for yourself. If you get stuck, visit keyword: BPS and click the **Power Help Center** for answers to commonly asked questions and tips on how to use the software. They also have live online technical support, message boards, and a newsletter. The forum is filled with friendly folks happy to assist.

PowerTools isn't just the equivalent of adding cruise control to your car — it is like going from a manual transmission to an automatic!

Contributed by Becky Fowler (screen name: BeckyFowlr)

Meet Becky

Becky Fowler (screen name: *BeckyFowlr*) is a consummate community leader, gifted teacher, and expert member. Becky makes her home in Illinois, though I'm happy to say her virtual home is with me in The VirtuaLeader Academy. Becky is always ready with friendly words and supportive gestures. Thank you, Becky!

Watching with PowerKids   :) :) c   Win only

. . . or how to have eyes in the back of your head

The Internet isn't always the safest place for children. You've seen it in the news, you've read it in the papers, and now's the time to do something about it. *PowerKids* is currently the only add-on software designed for kids aged 12 through 17. Another one of BPS Software's creations, this add-on is a light version of their popular PowerTools, with the addition of complete customization of parental controls for online sessions and the Web.

Beyond sporting many of PowerTools features, PowerKids enables you to set specific limits on the amount of time each screen name can spend online. That is further broken down into limits that can be set on each session, day, or billing period. In addition, there are powerful auditing tools, which enable you to track time online, where it is spent, and the charges accrued.

As with most of BPS Software's programs, PowerKids does have a small registration fee which includes free upgrades within the version (usually about a year's worth). Before you buy, you can preview a slightly limited version of the software. If you pay the registration fee all features are activated. Besides providing protection for children, PowerKids may also be a good buy for businesses that use America Online but don't want their employees to abuse it. The preview version's free, so there's no reason not to try it out! Full details and the download can be found in the BPS Software Forum at keyword: BPS.

Please note that this tip was written before the actual software became available. As with any dynamic software, there may be changes to the features described above by the time you try it out yourself. But BPS Software always provides excellent help resources, not to mention an entire forum of helpful folks happy to answer your questions and hear your suggestions. Just visit keyword: BPS.

Contributed by Bradley Zimmer
(screen name: Bradley476)

Chatting with Gritty Snert   :) :) :) | Win 3.0 only

. . . or how to repel the pests

Just what is a snert? Its meaning is about as pleasant as it sounds: a chat room pest who tries to intentionally ruin the chat for others. As we described in Chapter 5, you can use the AOL software to ignore these no-goodnicks while they are in the room with you, but if they leave and come back the Ignore command wears off. Enter an America Online add-on called *Gritty Snert* (see Figure 8.2).

Once installed, Gritty Snert gives you control over what you (or your children) see in chat rooms. You can ignore specific people, and then continue ignoring them for as long as you like. You can also filter out certain words (such as vulgarities), dice rolls, or anyone who sends a lot of text to the room in rapid succession (scrollers). Everything is fully configurable, naturally, so you can tailor the filters to meet your needs.

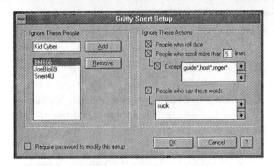

Figure 8.2 Gritty Snert gives you chat control (view from Windows AOL software version 3.0).

Gritty Snert is a great freebie. Well, actually, there is a cost — it is requested that you send a shotglass if you like it. But no nagging if you don't, and no registration. A Guide (Sean Stallings) who has seen and heard it all designed Gritty Snert to help his fellow members. More details can be found at keyword: GRITTY NEWS.

At this time, Gritty Snert only works with Windows AOL software version 3.0 and below, and only with the 16-bit client.

Using Window-To-Back   :) :) :)   Mac only

. . . or how to get through a window

Have you ever been stuck in a window? No, not the kind in a house — the kind on your computer. You know, like when you're uploading a file and the little window that shows your progress won't let you move to another window. Or when you're ordering flowers for your mother's birthday and you can't look up your Mom's phone number on the computer because you can't open a file or do anything other than stare at the ordering window. These windows are usually missing a title bar (the bar at the top of a window with the "racing stripes") and beep at you if you even attempt to click another window. They can make life online difficult, but there is a way around them with *Window-To-Back*.

Window-To-Back is a simple little utility. It does one thing, but it does it well. Once installed, you simply press a key (or three) and the window that is forefront on your screen is sent to the bottom of the stack, enabling you to move about freely. It doesn't close this window, and whatever you were doing isn't canceled. When you're ready to return to it, you simply click it again to bring it to the front, or select it from your **Window** menu within America Online.

Sounds simple, huh? I'd be lost without it. Give it a try by going to keyword: FILE SEARCH and searching on **Window FKey**. There are a number of different types, but they all do basically the same thing. Once downloaded, you can install it using an FKey installer (some are available online, too). An *FKey*, by the way, is one of those keys at the very top of your keyboard — **F1**, **F2**, **F3**, etc. You put Window-To-Back into action when you press one of these keys (the key varies).

This function is available only on the Mac. You can switch between windows on the PC by pressing **Ctrl** and **Tab** simultaneously, though that doesn't help you if you get stuck in a window.

Automating with Key Quencer :) :) | Mac only

. . . or how to get out of doing chores

Click, click, click, type type typetypetype type, click, type, click! Sound familiar? If you use America Online often at all, I'm sure you can recognize the sound of doing something you've done a hundred times before. Like doing the dishes, repetitive tasks become monotonous and lifeless, sucking away the fun and excitement of being online. But you can change that by automating things you do often with a shareware program known as *Key Quencer*.

Key Quencer is a *macro* utility (see Figure 8.3). Macros are files containing instructions on how to perform a series of tasks. Once a macro is created, you can use a single keystroke to put it into action, doing that once-repetitive task quickly and efficiently. They are a little bit like a dishwasher, only much cheaper and quieter.

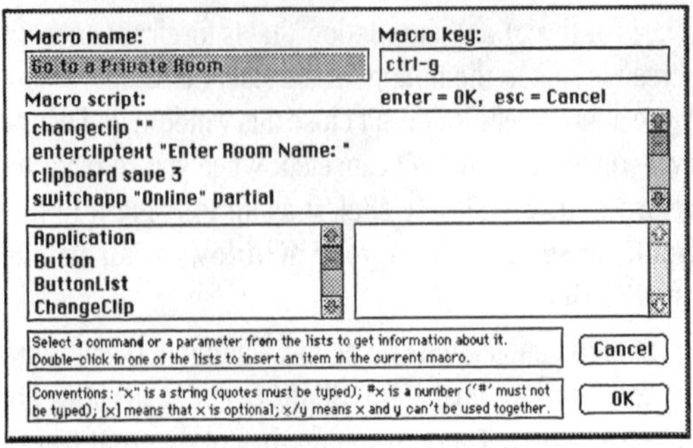

Figure 8.3 Creating a Key Quencer macro (view from the Mac).

You can do all sorts of things with Key Quencer, such as have it sign on for you and bring up your new mail first thing, or have it take you directly to a private room. You can even use it to display reminders to get offline and visit your Mom, or help you send her an e-mail. It is easy to use and versatile, offering lots of functions for those who need them. For those new to macro programs, there are pre-programmed macro files available online for Key Quencer to do things like help you delete or compose mail quickly. To find Key Quencer, go to keyword: FILE SEARCH, search on **Key Quencer**, and download the "Lite" version. Documentation is included. At this time, Key Quencer only works on the Mac.

Mailing with Claris Em@iler   :) :)   Mac only

... or how to manage your mail better

E-mail is a blessing and a curse. It is easy and convenient to use, with the ability to improve and clarify your communications. But its ease and convenience also mean you may receive far too much of it to actually read, understand, and digest, not to mention reply. Add to that multiple Internet and AOL accounts, each receiving e-mail, and you have a problem. The solution? Claris *Em@iler*.

Em@iler is a commercial program that manages your mail. The most powerful feature is its ability to sort, file, reply, and forward your new mail. If you go out of town for a weekend, Em@iler can automatically reply to those who e-mail you while you're gone. Upon your return, your mail is sorted into hierarchical folders based on name, subject—whatever you want. It works with America Online, Internet service providers, and other online services (though not the Web-based free mail services). It collects your mail from as many e-mail accounts as you have—and stores it all in one easy-to-access place.

Once you've purchased and installed Em@iler, use the **Easy Setup** wizard to configure it to send and retrieve e-mail. Once set up, you can check mail with Em@iler whenever you want—you can even schedule it.

Em@iler's documentation shows you how to do such things as schedule pickup and delivery times for your mail, create an address book, attach signature files, import and export addresses, save sent mail and read mail for a certain timeframe, and so on. More information is at http://www.apple.com/products/claris/clarisemailer.html.

Meet Sue

Sue Boettcher (screen name: *SueBD*) is an experienced member and community leader. She also has an interest in psychology (do you see a trend here?), and enjoys photography and music, not to mention computers. Thank you, Sue!

Contributed by Sue Boettcher(screen name: SueBD)

Tooling About with OneClick   :) :) | Mac only

. . . or how to make your own toolbars

Do you like the America Online toolbar at the top of the screen? It keeps important functions close at hand, it is easy to reach, and you can move it around the screen as you like. Now, wouldn't it be great if you could customize this toolbar? You can in AOL software version 4.0, but only to a limited extent. What if you need more control?

Use the commercially-available program that lets you create more toolbar-like windows. You have total control over what buttons do and where they go on these new toolbars. What is it? *OneClick* by WestCode Software.

OneClick is a bit like Key Quencer (described earlier in this chapter) in that it can record and use macros. But the OneClick macros are activated through buttons, rather than keystrokes. These buttons are placed on floating windows, like the America Online toolbar, that stay within reach for your convenience. You have complete control over the look and feel of these toolbars — they can be simple and plain, or fancy and detailed. And like Key Quencer there are OneClick toolbars already programmed and available online for your use. In fact, there are a lot of America Online-specific tools to help with mail, chat, navigation, and more. Plus making your own is simple and easy.

OneClick is available through the normal places you purchase software. It can also be ordered through the Web (which is what I did) at http://www.west-codesoft.com. At this time, OneClick is only available for Mac.

OneClick tips:

1. Use existing resources. There are many toolbars made specifically for America Online already available online. You'll find most of them by searching at keyword: FILE SEARCH for **OneClick**.

2. Follow examples. Use the library of examples, or examples from the preprogrammed toolbars available online. This is one of the best ways to learn.

3. Keep it small. The smaller your toolbars, the better. Don't crowd your limited screen "real estate" with toolbars that are overly large.

Companion Confessions

The moment of truth arrives. What kind of computer does the author really prefer? Well, I think I've been good up to this point. My companions and I have tried to present both computer platforms fairly, not letting either get too much attention when it wasn't warranted. But now that you know so much about me, and the end is drawing near, I think it is about time you knew the truth. I'm actually a stark-raving, madly-in-love, card-carrying, proud-to-be-an-American owner of a splendiferous Apple Macintosh (actually four Macs, but who's counting?). So, as such, my confessions about add-ons are mostly Mac-oriented. I'm sure you understand.

1. **Finding add-ons.** As you may have already observed, Mac add-ons are hard to come by. It isn't often you'll hear them discussed over coffee, or debated about in a chat room, so it becomes much more important that you know where to find them. My favorite hunting ground is the **America Online Add-Ons** library in the Mac Utilities Forum.

2. **Using Window-To-Back.** An absolute essential, Window-To-Back lets me put that pesky order form window in the background while I check my mail for the shipping address, or avoid having to restart my computer when it gets too fond of one window. I think this should be built right into the system.

3. **Using OneClick.** OneClick has been invaluable in making America Online work for *me*. In the past, I have had toolbars all around the perimeter of my screen, helping me navigate to often-visited places faster, sort my mail and files, and keep in contact with my friends and colleagues. I've also taken advantage of the various member-created toolbars available in the America Online libraries. I've even made specialized toolbars for times when I play games on America Online or other "labor-intensive" tasks.

APPENDIX A

SMILE WHEN YOU SAY THAT: SMILEYS AND OTHER EMOTICONS

Here's a language everyone can master: Smiley!

When you're online, people can't see the smile on your face when a long-lost friend finds you. Nor can they hear the pain in your voice when that same friend remembers you owe him money. So we have Smiley. For the linguists out there, Smiley is a pictographic language — for the rest of us: think of it as a bunch of cute pictures. Smileys are made up of nothing more than typographic characters, the ones on everyone's keyboard. Chances are you've seen smileys already. They are everywhere you go on America Online — in chats, Instant Messages, message boards, e-mail, and even articles. The most basic smiley has eyes (a colon) and a smile (a close parentheses) like that shown in Figure A.1 .

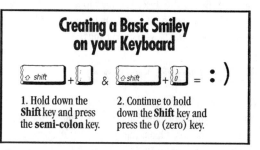

Creating a Basic Smiley on your Keyboard

1. Hold down the **Shift** key and press the **semi-colon** key.

2. Continue to hold down the **Shift** key and press the 0 (zero) key.

Figure A.1 The keystrokes needed to create a simple smiley.

Can't see the face? Tilt your head to the left and look at it again. Smileys build off the idea that simple letters, numbers and punctuation can take on new meaning when viewed in a different light. It is a bit like seeing a fly-ing elephant when you looked up at the clouds as a child.

Smileys convey the feelings and characteristics that normally accompany our words. They enrich, clarify, and strengthen our communications, bringing people to life even through the starkness of the computer screen.

But don't get the wrong impression. America Online members are not a bunch of goofs sitting around smiling at one another all day (well, not all day). Smileys are just one aspect — albeit a happy one — of the language. Other emotions like anger, passion, frustration, sarcasm, and sadness also have corresponding icons — in fact, we aptly term these emoticons.

Throughout this appendix I will be using smileys and other emoticons just as I would online. Watch where they fall, how they are used, and which ones are chosen. While my personal style is by no means the standard, it is close enough to give you a little taste of what I affectionately term *emotica*. ; >

Top Ten Smileys and Emoticons

While there are many smileys and countless variations, only a few are used with any consistency or depth of meaning. Below I've described the top ten popular smi-leys and emoticons on America Online, along with com-mon variations and how-to instructions.

1. The Classic Smiley :)

Regardless of where you go online, the Classic Smiley is a universal symbol of cheerfulness. You'll find it in e-mail, Instant Messages, chats, and even official correspon-dence from corporate America Online. It is used liberally as it conveys a lightness and good-naturedness that can be hard to express solely in words. It has been over-used at times — some tend to type it after every sentence or after delivering bad news. If you find yourself doing this, try a variation (there are several in this appendix). If you do find yourself smiling, use the Classic Smiley — you'll find that even online, smiles are infectious.

To create: Hold down the **Shift** key and type : (to produce a colon) and then hold down the **Shift** key and press the **0** (**zero**) key (to produce a close parentheses). :)

2. The Big Smiley :D

When the Classic Smiley seems too vague or weak, show some teeth with the Big Smiley. Research into smiles has shown that showing teeth is an indicator of a stronger feeling of happiness and a genuine expression of good tidings (no kidding). The Big Smiley radiates joy, laughter, and sincere affection. Use it sparingly for the best effect. Oh, and like real smiles, using the Big Smiley can actually improve your mood.

To create: Hold down the **Shift** key and press the : key (to produce a colon). Then hold down the **Shift** key and press the **D** key (to produce an uppercase *D*). : D

3. The Wink ;)

With a wink and a smiley ;) you can show you've got style. While winks are often thought of as flirtatious when done off the computer, they are mostly used online to express humor or sarcasm. You'll find them appearing after jokes as a reminder to laugh. Without the wink, a sarcastic comment can be taken seriously, destroying the mood or even a friendship. For the flirts out there, just avoid jokes or sarcasm when you wink for maximum effect. Try the impish wink ; > when you're really being naughty (but nice).

To create: Press the ; key (to produce a semicolon) and then press **Shift+0** (to produce an end parentheses). ;)

4. The Grimace :/

The Grimace conveys a variety of feelings, from sadness and resignation to remorse and frustration. It does not imply an intensity of feeling, however. Use it when something is bothering you, or when you feel you'd normally let out a sigh. A variation is : \ , with no additional meaning attached. You may also see : | , which conveys a similar feeling but one even less intense — I always think "glum" when I see that one.

To create: Hold down the **Shift** key and press the : key (to produce a colon). Then hold down the **Shift** key and press ? (to produce a slash). : /

5. The Little Pout :<

While the Little Pout is most often used when feeling petulant or deprived (whether serious or playful), it can express the full gamut of less intense negative emotions. I must admit I use this fairly often when something isn't quite going my way. : <

To create: Hold down the **Shift** key and press the : key (to produce a colon). Then hold down the **Shift** key and press , (to produce an open bracket). : <

6. The Classic Frown :(

A frown is simply a smile turned upside down, or in this case, flip-flopped. And like smiles, frowns are just as necessary to convey our feelings to others. Use the Classic Frown to express your genuine displeasure or sadness. It is more negative than either the Grimace or the Little Pout, and carries with it a stronger statement. If your feelings go beyond the Classic Frown, you may want to leave emoticons out entirely and express yourself in carefully chosen words instead. Emoticons of any sort tend to evoke familiarity, which can downplay intensity.

To create: Hold down the **Shift** key and press the : key (to produce a colon). Then press **Shift+9** to produce an open parentheses. : (

7. The Tongue :p

The Tongue is really quite innocent — imagine a child sticking out their tongue at someone and you've got the picture. The Tongue is used as a response to teasing or playful harassment, or even as an expression of embarrassment. It is rarely taken in offense, though you should take care to use it appropriately. Variations are the Bigger Tongue : P , the Bronx Cheer :pPpPpP~ , and the French Kiss :pd: (which isn't quite so innocent).

To create: Hold down the **Shift** key and press the : key (to produce a colon). Then press the **P** key (to produce a lowercase *p*). :p

8. The Kiss :*

Just as the same kiss in urban Europe and rural America have different meanings, so does the Kiss on America Online. Rarely used as a greeting with acquaintances, the Kiss is more often exchanged between close friends or significant others. It carries a feeling of familiarity, so it is not often used when flirting with strangers. Even so, there are subcultures within the America Online community that have different rules. Observe your environment, be true to yourself, and be considerate. A variation is the Long Kiss : * * * * * .

To create: Hold down the **Shift** key and press the : key (to produce a colon). Then press **Shift+8** to produce an asterisk. : *

9. The Shocked Expression :o

The Shocked Expression is used to convey mild surprise or shock. I often use it when someone says something I'd never have expected to "hear" online, or when something unlikely happens. A variation is the Hair-On-End Shocked Expression ===:o (those dashes are my "hair" standing straight up in shock—I have long hair).

To create: Hold down the **Shift** key and press the : key to produce a colon. Then press the **O** key to produce a lowercase *o*. :o

10. The Quiet One :x

The Quiet One has two different meanings, though both imply that the user is not "talking." The first is to indicate that they are hushing up, perhaps in deference to a story being recited or as an indication their feelings have been hurt. The second is used when something was "spoken" that was better left alone, such as when a bad joke was made or when something hurtful was done. : / This last takes some experience to use and interpret correctly.

To create: Hold down the **Shift** key and press the **:** key (to produce a colon) and then press the **X** key (to produce a lowercase *x*). : x

The America Online Nose Job

Glance back through the top ten smileys on the previous pages and you'll notice none have noses. Eyes and mouths abound, but not a nose in sight. Take the Classic Smiley — without the nose it appears as :) but with the nose it looks like : -) . This noseless face is the America Online "dialect" of smileys. Before you look down your nose at our custom, consider that it is faster and easier to type a smiley sans nose. Besides, few of us wish to stick our noses in other people's screens. ;)

All puns aside, the beakless smiley is a hallmark of the veteran America Online member. But if you wish to show off your nose, rejoice in your olfactory organs by including them in all your smileys. The classically straight-and-narrow nose as seen in the Classic Smiley above : -) is but one example. Consider the "turn-up" nose : ^) , the clown nose : o) , or even the pierced nose : ?) . Whatever your preference, use it consistently in each smiley you display. No one will know you picked your own nose. : D

The Complete Smiler

As you can imagine, once folks realized the potential for communication (and miscommunication) in smileys, new smileys flew out of their keyboards and onto the screens of unsuspecting members. Though some claim there are hundreds of smileys, most of these really stretch the imagination. Following are fifty smileys from my personal collection of emotica that you can actually identify and use (at least occasionally). Just remember that, unlike the Top Ten America Online Smileys, these aren't as recognizable and you may need to explain them. But they make great conversation starters. :>

>:(= I'm angry or annoyed.

:~(= I'm crying.

:t = I'm cross.

:s = I'm confused.

:c = I'm pouting (and I'm going to trip over my lower lip).

:r = I'm giving you a raspberry.

:Y = I'm whispering.

:V = I'm shouting!

:@ = I'm screaming!

:9 = I'm licking my lips.

:+ = I'm pursing my lips.

:6 = I'm making a face of distaste.

:$ = I'm wearing braces.

:T = I'm trying to keep a straight face.

:& = I'm tongue-tied.

:<> = I'm bored (a yawn).

|) = I'm sleeping.

8) = I'm wearing glasses.

B) = I'm wearing sunglasses/shades.

:{) = I have a mustache.

O.o = I'm raising an eyebrow.

O.O = My eyes are opened wide.

:k = I'm chewing on my lower lip.

O:> = I'm an angel (for innocent remarks).

}:> = I'm a devil (for lewd remarks).

<:) = I'm bald.

") = I have one black eye.

X(= I'm a Dead Head.

*:o) = I'm clowning around.

[:] = I'm a robot.

Southpaws

Left-handed? Show off your orientation proudly with lefty smileys. Just reverse the order and characters of your favorite smileys so they read from right to left rather than left to right. For example, the Classic Smiley :) can be easily translated into (: . You can't convert every smiley—not all characters have mirror-image equivalents—you can create new smileys that most folks would never think of. Consider the Super Smiley C: , the Queen (:E , or the Mouse <:3 . One caveat: if you use the Southpaw Smiley dialect, be sure to use it consistently or folks may think your head is exploding <: when you're really just grinning. :>

:! = I'm smoking.

:? = I'm smoking a pipe.

:Q = I'm smoking and talking at the same time.

K:p = I'm wearing a propeller beanie.

d:) = I'm wearing a cap.

[:) = I'm wearing a headset.

8:) = I'm wearing a bow.

:)X = I'm wearing a bow tie.

:P~~~~~ = I'm drooling.

*<|:o>D = I'm Santa Claus.

:[= I'm a vampire.

:© = I'm a lawyer.

:=} = I'm a baboon.

<:| = I'm a dunce.

(:) = I'm an egghead.

P> = I'm a pirate.

=) = I'm a troublemaker.

:)) = I'm really happy (or I have a double chin).

:`) = I'm embarrassed.

%) = I've seen too many smileys today.

Have You Hugged Your Computer Today?

While I don't recommend hugging your computer (the cables can really get in your way), hugging is an established and common way of greeting friends on America Online. How can you hug through the modem? Imagine what two arms outstretched and ready to hug look like. Conveniently, a curly bracket { bears a striking resemblance to this. Now type them around the name of the person you want to hug {{{Jennifer}}} and you have an online hug. The more hugs, the more affection you feel. If you see the square brackets used [[[George]]], this often signifies a masculine hug given from male to male. Beware of hugging those you do not know. If you enjoy hugs, make your own special hugs using brackets, kisses, and so on. My favorite? The Angel Hug with airy, light hugs: { { { { Varian } } } }.

You've got personality!

Do the Classic Smileys leave you uninspired? Does your true self beg to be recognized and celebrated in all its variety? Do you feel you would reign supreme online if only you could express yourself clearly? You need wait no longer, my friend. Yes, you too can have personalized smileys that light up the screen and convey your dazzling individuality to the world. And for a limited time only, we'll throw in a 300 bps modem! ;>

Well, maybe you won't get a modem, but you *can* personalize your smileys. Include your individual style or characteristics and add depth to your online communications. If you have a mustache, you can add a mustache to *all* your smileys with the open curly bracket : { > . Try on some of these other ideas or create your own!

On the head

== = Long hair ==:)   # = Short hair #:)

[= Headset [:)   d = Cap d : >

E] = Cowboy hat E] :)   <} = Wizard's hat <} ; >

< | = Witch's hat < | ; >   O = Angel's halo O ; >

} = Devil's horns } ; >   8 = Bow 8 :)

On the face

8 = Glasses 8)   B = Sunglasses B)

{ = Mustache : { >   [= Handlebar mustache : [>

! = Cigarette : !   ? = Pipe : ?

Below the face

> = Goatee :) >   X = Bow tie :) X

Anything else is probably too naughty for this book! ; >

Be shy and bold

You can add some flare without showing quite so much of your self by using *styled text* for your smileys. You can crack a big bold **:D** or choose an unusual type face for contrast ;) (Frutiger) and while it is beyond the budget of this book, you can even give your shocked expression a shock of red hair! ==:o All you need is the AOL 4.0 software, where the chat rooms give you the power to spice up your smileys. You can select a font, add **bold**, *italic,* and/or underline in any **_combination_**. Just remember that folks using older versions of the AOL software will see the same familiar :) .

Inventing new smileys

Do you have an idea for the next great smiley masterpiece, or perhaps just a new way to express a feeling?

Indulge your creativity and invent a smiley! Begin by typing out all the characters you can generate (don't forget the **Shift** key), print it out, turn the paper 90 degrees clockwise, and take a good look. Do they remind you of anything? Free associate, and don't let your aesthetic sensibilities get in your way yet. Use your creativity to put together faces and bodies. Just remember that smileys are by no means an exact science and that their success relies upon recognizable features and patterns. :)

Every Little Smile

My friend Vicki sent me this story, along with a smile:

Mark was walking home from junior high one day when he noticed the boy ahead of him had tripped and dropped a stack of books, a couple of sweaters, and a small cassette recorder. Mark knelt and helped the boy pick up the scattered articles. As they were going the same way, he carried part of the burden. As they walked, Mark learned the boy's name was Bill and that Bill loved video games and history. He also discovered that he was having trouble with school and that he had just broken up with his girlfriend. They arrived at Bill's home first and Mark was invited in. The afternoon passed pleasantly with a few laughs. They continued to bump into one another around junior high and high school. Three weeks before graduation, Bill spoke to Mark of the day years ago when they had first met. "Did you ever wonder why I was carrying so many things home that day?" asked Bill. "You see, I cleaned out my locker because I didn't want to leave a mess. I had some of my mother's sleeping pills and I was going home to commit suicide. But after we spent time together talking and laughing, I realized that I would have missed that time and others that might follow. So you see, Mark, when you picked up those books, you did a lot more — you saved my life."

No smile, no hello, no helping hand is too small.

ASCII Art

Though faces remain the most familiar and recognizable shapes — online and off — there are hundreds of other pictures and representations you can use to express yourself online. Known collectively as *ASCII Art*, this term refers to the fact that all components of the "artwork" are from the ASCII (American Standard Code for Information Interchange) set of characters. Well-known examples include the rose @>—`—,—-, the fish <:))>< , and refreshments: YYY (glasses of wine), c{-} (a mug of beer), c[~] (a cup of cocoa), \&&&&/ (a bowl of pretzels), and |> |> |> (slices of pizza). There is also the arrow <-- which is used in chat to refer to oneself in the third person, whether as a statement or in response to a question (for example, Jennifer: <-- still here).

Though the examples we've seen so far have been simple, ASCII Ärt really does deserve its name. More complicated images range from multiline line drawings, lettering, pictures, and even miniaturized text-to-art (see Figure A.2). Many are beautiful, some are weird, and a few are even useful.

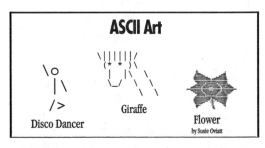

Figure A.2 Examples of ASCII Art.

You should remember three important things about using multiline ASCII Art in a chat room. First, you need to be able to send the lines to the screen quickly for maximum effect. To aid in this, consider a macro program (several are discussed in Chapter 8). Second, large ASCII Art can be disruptive to a conversation. Display it only when appropriate to the chat. Last, if you see a piece of art you'd like to use, don't just take it — ask the artist if art you'd like to use, don't just take it—ask the artist if you may also use it. Many collections of ASCII Art within AOL libraries have been donated to the general public.

Body Language

Cute pictures can only take you so far if your goal is true comprehension. If you type : / in response to a bad joke, does this mean you are groaning at the poor attempt at humor, or that you're sighing because it struck a raw nerve? While a true groan or sigh would be the ideal and one day we'll be able to transmit even these while online, for now the next best thing is the words themselves. You could just type out *groan* or *sigh*, but these disembodied words get confused with your chat and other dialogue. Thus, to denote our actions and body language, we use special characters around the text.

On America Online, there are two primary methods used to express body language:

1. Use two or more colons around your words: ::groan:: or :::::sigh:::::.
2. Use a set of brackets around your words: <groan> or <sigh>.

The first method is used almost exclusively on America Online, and I suspect it was invented here. The second is more widely used across the Internet and even has its own shorthand: for example, <s> stands for *smile*, <g> stands for *grin*, and <vbg> stands for *very big grin*.

Some quiet people are known to communicate almost exclusively through smileys and emoticons, much as they do through facial expressions and body language in the 3D world. Others tend to use these online devices sparingly. Either way, smileys and emoticons are useful for expressing nonverbal actions in this nonvisual world. If you learn nothing else from me, remember this: Smile— it makes people wonder what you're up to. O;>

APPENDIX B

GMTA: SHORTHANDS AND NETIQUETTE

GMTA! Great Minds *do* Think Alike online . . . especially when it comes to communication. In addition to the Smiley language and other emotica, the America Online community has its own system of shorthands and netiquette (*'Net + etiquette*). So, all you Great Minds out there (isn't everyone reading my book a Great Mind?), put on your thinking caps and join me as we explore America Online shorthands and netiquette.

Can You Take a Letter?

Throw out your steno pads! This is shorthand for the electronic age. To keep up with fast-paced, quick-witted online conversations, common phrases are converted into a shorthand to reduce the stress on our keyboards (not to mention our wrists). These online shorthands are simply acronyms — words formed from the first letters of phrases. Some you may already recognize, like *FYI* (For Your Information) or *SNAFU* (Situation Normal: All Fudged Up). But most shorthands stand for popular expressions in online chats, like *AFK* (Away From Keyboard) or *LOL* (Laughing Out Loud). There are many online shorthands, though most you will only see about as often as I get a cheap phone bill. Below are the most popular shorthands used on America Online, followed by a full list.

LOL (Laughing Out Loud)

We love to laugh! All across America Online, you'll "hear" bursts of laughter in the form of *LOL*! It is used generously in chats, Instant Messages, and e-mail, and usually in the company of smileys. Its cousins are the stronger *LHOL* (Laughing Heartily Out Loud), the down-and-dirty *ROFL* (Rolling On Floor Laughing), the more exuberant *ROFLMAO* (Rolling On Floor Laughing My Arms Off), and the simple *OTF* (On The Floor). You may even see *LOLOL!* or *LOLOLOL!* — these are not mere snickers or bursts, but full-bellied peals of laughter that ring through the room. Feel free to join in and remember: They're not laughing at you, they're laughing *with* you!

Example: *LOL! Did you really say that to her? ;)*

AFK (Away From Keyboard)

Unlike face-to-face conversations where you *know* your partner has wandered off in search of the facilities, it is really hard to tell when folks online leave their keyboards for a moment. To save folks the embarrassment of talking to an empty chair for ten minutes, folks on America Online type *AFK* when they're leaving the keyboard, even if only for a minute or two. If you plan to be away for longer, perhaps even if you intend to sign off and return, you can use *BRB* (Be Right Back), *BBIAB* (Be Back In A Bit), or *BBL* (Be Back Later). When you return, simply type *BAK* (Back At Keyboard) to let folks know you've returned.

Example: *AFK (to let my dog Kippi out).*

BTW (By The Way)

General expressions find their way into shorthand just as easily. *BTW* (By The Way) is used when you want to pass on bits of trivia or just share some news. Close cousins are *FYI* (For Your Information), *FYA* (For Your Amusement), and *FWIW* (For What It's Worth). Don't be surprised if old expressions find their way into new short-hand, too. Think *DYK* (Did You Know . . .) will catch on?

Example: *BTW, did you know it's Dave's birthday?*

IMHO (In My Humble Opinion)

America Online members are nothing if not opinionated. *IMHO* (In My Humble Opinion) occurs frequently, as does *IMO* (In My Opinion) and the ever-so-modest *IMN-SHO* (In My Not So Humble Opinion). And, of course, when your opinions coincide, you can use *GMTA* (Great Minds Think Alike).

Example: *IMHO, this software needs more work. :/*

J/K (Just Kidding!)

If an opinion was overboard, you may see it followed shortly by *J/K* (Just Kidding). It either means they forgot to wink or they realized their comment might result in virtual harm if taken seriously.

Example: *j/k! I'd never really do that!*

Online Shorthand A–Z

Here's the full list of common shorthand for your reference. How many can you use in one sentence? j/k! ;)

ADN = Any Day Now

AFAIK = As Far As I Know

AFK = Away From Keyboard

AFKFAS = Away From Keyboard For A Second

BAK = Back At Keyboard

BBIAB = Be Back In A Bit

BBL = Be Back Later

BBS = Bulletin Board System

BFN = Bye For Now

BRB = Be Right Back

BRBBYCS = Be Right Back Before You Can Spit

BTW = By The Way

CUL8er = See You Later

CYA = See Ya

DIIK = Darned If I Know

DITYID = Did I Tell You I'm Distressed?

DH = Dear (or Dratted) Husband

FAIK = For All I Know

FAQ = Frequently Asked Questions

FITB = Fill In The Blank

FWIW = For What It's Worth

FYA = For Your Amusement

FYI = For Your Information

GA = Go Ahead

GD&R = Grin, Duck and Run

GIGO = Garbage In, Garbage Out

GIWIST = Gee, I Wish I Had Said That

GMTA = Great Minds Think Alike

GTRM = Going To Read Mail

HAND = Have A Nice Day

HHOK = Ha Ha, Only Kidding

IAE = In Any Event

IC = I See

IMHO = In My Humble Opinion

IMNSHO = In My Not So Humble Opinion

IMO = In My Opinion

INAE = I'm Not An Expert (but . . .)

IOW = In Other Words

J/K = Just Kidding

K = OK

KISS = Keep It Simple, Silly

L8R = Later

LD = Later, Dude

LHOL = Laughing Heartily Out Loud

LMAOADCWHM = Laughing My Arms Off And Don't Care Who Hears Me

LOL = Laughing Out Loud

LSHISOS = Laughing So Hard I Spit On (the) Screen

LSHMSH = Laughing So Hard My Sides Hurt

LTNS = Long Time No See

MorF = Male or Female?

NIFOTC = Naked In Front Of The Computer

NIFOTC = Not In Front Of The Children

O&O = Over and Out

OIC = Oh, I See

OTF = On The Floor

OTOH = On The Other Hand

OTTOMH = Off The Top Of My Head

P* = Prodigy

POV = Point Of View

ROFL = Rolling On Floor Laughing

ROFLMAO = Rolling On Floor Laughing My Arms Off

ROTFL = Rolling On The Floor Laughing

RSN = Real Soon Now

RTFM = Read The Freakin' Manual

SNAFU = Situation Normal: All Fudged Up

SNERT = Sexually Nerdishly Expressive Recidivistic Troll

SO = Significant Other

SOL = Smiling Out Loud (or you're outta luck)

TANJ = There Ain't No Justice

TANSTAAFL = There Ain't No Such Thing As A Free Lunch

TIA = Thanks In Advance

TLIKAI = The Last I Knew About It

TLK2UL8R = Talk To You Later

TMFOOMM = Taking My Foot Out Of My Mouth

TTFN = Ta Ta For Now

TTYL (or *TTUL*) = Talk To You Later

TXS (or *TNXS*) = Thanks

WB = Welcome Back

WTG = Way To Go

WU = What's Up?

WYSIWYG = What You See Is What You Get

YSR = Yeah Sure Right

The success of online shorthand relies on recognition. Most folks that you meet understand that *LOL* means Laughing Out Loud, but how many know *BAG* stands for Busting A Gut? If you're intent on creating your own shorthand, do so with finesse and flair, but be prepared to explain your creations often. Remember: *IMHO, TBC RTTR ETU, FWIW*! (Translation: In my humble opinion, the best conversations are those that are easiest to understand, for what it's worth.)

The Virtues of Longhand

I don't know the history behind the word "longhand," but I know for certain that typing lengthy words and sentences requires "long hands" — literally. Even so, there are some obvious advantages to taking the time to type words out and avoiding online shorthand altogether. When you are in an unfamiliar chat room, or speaking with someone who hasn't learned the shorthand, be kind and type in longhand. And if you're trying to impress someone, or just show your respect, let them know that they are worth the extra time and effort it takes to type out words fully. Shorthand is the online equivalent of slang, so use it judiciously.

The Language of AOL's Subculture

The America Online community is a highly developed subculture, with its own language, legends, and, yes, strange behaviors. And to those unfamiliar with America Online, a *poof* could be a highly flammable hairstyle, or **you** could mean that I see stars when I look at you. As odd as they look, these are common words and devices with meanings unique to our community:

Re's or *Rehi*! = Hello again!

::poof:: = Leaving or signing off.

(oh) = Words in parentheses like this often denote thinking out loud or an annotation to comments.

wrd=word = A correction to a misspelled word.

CAPS = Shouting or very strong emphasis.

word = Emphasis on a word.

Netiquette

I've hinted at this netiquette stuff throughout the book, though I must admit I was sometimes sneaky about it. Now that you're here, though, I must make a confession: Netiquette (etiquette on the 'Net and specifically America Online) has been one of my passions since I first discovered the online world. And yes, I am that seemingly mild-mannered, bespectacled woman with the *Netiquette* screen name lurking about in search of situations calling for netiquette. But make no mistake: I don't wear white gloves, and I definitely don't condone closed minds.

Netiquette isn't about a bunch of fussy rules and staid dictates. Rather, netiquette revolves around one simple idea. Behind the monitors, dancing phosphor words, and roar of the modems are flesh-and-blood human beings not unlike you. Everyone has feelings to respect, opinions to share, and personalities to express.

Sound simple? It is. Even so, the uniqueness of the online experience creates situations that common sense cannot comprehend, let alone answer for. So allow me to don my netiquette hat for a bit and share some of netiquette's solutions for sticky online situations.

CAN YOU READ THIS?

Got your attention, didn't I? While all capital letters may be eye-catching, they are difficult to read and equate to shouting online. Use them cautiously. If you see another member using all caps constantly, ask them politely not to and give a reasonable explanation. Making someone feel embarrassed about typing in all capital letters is as rude as using them yourself. Keep in mind that new members often have their **Caps Lock** key stuck in the on position without realizing it, too.

Screen name game

Your screen name precedes you and offers a first impression, so choose one carefully. It can be your biggest asset if open and descriptive. It can also bar your way if dubious or offensive. Avoid numbers and indecipherable abbreviations; these are hard for your newfound friends to remember and may result in misdirected e-mail. See the tip "Choosing a Screen Name" in Chapter 2.

Just Jennifer

Although I have many screen names, my absolute favorite is *Jennifer*. It is often assumed that I've been on America Online since day one and that I was the first to create Jennifer, but in fact I got it long after I originally arrived. When I wasn't able to create it right away (someone else was using it), I bided my time until it was deleted. Then I waited the six months, keeping careful track of the time (screen names usually become available to create again six months after deletion). I made it well known that I wanted this name — I told all my friends, informed my colleagues, and even tried to request it from Member Services. Perhaps I drove them a bit crazy, but no one ever complained. I kept trying for it and never gave up. Finally, in spring of 1994, I was able to create it for myself. With millions of members online, many good screen names are taken, but there is a perfect screen name out there for you, too.

E-mail etiquette

Many members come to America Online for the e-mail features, but stay for the community. When composing e-mail, shoot for an accurate subject line. *Hi* or *No Subject* is unlikely to inspire mad dashes for your letter. For important or detailed correspondence, use the **Forward** button to send along a copy of the letter you are replying to. Use this with care, though; a long chain of forwards can propagate unwittingly and makes reading tedious.

Remember also that e-mail will collect in your recipient's mailbox if they are not online when sent. Thus, while a few letters sent over the course of a couple days seems natural to you, the recipient may feel overwhelmed when they open their mailbox to hoards of letters. If you find you have just "one more thing to say," unsend your previous e-mail and write one note that covers everything. See Chapter 4 for help on using your e-mail.

The boardwalk promenade

If you enjoy exchanging words, the message boards are a veritable haven. These collections of public messages cover just about every topic imaginable and some that aren't. Be forewarned that the fascinating nature of board discussions can lead to overreaction. Keep your cool and remember feelings can be as easily hurt online as offline.

Chatter matters

Intriguing message board discussions will often whet your appetite for chats. It is in chat and conference rooms that your online persona will form most quickly; be sure that it is what you wish to convey. Avoid short-changing your conversation with poor typing or inane comments. You are what you type here. You'll do best by leaving sexual references behind; not only are they frowned upon by the online community, they are often prohibited under America Online's Terms of Service. For freedom of speech, create a private room and let it rip.

Protocol

You've been invited to a conference on the ever-present *Fibrous Umbilicus* (belly-button lint). You arrive to a full house — the conference room is at its maximum of 48. But before you manage to type out your exuberant hello, you notice that others are typing nothing more than /s and ?s. You begin to wonder if you accidentally entered the monthly meeting of National Punctuation Club. Then you receive an Instant Message informing you that this conference uses *protocol*. Protocol at a belly-button lint conference? What is this?

Protocol is a system used in busy conferences, particularly those where folks ask questions and expect answers. Without protocol, chaos reins: Extraneous chat hides and scrolls the answers, general questions and comments are confused with those intended for individuals, and topics drift out of reach before they can be read. The basic idea behind protocol is the less said, the better. If you want to ask a question or make a comment, you type a question mark (?) or an exclamation point (!) rather than blurting it out. Someone then keeps track of all the questions and comments folks are waiting to make and places their name in a *queue*. The queue is the virtual equivalent of waiting in line. When your turn comes, you are prompted to ask your question or make your comment. Don't mistake seeing your name in the queue as a prompt to speak — you'll be called directly when it is your turn. Once you begin speaking, no one else speaks until you are done, which you signal by typing **/ga** or **/done**. It is considered very rude to "break" protocol by barging ahead when it is not your turn. But don't fear, almost every conference that uses protocol will let you know almost as soon as you enter the door (just make sure your Instant Messages aren't blocked). So you can talk about belly-button lint, or whatever else tickles your fancy, with complete confidence and rapt attention from your audience. Would could be better?

Instant Messages or Intruding Menaces?

Instant Messages, also known as IMs, are the best way to communicate one-on-one with all the friends you've made in chat rooms. IMs give you the ability to immediately call upon someone if they are online, but keep in mind that being online doesn't equate to being able to chat. If you have someone in your Buddy List, don't IM them as soon as they come online unless it is urgent. Be considerate and patient; start IM conversations with an inviting hello and end them with a farewell.

There are many amazing and diverse worlds to discover online. Yet wherever you go, one principle is held in the highest regard — respect. Ignore respect and you'll be lucky to catch even a glimpse of the richness of online communication.

If you know of a matter of netiquette I've left out, feel free to e-mail me the details at my *Netiquette* screen name. I love to discuss the finer points of online culture.

VirtuaLingo Glossary

The VirtuaLingo Glossary is a comprehensive glossary of the terms heard in the many gathering places around America Online. This is the full and unabridged version, complete with all the technical terms, jargon, and slang you could want, in addition to useful (and trivial) information — network phone numbers, filename extensions, leader uniforms, and assorted tips and techniques included. A very special thank you goes to George Louie, who has co-authored this glossary with me since its inception over four years ago.

800 & 888 numbers

America Online provides 800 and 888 numbers, at a modest hourly rate, to U.S. and Canadian members who are without local access numbers. Additional information on these numbers can be found at keyword: ACCESS. For more information, see "Using 800 Access Numbers" in Chapter 1. *See also* access number *and* AOLnet.

$im_off/$im_on

Commands for ignoring Instant Messages (IMs). Sending an IM to the screen name: *$im_off* blocks incoming IMs. Conversely, sending an IM to *$im_on* allows you to receive IMs again. To execute the command, simply click the **Available?** button. This command ignores all incoming IMs — to block an individual only, type **$im_off**, a space, and then their screen name. Confirmation in the form of a dialog box is sent when turning IMs on or off. If members try to send you an IM or use the **Available?** button on the IM window, they will be told that you "cannot currently receive Instant Messages." For more information, see "Blocking

Instant Messages" in Chapter 5. *See also* IM; *contrast with* ignore *and* parental chat controls.

<< and >>

Symbols used to quote text in lieu of quotation marks; they are often used in e-mail and posts. Members using Windows AOL software 2.5 or higher, or Mac AOL software 3.0 or higher, can get automatic quoting simply by selecting a block of text in an e-mail, and then clicking **Reply**. Mac AOL software 4.0 users can also add quoting to any text by first copying it and then pasting while holding down the **Option** key. *See also* e-mail post.

//roll

Command for rolling dice. When entered in a chat or conference room, America Online's host computer will return a random result for two six-sided dice to the room. For example:

```
OnlineHost : NumbersMan rolled 2
6-sided dice: 2 4
```

The command can also be used to roll other types and quantities of dice. The full syntax of the command is **//roll -diceXX -sidesYYY** (where XX is 0-15 and YYY is 0-999). Be sure to include the spaces. It is considered rude to roll dice in Lobbies or other public chat areas (with the exception of the Red Dragon Inn, sims, and other special game rooms). This command is often used when role-playing or in lieu of "drawing straws." *See also* chat room, OnlineHost, *and* sim.

/ga

Common shorthand for "go ahead," often used during conferences with protocol. Additional information on use is available in Appendix B. *See also* protocol.

abbreviations

Acronyms for common online phrases used in chat, IMs, and e-mail. Examples include LOL (Laughing Out Loud) and BRB (Be Right Back). A comprehensive list of abbreviations is available in Appendix B. *See also* chat *and* shorthand; *contrast with* body language *and* emoticons.

access number

A phone number (usually local) your modem uses to access America Online. To find an access number online, go to keyword: ACCESS. If you aren't able to sign on to America Online, see "Finding Local Access Numbers" in Chapter 1. *See also* 800 number, AOLnet, SprintNet, *and* node.

address

There are two types of addresses you'll hear about on America Online and the Internet. The first is an e-mail address, which allows you to send an e-mail to anyone on America Online, the Internet, and just about any other online service. You can look up addresses for America Online members at keyword: MEMBERS, and addresses for Internet denizens at various places on the World Wide Web. More information is available in "Finding Internet Addresses" in Chapter 7. The second is a location address for information on America Online or the Web, which is better known as an URL. An example of an address on America Online is `aol://1722:help`, which takes you to Member Services when entered into the keyword window. On the Web, the address `http://members.aol.com/jennifer/` takes you to Jennifer's home page. More information is available in "Finding URL Addresses" in Chapter 3. *See also* e-mail, e-mail address, Internet, URL, *and* World Wide Web.

Address Book

An AOL software feature that allows you to store screen names for easy access. Your Address Book may be created, edited, or used through the Address

Book icon available when composing mail. You can also create or edit them with the **Edit Address Book** or **Address Book** option under the **Mail Center** button on the toolbar. See "Keeping an Address Book" in Chapter 4.

Adobe Acrobat

Commercial software that allows you to create and/or view Portable Document Format (PDF) documents that retain their original appearance across computer platforms when read with the freely distributed Adobe Acrobat Reader.

AFK

Common shorthand for "Away From Keyboard." It's most often used in chat and IMs when it's necessary to leave the keyboard for an extended length of time. There are few valid reasons for going "AFK," but taking your pet hamster out for a walk is one of them. Upon return, "BAK" is used, meaning "Back At Keyboard." For a complete list of shorthand, see Appendix B. *See also* shorthands, abbreviations, *and* chat; *contrast with* body language *and* emoticons.

Alt key

A special function key on the PC keyboard. Usually located near the space bar, you'll find the letters *Alt* printed on it. Holding down the **Alt** key while another key is pressed often activates a special function. For example, **Alt+H** brings up the Offline Help in the Windows AOL software. (Note: Some Macintosh keyboards also have a key labeled **Alt**, but this is primarily for use when operating a PC emulator on the Mac and is otherwise defined as the **Option** key.) *See also* Control key, Command key, *and* Option key.

alphanumeric

Data or information consisting of the letters of the alphabet A through Z (upper- and lowercase), the digits *0* through *9*, punctuation marks, and other keyboard symbols.

America Online, Inc. (AOL)

The nation's leading online service, headquartered in Virginia. Founded in 1985 and formerly known as Quantum Computer Services, America Online has grown rapidly in both size and scope. America Online has over 12 million members and hundreds of alliances with major companies. America Online's stock exchange symbol is AOL. To contact America Online headquarters, call 1-703-448-8700 or use 1-800-827-6364 to speak to a representative, or use 1-800-827-6364 to speak to a Member Services representative. *See also* America Online; *contrast with* CompuServe, eWorld, Microsoft Network, *and* Prodigy.

analog

A transmission mode in which information is converted to a continuously variable signal. Commonly a representation of variations in intensity, such as sound and light. The information on an old-fashioned black vinyl recording is analog, as the movement of the phonograph needle within the grooves copies (more or less) the movement of the original vibrating string. Digital information represents the same vibrations as a series of measurements — capturing the position of that string many times as it is vibrating. Computers commonly use information in digital form, as the numbers that comprise the information are easy to store and manipulate. *Contrast with* digital.

AOL

Abbreviation for America Online, Inc. Occasionally abbreviated as AO. *See also* America Online, Incorporated.

AOL Instant Messenger

Software that allows people with Internet accounts to send and receive Instant Messages from America

Online members. Once a person has downloaded, installed, and registered the AOL Instant Messenger software, America Online members will be able to add them to their Buddy List and send Instant Messages to them as if they were using America Online rather than another service or ISP. For more information, see "Using AOL Instant Messenger" in Chapter 7. *See also* IM.

AOL NetFind

America Online's exclusive Internet directory and search service available at http://www.aol.com or at keyword: AOL NETFIND. It was created through America Online's partnership with Excite, Inc. See "Surfing with AOL NetFind" in Chapter 3 for more information.

AOL Radio

A forthcoming feature on America Online similar to Progressive Network's RealAudio. AOL Radio will allow members to listen to real-time broadcasts of news, music, and advertisements.

AOL Slideshows

An America Online-exclusive presentation consisting of a series of images, animation, and sound. AOL Slideshows take advantage of streaming technology to begin playback without having to wait for the entire slideshow to download. Slideshows are only available for version 3.0 or later. See keyword: SLIDESHOWS for examples and more information.

AOL Talk

A future feature on America Online, which will allow members to talk to other members in real time through America Online. AOL Talk will probably require AOL software 4.0, a microphone and sound card, and a 28.8 Kbps or better modem connection, to be useful.

AOL.com

America Online's home page on the Web located at `http://www.aol.com`.

AOLiversary

A date celebrated yearly on which a member first became active on America Online. Considered an accurate yardstick by some to determine their state of addiction. *See also* AOLoholic.

AOLnet

America Online's own packet-switching network that provides members with up to 56,600 bps local access numbers. To use this network, you must have Windows AOL software 2.5 (or higher), or Mac AOL software 2.5.1 (or higher). If you have a version below 3.0 of either software, you may need the AOLnet CCL file available at keyword: AOLnet. AOLnet numbers are located across the country. For members who do not have a local access number, there is also an 800 number that is more affordable than most long-distance fees. An alternative is to sign on to America Online through an Internet or ISP (Internet service provider) connection. To find AOLnet local access numbers, go to keyword: AOLnet. *See also* 800 number, packet-switching, *and* access number; *contrast with* SprintNet.

AOLoholic

A member of America Online who begins to display any of the following behaviors: spending most of their free time online; thinking about America Online even when offline (evidenced by the addition of shorthands to non-America Online writings); attempting to bring all their friends and family online; and/or thinking America Online is the best invention since the wheel. A 12-step plan is in development. Many, but not all AOLoholics, go on to become community leaders. If you fit this description, see keyword: LEADERS. *See also* community leader *and* member.

ARC

Short for archive, this is an older compression utility which was the PC standard prior to ZIP. This utility will compress one file, or multiple files, into a file (called an *archive*), which will make for shorter transferring while uploading or downloading. Some older files online are still packaged in the ARC format. More on file compression is available in "Decompressing and Installing Files" in Chapter 6. *See also* archive, file, file compression, PKZip, ShrinkIt, *and* StuffIt.

archive

1. A file that has been compressed with file compression software. *See also* file, file compression, ARC, PKZip, *and* StuffIt.

2. A file that contains message board postings that may be of value, but have been removed from a message board due to their age, inactivity of topic, or lack of message board space. These messages are usually bundled into one document, and placed in a file library for retrieval later. *See also* file *and* library.

article

A text document intended to be read online, but may be printed or saved for later examination offline. Usually articles are less than 25K in size. For more information, see "Saving and Printing Windows" in Chapter 6. *See also* document; *contrast with* file.

asbestos

A flame retardant. Used as a modifier to anything intended to protect one from flames. For example, "donning asbestos underwear." This is usually used just before saying something that is expected to produce flames. Contrary to popular belief, hamsters are not flame retardant, and system slowdowns can be attributed to the increased number of flames. *See also* flame.

ASCII

Acronym for American Standard Code for Information Interchange. ASCII is the numeric code used to represent computer characters on computers around the world. Because only seven bits are used in ASCII, there are no more than 128 (2^7) characters in the standard ASCII set. Variations of ASCII often extend the available characters by using an 8-bit means of identifying characters and thus may represent as many as 256 characters. The standard ASCII code set consists of 128 characters ranging from 0 to 127. America Online supports characters 28–127 in chat areas, IMs, and message boards. (Pronounced "ask-key.") *See also* ASCII text.

ASCII Art

Pictures created with no more than the 128 ASCII characters. ASCII Art can be humorous, entertaining, or serious. It is popular in some chat rooms. Some members find it disruptive when large ASCII Art is displayed in a chat room, so you are advised to ask before scrolling it. More details on ASCII Art are available in Appendix B. *See also* ASCII *and* ASCII text.

ASCII text

Characters represented as ASCII. Sometimes called "plain text;" this is compatible with all platforms represented on America Online. *See also* ASCII; *contrast with* rich text.

Ask The Staff button

A button available in file libraries that takes you to the Download Info Center, which offers a great deal of information about libraries and allows you to send a note to the managers of the library. Note that it doesn't send a note to the uploader, only the library managers (often a forum leader or assistant). The Download Info Center is also available directly at keyword: INFO CENTER. *See also* download *and* library.

asynchronous

> Data communication via modem of the start-stop variety where characters do not need to be transmitted constantly. Each character is transmitted as a discrete unit with its own start bit and one or more stop bits. America Online is asynchronous. *See also* synchronous.

attached file

> A file that hitches a ride with e-mail. Be the file text, sound, or pictures of your hamster "Bruno," it is said to be attached if it has been included with the e-mail for separate downloading by the recipient (whether addressed directly, carbon copied, or blind carbon copied). E-mail that is forwarded will retain any attached files as well. Files are usually attached because the information that they contain is either too long to be sent in the body of regular e-mail or is impossible to send via e-mail, such as with software programs. Multiple files may be attached by compressing the files into one archive and attaching the archive to the piece of e-mail with the Attach File icon. More information is available in "Attaching Files to Mail" in Chapter 4. *See also* archive, download, e-mail, *and* file.

auditorium

> Auditoriums are specially equipped online "rooms" that allow large groups of America Online members to meet in a structured setting. An auditorium is divided into two parts: the stage, where the emcee and the guest speaker(s) are located, and the chat rows, where the audience is located. Upon entering an auditorium, a member is assigned to one of the chat rows, consisting of up to 15 other audience members. Audience members in the same row may talk to each other without being heard by those on stage or by those in other rows. Nothing said in the audience can be normally heard by anyone on stage, although anything said on stage can be "broadcast" and heard by everyone in the audience. The *OnlineHost* broadcasts important information

throughout the conference. The emcee moderates the conference and broadcasts more specific information. You can tell the difference between what is said on stage and what is said in your chat row because what is said in your chat row is preceded by a row number. More information on auditoriums can be found at keyword: AOL LIVE or in "Using Auditoriums" in Chapter 5. *See also* emcee *and* OnlineHost; *contrast with* chat room *and* conference room.

Automatic AOL

An automated feature that can send and receive your e-mail and files, as well as receive newsgroup postings. It is also known as FlashSessions on some older AOL software versions. Auto AOL can be set up to run at any time, including while you are online. It is accessible under your Mail menu. More information is available in "Reading Mail Offline" in Chapter 4. *See also* e-mail, file, flashmail, *and* newsgroup.

avatar

A graphical representation or depiction of a person used in online games or chat rooms. Avatars are usually customizable, have limited animated actions or expressions, and interact with other avatars. *See also* People Connection, chat room, *and* conference room.

bandwidth

A measure of the amount of information that can flow through a given point at any time. Technically, bandwidth is the difference, in hertz (Hz), between the highest and lowest frequencies of a transmission channel. However, as typically used, it more often refers to the amount of data that can be sent through a given communications circuit. To use a popular analogy, low bandwidth is a two-lane dirt road while high bandwidth is a six-lane superhighway

bash

A get-together or party of America Online members in a particular area. Members who attend are often referred to as bashees, and popular bashes are the Big Apple Bash (in NYC) and the Texas Bash. Information on bashes can usually be found in "The Quantum Que," a community message board available at keyword: QUE.

basher

A particularly vile form of snert. A basher will usually target a certain group and harass them for the basher's pleasure. This usually takes place in a People Connection chat room dedicated to that group, but may also occur in conference rooms. *See also* snert, People Connection, chat room, *and* conference room.

baud rate

A unit for measuring the speed of data transmission. Technically, baud rates refer to the number of times the communications line changes states each second. Strictly speaking, baud and bits per second (bps) are not identical measurements, but most nontechnical people use the terms interchangeably. *See also* bps.

BBS (Bulletin Board System)

A system offering information that can be accessed via computer, modem, and phone lines. While that definition technically includes America Online, BBSs are typically much smaller in size and scope. Most BBSs maintain message boards and file libraries and some feature Internet access, newsfeeds, and online games. For more information online, go to keyword: BBS. BBSs are sometimes abbreviated as simply "board," and should not be confused with message boards on America Online. *Contrast with* message board.

beta test

A period in a new product or service's development designed to discover problems (or "bugs") prior to its release to the general public. America Online often invites members to beta test its new software. If you are interested in beta testing AOL software, you may be able to apply at keyword: BETA APPLY. Hamsters are notoriously bad beta testers; the bugs distract their attention. For more information see "Becoming a Beta Tester" in Chapter 6. *See also* bug.

blind carbon copy (bcc)

A feature of the America Online e-mail system that allows you to send e-mail to a member or members without anyone other than you being aware of it. To blind carbon copy, simply place parentheses around the screen name(s). For example, (JoeShmo) or (JoeShmo, HughHamstr). Members on Mac AOL software 3.0 and higher can use the small pop-up menu to change an address to BCC. Geos AOL software users will need to use two parentheses, as in ((JoeShmo)) or ((JoeShmo, HughHamstr)). When a blind carbon copy is made, it is said to be bcc'ed. See "Blind Carbon Copying" in Chapter 4 for more information. *See also* e-mail; *contrast with* carbon copy.

board

An abbreviated reference to a message board or bulletin board service (BBS). *See also* message board *and* BBS.

body language

An online expression of physical movement and nonverbal emotions through text. Two popular methods have developed on America Online: colons (:::yawning:::) and brackets (<yawning and trying to stay awake for ten straight hours in front of a monitor>). See Appendix A for more information on body language. *See also* chat; *contrast with* abbreviations, emoticons, *and* shorthand.

Boolean search

A search that uses logical operators from Boolean algebra to narrow the number of matches. For example, a search in the classifieds for "car" would yield many matches, but not exactly what you want. A search for "car and brown and (Firebird or TransAm)" would help you find exactly what you are looking for. Most searches on America Online are Boolean searches and use the following Boolean operators: *and*, *or*, *not*. See "Searching with Skill" in Chapter 6 for more information.

bounce

Something that is returned, such as e-mail. For example, e-mail sent to recipients outside America Online may bounce and never make it to its intended destination, especially if it was not addressed correctly. Sometimes users who are punted will refer to themselves as bounced. *See also* e-mail *and* punt.

bps (bits per second)

A method of measuring data transmission speed. Currently, 1200 bps through 56K are supported on America Online (see keyword: AOLnet for more information). *See also* baud.

BRB

Common shorthand for "Be Right Back." It is used by America Online members when participating in chat/conference rooms or talking in IMs (Instant Messages). For a complete list of shorthand, see Appendix B. *See also* shorthands, abbreviations, *and* chat; *contrast with* body language *and* emoticons.

browse

To casually explore rather than examine in detail. Typically used in reference to message boards and file libraries. Browsing information online without a specific target is one prominent trait of a budding AOLoholic. *Contrast with* search.

browser

A way of accessing the World Wide Web. On Mac AOL software 3.0 and Windows AOL software 2.5 and higher, this is an integrated component of the software. On Mac AOL software 2.6 and 2.7, it is a separate piece of software. More information is available in "Browsing the World Wide Web," "Purging Your Web Cache," and "Using Alternate Web Browsers" in Chapter 7. *See also* Favorite Place, Internet, page, Personal Filing Cabinet, site, *and* World Wide Web.

BTW

Common shorthand for "By The Way." It is used in IMs, chat/conference rooms, e-mail, and message postings. A complete list of shorthands is available in Appendix B. *See also* shorthands, abbreviations, *and* chat; *contrast with* body language *and* emoticons.

buddy

A friend or family member who has an America Online membership or is using AOL Instant Messenger, and has been added to your Buddy List. More information on buddies is available in "Using Buddy Lists" in Chapter 5. *See also* AOL Instant Messenger *and* Buddy List.

Buddy List

A special list that stores your "buddies" (screen names of friends, family members, coworkers, and so on) and informs you when they sign on or off America Online. You add (or remove) buddies yourself, and can define several groups of buddies as you like. The Buddy List is a feature of the Windows AOL software and Mac AOL software 3.0 software. See "Using Buddy Lists" in Chapter 5 for more information. *See also* buddy *and* invitation.

bug

A problem or glitch in a product, be it software or hardware. A bug may be referred to jokingly as a "feature." You can report a problem with AOL software or services by going to keyword: HELP, clicking **Error Messages**, and clicking the **Ask The Staff** button.

bulletin board

See message board *and* BBS.

cache

A portion of a data storage device, RAM, or processor, set aside to temporarily hold recently accessed or frequently accessed information. By saving the information locally, performance is improved because it is quicker to receive the information from the cache than from the original source. For example, America Online's client software saves the artwork and icons for areas that you visit so that they don't need to be downloaded every time. See "Purging Your Web Cache" in Chapter 7 for more information on the Web browser cache.

carbon copy (cc)

A feature of the America Online e-mail system that allows you to address e-mail to a member for whom the e-mail is not directly intended or is of secondary interest. The primary addressee(s) are aware that the copy was made, similar to the carbon copy convention used in business correspondence. As such, the members carbon copied are not usually expected to reply. When a carbon copy is made, it is said to be cc'ed. Also known as a courtesy copy. *See also* e-mail; *contrast with* blind carbon copy.

Center Stage

See auditorium.

channel

This is the broadest category of information into which America Online organizes its content. See keyword: CHANNELS for an interactive list or CHANNEL GUIDE for listings of the areas within each channel. At the time of this writing, these are the channels for the different areas online:

AOL Today

Computing

Entertainment

Families

Games

Health

Influence

Interests

International

Kids Only

Lifestyles

Local

News

Personal Finance

Research & Learn

Shopping

Sports

Travel

Workplace

Member Services

People Connection

chat

To engage in real-time communications with other members. America Online members that are online at the same time may chat with each other in a number of ways: Instant Messages (IMs), chat/conference rooms, and auditoriums. "Chatting" provides immediate feedback from others; detailed discussions are better suited toward message boards, and lengthy personal issues are best dealt with in e-mail if a member isn't currently online. Chapter 5 has more information on chatting. *See also* Instant Message, chat room, conference room, *and* auditorium; *contrast with* message board *and* e-mail.

chat rooms

Online areas where members may meet to communicate and interact with others. There are two kinds of chat areas: public and private. Public chat areas can be found in the People Connection area (keyword: PEOPLE) or in the many forums around America Online (see keyword: AOL LIVE for schedules). Public rooms may be either officially sanctioned rooms or member-created rooms (which are listed separately). All public rooms are governed by America Online's Terms of Service (TOS) and are open to anyone interested. Private chat rooms are available from most chat areas and are open only to those who create them or know their names and meeting times. All chat rooms accommodate at least 23 members, while some of the chat areas in forums other than People Connection may hold up to 100 members. Those chat rooms that can be created by members (both public and private) must have names with no more than 20 characters, beginning with a letter, and containing no punctuation. Beware that Stratus hamsters have been known to escape and surprise unsuspecting members in chat rooms. See Chapter 5 for "Finding Chats" and "Creating Chat Rooms." *See also* private room, chat, host, Guide, TOS, *and* People Connection; *contrast with* auditorium *and* conference room.

chat sounds

Sounds may be played and broadcast to others in chat areas by typing {S <sound>} and sending it to the chat area. Be sure to type it exactly as shown and insert the exact name of the sound you wish to play where <sound> appears in the example. For example, {S Welcome} will play America Online's "Welcome" sound in a chat area. Please note also that Geos AOL software users cannot hear chat sounds, nor can those without sound capabilities. More information on chat sounds is available in "Playing Sounds in Chat Rooms" in Chapter 5. *See also* chat room *and* library.

CIS

Short for CompuServe Information Service. *See also* CompuServe; *contrast with* America Online, eWorld, Microsoft Network, *and* Prodigy.

client

A computer that requests information from another. On America Online, your computer is generally the client and the Stratus is the host. Also an abbreviation of *client software*. *See* client software. *Contrast with* host (1).

client software

A software program needed in order to communicate with host/server computers on a network. The AOL software installed on your computer(s) is the *client*, and is necessary for connection and use of the AOL service. *See* client. *Contrast with* host.

close box

The small box in the upper-right corner of your window (in Windows) or the upper-left corner (on the Mac). Clicking this box closes the window. Not to be confused with a shoe box, boom box, or even clothes box. *See also* window; *contrast with* zoom box.

club

See forum.

Command key

A special function key on the Mac. Usually located near the space bar, you'll find printed on it either an open Apple symbol or a clover-leaf symbol (or both). Holding down the **Command** key while another key is pressed will often activate a special function. A list of special functions available in the AOL software is in "Taking Keyboard Shortcuts" in Chapter 3. Also known as the Open-Apple key. *See also* Control key, Option key, *and* Alt key.

community leader

America Online members who volunteer in the various forums and areas online. They usually work from their homes, not America Online headquarters; hence they have been known as *remote staff* in the past. They serve as guides, hosts, forum leaders/assistants/consultants, and so on. With partners, the community leaders are usually those who do not work on the premises of the partner's offline physical location, whereas those partner employees who do are known as corporate staff. To learn more, see keyword: LEADERS. *See also* Guide, host, partner, *and* uniform; *contrast with* corporate staff *and* inhouse.

compression

See file compression.

CompuServe (CIS)

A large, established commercial online service similar to America Online. While CompuServe Information Service (CIS) has more databases available, their service is priced higher and uses different software than America Online. CompuServe has been acquired by America Online and "positioned" as a business-oriented service. *Contrast with* America Online, eWorld, Microsoft Network, *and* Prodigy.

conference room

A specific kind of chat area found in forums all around America Online where members can meet, hold conferences, and interact in real time. Conference rooms can hold up to 48 or 100 members at any one time (depending on location) and are located outside of the People Connection.

Currently, there are over 600 public conference rooms with more being added all the time. Often special events are held in these rooms, and a protocol system may be used to make them proceed smoothly. Hosts or moderators often facilitate the discussions and conferences here. Hamster sightings are less frequent in these rooms. *See also* host, moderator, *and* protocol; *contrast with* chat room *and* auditorium.

Control key

A special function key, usually located on the bottom row of keys, you'll find printed on it either **Ctrl** or **Control**. Holding down the **Control** key while another key is pressed will often activate a special function on the PC. A list of special functions available in the AOL software is in "Taking Keyboard Shortcuts" in Chapter 3. Mac keyboards also have a key labeled Control, but it generally behaves differently — in the Mac AOL software 4.0, holding down the **Control** key while clicking in a window often produces a special menu. *See also* Command key, Option key, Alt key, *and* Open-Apple key.

corporate staff

Members who are usually company or partner (information provider) employees and work at the corporate offices of the company. In-house America Online, Inc. staff is often referred to in this manner as well. *See also* in-house *and* partner; *contrast with* community leader.

cracker

One who violates security. Coined by hackers in the 1980s in defense against the growing assumption that all hackers are malevolent. A password scammer is a cracker. *See also* password scammer; *contrast with* hacker, phisher, *and* snert.

cross-post

To make the same message in several folders, message boards, or newsgroups. Overuse of this is bad netiquette, and may result in having your posts hidden (if on America Online) or your mailbox barraged with flaming e-mail(if on the Internet). *See also* flame, newsgroup, post, *and* spam.

CS Live

See Tech Live.

Customer Relations

America Online's Customer Relations Hotline is open 6 a.m. to 4 a.m. Eastern Time, seven days a week. You can reach them at 1-800-827-6364. *See also* Tech Live.

cyberpunk

First used to designate a body of speculative fiction literature focusing on marginalized people in technologically enhanced cultural "systems." Within the last few years, the mass media has used this term to categorize the denizens of cyberspace. Cyberpunks are known to cruise the information landscapes with alacrity, or lacking that, eagerness.

cyberspace

An infinite world created by our computer networks. Cyberspace is no less real than the real world, that is, people are born, grow, learn, fall in love, and die in cyberspace. These effects may or may not be carried over into the physical world. America Online is an example of cyberspace created through interaction between the energies of the members, community leaders, staff, and computers. *See also* online community.

daemon

An automatic program that performs a maintenance function on America Online. For example, a board daemon may run at 3 a.m. and clean up old posts on a message board. Rumored to stand for "Disk And Execution MONitor."

database

A collection of information, stored and organized for easy searching. A database can refer to something as simple as a well-sorted filing cabinet, but today most databases reside on computers because they offer better access. Databases are located all over America Online, with a prominent example being the Member Directory (keyword: MEMBERS). See the AOL Research & Learn channel (keyword: RESEARCH) for a large collection of databases. *See also* Boolean Search, Member Directory, *and* searchable.

Delete

An America Online e-mail system feature that allows you to permanently remove a piece of mail from any and all of your mailboxes. To use, simply select and highlight the piece of mail you wish to delete (from either your new mail, read mail, or sent mail) and click the **Delete** button at the bottom of the window. The mail will be permanently deleted and cannot be retrieved. Mail you have deleted without reading first will appear as "(deleted)" in the Status box of the sender. The Delete feature is useful for removing unneeded mail from your Old Mail box. Do not confuse this feature with the **Unsend** option, which will remove mail you've sent from the recipient's mailbox. *See also* e-mail *and* Status; *contrast with* Unsend.

demoware (demonstration software)

These are often full-featured versions of commercial software, with the exception being that the Save or Print features are often disabled. Some demos are only functional for certain periods of time. Like shareware, demonstration software is a great way to try before you buy. *Contrast with* freeware, public domain, *and* shareware.

department

See channel.

digital

A transmission mode in which information is coded in binary (or other numeric) form. This simplifies computation and information storage. Nearly all computers use this design (including PCs and Macs). Information (whether sound, image, or text) must be converted into digital format (numbers) before it can be used by the computer, and it must be converted back to its original form before humans can experience the results. *Contrast with* analog.

document

An information file, usually relating specific details on a topic. On America Online, these can be in the form of articles (which are read-only), or modifiable documents, usually created with the New (Memo) menu command within America Online. *See also* article *and* file.

DOD

Abbreviation for Download On Demand, a method of receiving artwork updates that was used prior to progressive artwork downloading, still used on Mac AOL software 2.7 and Windows AOL software 2.5 and lower. When you enter an area that includes new artwork, such as a logo or icon, it is automatically downloaded and stored on your computer, where it can be retrieved whenever you revisit that area. After you've visited an area once, you never have to wait for the artwork to download again. The difference between DOD and Smart Art (progressive artwork downloading) is that with DOD your computer is totally tied up while the download is in progress, and you do not see the artwork until the download has completed. *Contrast with* Smart Art *and* UDO.

domain

The equivalent of a "city" in an Internet address. In e-mail addresses, usually everything to the right of the @ symbol is referred to as the domain. For example, the domain name for America Online member addresses is *aol.com*. *See also* address, e-mail, e-mail address, *and* Internet.

DOS

Abbreviation for Disk Operating System (which every computer with a disk drive requires), it has commonly come to mean PC-DOS or MS-DOS (Microsoft). MS-DOS used to be the most widely used operating system for IBM PCs and compatibles. Pronounced "dahss." *Contrast with* OS/2, System, *and* Windows.

download

The transfer of information stored on a remote computer to a storage device on your personal computer. This information can come from America Online via its file libraries, or from other America Online members via attached files in e-mail. Usually, downloads are files intended for review once you're offline. You download graphics and sounds, for instance. Download is used both as a noun and a verb. For example, you might download a graphic file to your hard drive, where you store your latest downloads. Hamsters have been known to defect via downloads. More information on downloading is available in "Downloading Files" in Chapter 6. *See also* archive, attached file, download count, download manager, FileGrabber, *and* library.

download count

The download count refers to the number of times that a file has been downloaded. This is often used as a gauge of the file's popularity. While this may not be too significant for a new upload, it is a good indication of the popularity of files that have been around for a while. Often, however, the number of downloads is more reflective of the appeal of a file's name or description rather than of its content. Note that a newly uploaded file will always have a download count of 1, even though it hasn't been downloaded yet. So to divine the true number of downloads, always subtract one from the total. Also, if the system is slow, the download count visible at the top level of the library may not update immediately. More information is available in "Listing Library Files" in Chapter 6. *See also* file, library, *and* download.

download manager

An AOL software feature that allows you to keep a queue of files to download at a later time. You can even set up your software to automatically sign off when your download session is complete. You can schedule your software to sign on and grab files listed in the queue at times you specify. *See also* Automatic AOL, Personal Filing Cabinet, download, *and* file. See "Using the Download Manager" in Chapter 6 for more information.

e-mail

Short for electronic mail. One of the most popular features of online services, e-mail allows you to send private communications electronically from one person to another. No wasted paper, leaky pens, or terrible tasting envelope glue involved! E-mail is usually much faster and easier to send than ordinary mail; the shortcomings are that not everyone has an e-mail address to write to and your mail resides in electronic form on a computer system, although e-mail is considered as private and inviolable as regular U.S. Mail. With America Online's e-mail system, mail can be sent directly to scores of people, carbon copied, blind carbon copied, forwarded, and even include attached files. E-mail can also be sent (and forwarded) to any other service that has an Internet address. On versions 3.0 and higher, there is no limit to the size of mail that can be sent and received. On lower versions of the AOL software, mail can be sent and received up to 32K. See keyword: MAIL CENTER or Chapter 4 for more information. *See also* attached file, blind carbon copy, carbon copy, Delete, e-mail address, flashmail, gateway, Ignore, Keep As New, mailbomb, massmail,

Personal Filing Cabinet, return receipt, *and* Status; *contrast with* snail mail, message, *and* IM.

e-mail address

A cyberspace mailbox. On America Online, your e-mail address is simply your screen name; for folks outside America Online, your address is your screen name with *@aol.com* after it. For example, if our friend Sharon wants to e-mail us from her Internet account, she can reach us as `jennifer@ aol.com` or `numbersman@aol.com`. *See also* address, e-mail, *and* screen name.

Easter egg

A hidden surprise in software often left in at the whim of the programmers (sometimes the Easter egg is a photo of the programmers themselves). Both Macintosh and Windows applications have Easter eggs. There are also some Easter eggs scattered around America Online but be forewarned they come and go as quickly as chocolate bunnies on Easter Sunday.

emcee

A member who has been trained to moderate and host events held in auditoriums. *See also* auditorium; *contrast with* host *and* moderator.

emoticons

Symbols consisting of characters found on any keyboard that are used to give and gain insight into emotional states. For example, the symbol :) is a smile — just tilt your head to the left and you'll see the : (eyes) and the) (smile). The online community has invented countless variations to bring plain text to life, and you'll see emoticons used everywhere from chat rooms to e-mail. Emoticons, like emotions, are more popular in "face-to-face" chat. Some people consider them unprofessional or overly cute in correspondence. Regardless, they are one of the best methods of effective communication online. Emoticons may also be referred to as smileys, and collectively with other chat devices as shorthands. A brief list is available online at keyword: SHORTHANDS, but a more complete guide is available in Appendix A. *See also* shorthands *and* chat; *contrast with* abbreviations *and* body language.

encryption

The manipulation of data in order to prevent any but the intended recipient from reading that data. There are many types of data encryption, and they are the basis of network security.

ET (EST or EDT)

Abbreviation for Eastern Time. Most times are given in this format, as America Online is headquartered in this time zone. See "Understanding Time Zones" in Chapter 2 for more information.

eWorld

Apple Computer's now defunct online service. Based on America Online's client system, eWorld had stylized graphics, and extensive Apple support. eWorld opened to the public on June 20, 1994 and closed only a year and a half later. *Contrast with* America Online, CompuServe, Microsoft Network, *and* Prodigy.

FAQ

Short for Frequently Asked Questions. FAQs may take the form of an informational file containing questions and answers to common concerns/issues. These are used to answer questions that are brought up often in message boards or discussions. These files may be stored online in an article or archived in a file library. *See also* message board *and* library.

Favorite Place

A feature that allows you to "mark" America Online and World Wide Web sites you'd like to return to later. These Favorite Places are stored in your

Favorite Places list. Any World Wide Web site can be made a favorite place, as well as any America Online window with a little heart in the upper right-hand corner of the title bar. See "Using Favorite Places" in Chapter 3 for more details.

fax (facsimile)

A technique for sending graphical images (such as text or pictures) over phone lines. While faxes are usually sent and received with a stand-alone fax machine, faxes may also be sent to or from computers using fax software and a modem. In the past you could send a fax through America Online for a fee at keyword: FAX, but America Online has discontinued this service. *Contrast with* e-mail *and* snail mail.

file

Any amount of information that is grouped together on a computer as one unit. On America Online, a file can be anything from text to sounds and can be transferred to and from your computer via America Online. Collections of files are available in libraries for downloading, and files may be attached to e-mail. *See also* download, library, *and* software file; *contrast with* article.

file compression

A programming technique by which files can be reduced in size without changing their content. Files are usually compressed so that they take up less storage space, can be transferred quicker, and/or can be bundled with others. Files must be decompressed before they can be used, but the AOL software can be set to automatically decompress most files (check your Preferences). More information is available in "Decompressing and Installing Files" in Chapter 6. *See also* file *and* download.

file library

See library.

File Transfer Protocol

See FTP.

FileGrabber

A piece of software built into the AOL software that automatically decodes encoded data (also known as "binaries"), such as that found in some newsgroups. Besides making sure that your newsgroup preferences are set to allow you to decode files, you don't need to do anything else to use it — FileGrabber will automatically detect encoded data and ask you if you want to download the file. For more information, see the `aol.newsgroups.help.binaries` newsgroup. *See also* download, file, Internet, *and* newsgroup.

filename extensions

These are usually three-character codes found suffixing a filename, and are primarily used for PC files. A comprehensive list would take several pages, but here are some common extensions:

Text/Word Processor formats:

`.doc`	Microsoft Word document
`.hlp`	Help file
`.htm`	Hypertext Markup Language (World Wide Web) format
`.htx`	Hypertext document
`.lf`	Line Feeds added to text format
`.let`	Letter file, as to a friend (for example, `Friend.let`)
`.log`	America Online log file, usually text
`.mw`	MacWrite document
`.rtf`	Rich Text Format
`.txt`	Text document (usually plain text)
`.ws`	WordStar document
`.wp or .wpd`	WordPerfect document

Graphics formats:

.art	Johnson Grace ART
.bmp	OS/2 or Windows Bitmap
.eps	Encapsulated PostScript
.gif	Graphic Interchange Format
.jpg	Joint Photographic Experts Group (JPEG)
.mac	MacPaint (also .pnt)
.pic	Macintosh PICT
.pcx	Zsoft Paintbrush
.tif	Tagged-Image File Format (TIFF)
.wpg	WordPerfect Graphic

Compressed formats:

.sit	StuffIt (Mac AOL software 2.x or later can unstuff this automatically)
.zip	PKZip (PC/GEOS, Windows AOL software, and Mac AOL software v2.1 or later can unstuff this automatically)
.arc	Abbreviation for ARChive; similar to PKZip (PC/GEOS and Windows AOL software can unstuff this automatically)
.sea	Self Extracting Archive

Other formats:

.avi	Audio-Video Interlaced animation
.bat	Batch file; executable file; DOS
.bin	Binary program file; often a subdirectory name
.bmk	Windows Bookmark file; references Help segment
.com	Executable program file; DOS
.dat	Data file or subdirectory with data files
.dbf	DBase file

.dll	Dynamic Link Library; program files recognized by Windows
.exe	PC executable file, can be a self-extracting archive
.grp	Windows Program Group
.ini	Initialization file for Windows and other applications
.mac	Macro
.mov	QuickTime movie
.mpg	MPEG animation
.pdf	Adobe Acrobat Portable Document Format
.pm4	PageMaker version 4.x file
.slk	SYLK file
.sys	Device driver or System file
.wav	Windows sound file
.xlc	Excel chart
.xls	Excel worksheet

flame

Made popular on the Internet, this means to chat, post messages, or send e-mail about something that is considered inflammatory by other members, and may cause fires among those who read and respond to it. "Flaming" may spark a lively debate when selectively and appropriately used. More often, it will cause misunderstandings and divided parties. Harassment and vulgarity are not allowed on America Online, and if you see this occurring, you may report the occurrence at keyword: TOS. *See also* asbestos, chat, message board, e-mail, *and* TOS.

flashmail

This is a feature of the AOL software that allows you to save your outgoing e-mail to your hard disk to send at a later time, or save your incoming e-mail so that you can look at it later, online or offline. These e-mails are stored in your Personal Filing Cabinet. Note: On newer versions of the AOL software, the term "flashmail" is no longer used and "FlashSessions" are now "Automatic AOL sessions." More information is available in "Reading Mail Offline" in Chapter 4. *See also* Automatic AOL *and* e-mail.

form

A window for an area online, usually comprised of a text field, a list box (scrollable), and one or more icons. Often special artwork will be placed in the form as well, as in a logo. Examples of forms include Star Trek Club (keyword: TREK) or MTV Online (keyword: MTV). *See also* icon *and* window.

format

To organize information into a particular style, size, or makeup. On America Online, you *format* text using the various buttons in the Format toolbar at the top of most windows that allow text input. More information is available in "Setting Your Style" in Chapter 2. *See also* rich text.

forum

A place online where members with similar interests may find valuable information, exchange ideas, share files, and get help on a particular area of interest. Forums (also known simply as areas or clubs) are found everywhere online, represent almost every interest under the sun, and usually offer message boards, articles, chat rooms, and libraries, all organized and accessible by a keyword. Forums are moderated by forum hosts or forum leaders. For example, in the Macintosh Computers & Software channel, each forum has a forum leader (denoted by *AFL* at the beginning of their screen name), and is assisted by Forum Assistants (denoted by *AFA*) and often assisted even further by Forum Consultants (denoted by *AFC*). *See also* form *and* keyword.

freeware

A file that is completely free and often made available in libraries of online services like America Online for downloading. Unlike public domain files, the author retains the copyright and you are not allowed to modify it. Since the author or programmer usually posts freeware and the user downloads it, distribution is direct and nearly without cost. Users are generally encouraged to make copies and give them to friends, even post them on other services. Check the file's documentation for limits on use and distribution. *See also* file, shareware, *and* public domain.

FTP

Abbreviation for File Transfer Protocol. A method of transferring files to and from a computer that is connected to the Internet. America Online offers FTP access via the keyword: FTP, as well as personal FTP sites at keyword: MY PLACE. More information is available in "Downloading Files Through FTP" in Chapter 7. *See also* Internet, World Wide Web, *and* home page; *contrast with* library.

Fwd:

Short for *forward* as in forwarding e-mail to someone. *See also* e-mail.

gateway

A link to another service, such as the Internet or a game (Dragon's Gate). Gateways allow members to access these independent services through America Online. They are used both as a noun and a verb. It is also rumored that the celestial gateway to Heaven is hidden somewhere online. *See also* Internet.

Geos AOL software

The PC platform's DOS version of the AOL client software, based on the GeoWorks graphical operating system. The current version is 1.6a, although a special 2.0 version exists for GEOS users. America

Online has no plans to continue upgrading this software, but members may continue using the current versions for the time being. May also be referred to as PC/GEOS, PCAO, or GAOL, GEOS. *Contrast with* Mac AOL software *and* Windows AOL software.

GIF (Graphic Interchange Format)

A type of graphic file that can be read by most platforms; the electronic version of photographs. The GIF format was developed by CompuServe as a standard for sharing graphical information across platforms (any with graphical display abilities). GIFs can be viewed with your AOL software or with a GIF viewer utility, which are located at keyword: VIEWERS. Member GIFs are also located in the Portrait Gallery (keyword: GALLERY). The *G* in *GIF* should not be pronounced like the brand of peanut butter, but rather like *gift*. See "Using Picture Gallery" and "Editing Graphic Files" in Chapter 6.

Gopher

A feature of the Internet that allows you to browse huge amounts of information. The term implies that it will "go-pher" you to retrieve information. It also refers to the way in which you "tunnel" through the various menus, much like a gopher would. More information is available in "Digging with Gophers" in Chapter 7. *See also* WAIS *and* Internet; *contrast with* newsgroups *and* World Wide Web.

GPF

Abbreviation for General Protection Fault. If you get a GPF error, it means that Windows (or a Windows application) has attempted to access memory that has not been allocated for its use. GPFs are the scourge of Windows AOL software everywhere. If you experience a GPF while using Windows AOL software, write down the exact error message, then go to keyword: GPF HELP for assistance. (Note: As you may have guessed, GPFs occur only on PCs with Microsoft Windows installed.) *See also* bug.

GUI

Graphical User Interface. Some examples of GUIs include the Mac Operating System, OS/2, and Windows. *See also* operating system, system, OS/2, *and* Windows.

Guide

Experienced America Online members who have been specially chosen and trained to help other members enjoy their time online. All on-duty Guides wear "uniforms" — the letters *Guide* followed by a space and a two- or three-letter suffix in all caps. If you would like to apply to become a Guide, send a request to the screen name: *GuideApply* or ask a Guide for a copy of the application. Applicants must be at least 18 years of age, have an account that has been active six months or more, and be a member in good standing (no TOS or billing problems). To offer a compliment or lodge a complaint against a Guide, send e-mail to *Guide MGR*. *See also* Lobby *and* uniform; *contrast with* host *and* moderator.

gullible

Anyone who believes there are really hamsters on America Online. But seriously, the hamsters scattered throughout this glossary are just pranksters. The authors take no responsibility for their actions. We really don't know how they get in here.

hacker

Not to be confused with hamsters, hackers are self-taught computer gurus who take an unholy delight in discovering the well-hidden secrets of computer systems. Blighted by a bad reputation of late, hackers are not necessarily those who intend harm or damage. There are those, however, who feed upon the pain inflicted by viruses. For more information, see "Staying Safe Online" in Chapter 1. *See also* password scammers, phishers, *and* virus.

hamster

Unbeknownst to most users, America Online's host computers are actually powered by these small, efficient creatures with large cheek pouches. They are notorious for being temperamental workers. When things slow down or troubles mount online, it is a sure sign that an America Online employee forgot to feed the hamsters. *See also* host *and* Stratus.

handle

An outdated term for your electronic *nom de plume*, better known as a screen name. *See also* e-mail address *and* screen name.

header

The information at the top (or bottom) of e-mail received from the Internet, which contains, among other things, the message originator, date, and time. Headers can also be found in newsgroup postings. *See also* e-mail, Internet, *and* newsgroup.

help room

Online "rooms" where members can go to get live help with the AOL software/system as well as assistance in finding things online. There are a number of these scattered around the service. See "Getting Help" in Chapter 1 for details. *For more information on the Tech Live help rooms, see* Tech Live. *See also* Guide, Help, *and* MHM.

home page

1. The first "page" in a World Wide Web site.

2. Your own page on the Web. Every member on America Online can now create his or her own home page — see keyword: MY HOME PAGE or "Creating Your Own Web Pages" in Chapter 7 for more information.

3. The page you go to when you first enter the Web.

See also browser, Favorite Place, page, site, URL, *and* World Wide Web.

host

> 1. The America Online computer system, affectionately referred to as the Stratus (which is actually an outdated term, but it is particularly tenacious). *See also* Stratus.

> 2. An America Online community leader who facilitates discussion in chat rooms. These are usually chat-fluent, personable individuals with particular expertise in a topic. You can find hosts all over the system, and they will often be wearing "uniforms" — letters in front of their names (usually in all caps) to designate their forum. More information is available in "Recognizing Hosts" in Chapter 5. *See also* Guide, chat room, conference room, *and* uniform.

hot chat

> A safe, euphemistic term that means to chat about (read "flirt") and engage in the popular online dance of human attraction and consummation, virtually, of course, and usually in private rooms or IMs. Unfortunately, hamsters are prone to this activity but usually only on Mondays, Wednesdays, and Fridays in the early morning hours, for reasons man has yet to fathom.

hot list

> *See* Favorite Places.

html

> Acronym for Hypertext Markup Language. This is the language used in creating most Web pages and is interpreted by your Web browser to display those pages.

http

> Acronym for Hypertext Transport Protocol.

icon

> A graphic image of a recognizable object or action that leads to somewhere or initiates a process. For

example, the icons in the Compose Mail window may lead you to the Address Book, allow you to attach a file, send the mail, or look up help. Icons are activated by clicking them with a mouse; some may even be used with keyboard shortcuts. More information is available in "Understanding Buttons" in Chapter 3. *See also* keyboard shortcuts.

Ignore

1. Chat blinders; a way of blocking a member's chat from your view in a chat/conference room window. Ignore is most useful when the chat of another member becomes disruptive in the chat room. Note that the Ignore button does not block or ignore IMs from a member — it only blocks the text from your own view in a chat or conference room. For details, see "Ignoring Chatters" in Chapter 5. *See* $im_off/$im_on *for instructions on ignoring IMs*.

2. An AOL software e-mail system feature that allows you to ignore mail in your New Mail box, causing it to be moved to your Old Mail box without having to read it first. To use, simply select and highlight the piece of mail you wish to ignore in your New Mail box and then click the **Ignore** button at the bottom of the window. Mail you have ignored without reading first will appear as "(ignored)" in the **Status** box. *See also* e-mail *and* Status.

IM (Instant Message)

America Online's equivalent of passing notes to another person during a meeting, as opposed to speaking up in the room (chat) or writing out a letter or memo (e-mail). Instant Messages (IMs) may be exchanged between two America Online members signed on at the same time and are useful for conducting conversations when a chat room isn't appropriate, available, or practical. For details, see "Sending Instant Messages" in Chapter 5. IMs may be ignored (*see* $im_off/$im_on). It is also possible to send an IM to yourself, and this is often used as a therapy exercise for recovering AOLoholics. IM is used as a noun ("I have too many IMs!") or a verb

("I'm IMing with him now"). Internet users can also send and receive Instant Messages if they download and install the free AOL Instant Messenger program (see keyword: AIM). *See also* IMsect.

Keyboard shortcuts for IMs (on Mac AOL software):

Command+I (to bring up a new IM window)

Command+Return or **Enter** (to send the IM)

Keyboard shortcuts for IMs (on Windows AOL software):

Ctrl+I (to bring up a new IM window)

Ctrl+Enter (to send the IM)

Keyboard shortcuts for IMs (on Geos AOL software):

Ctrl+I (to bring up a new IM window)

Tab (to **Send** button) then **Enter** (to send the IM)

history

In the context of AOL software version 4.0, this refers to the last 16–25 places you visited. This history list is found under the small arrow next to the keyword-entry box on the toolbar. You can clear your history list in your **Toolbar** preferences. More information on using the history list is available in "Using the Toolbar" in Chapter 3. *See also* toolbar.

IMsect

An annoying Instant Message (IM). These are usually from someone who insists on IMing you when you're busy, or when you've indicated you'd rather not talk in IMs. If this happens, you have the option of turning off your IMs completely (see *$im_off/$im_on* for directions). If someone persists in IMing you even though you've politely asked them to stop, this may be considered harassment and you should report it via keyword: TOS. *See also* IM.

in-house

Used to describe those employees who actually work at America Online's Virginia-based headquarters or one of the other satellite offices. May also be referred to as corporate staff. This is contrasted with community leaders, many of whom are actually volunteers and work from their homes. *See also* community leader *and* corporate staff.

insertion point

The blinking vertical line in a document marking the place where text is being edited. The insertion point may be navigated through a document with either the mouse or the arrow keys. Also called *cursor*.

Instant Messenger

See AOL Instant Messenger.

interactive

Having the ability to act on each another. America Online is interactive in the sense that you can send information and, based upon that, have information sent back (and vice versa). The chat rooms are an excellent example.

Internet

The mother of all networks is not an online service itself, but rather serves to interconnect worldwide computer systems and networks. The Internet, originally operated by the National Science Foundation (NSF), is now managed by private companies (one of which is America Online). America Online features the Internet Connection which includes access to USENET Newsgroups, Gopher & WAIS Databases, FTP, and the World Wide Web, plus help with understanding it all. To receive mail through the Internet gateway, you need to give others your Internet mailing address, which consists of your America Online screen name (without any blank spaces) followed by the @ symbol and *aol.com* (for example, jennifer@aol.com). To obtain more information about the Internet, use the keyword: INTERNET to go to the Internet Connection or see Chapter 7. For information about TCP/IP access to America

Online, see TCP/IP. *See also* address, browser, domain, FTP, gateway, Gopher, header, IRC, newsgroups, page, site, URL, *and* WAIS.

Internet Explorer

See Microsoft Internet Explorer.

invitation

A request by another member to join a chat or visit an area on America Online, service made possible by a special feature of the software available on Windows AOL software and Mac AOL software 3.0. To invite someone, add them to your Buddy List, select their name, and click the **Invite** button. You will then be prompted to fill in the information regarding the invite. Note that you may need the address (or URL) or an area in order to invite someone to it. For more information see "Using Buddy Lists" in Chapter 5. *See also* address, buddy, Buddy List, *and* URL.

IRC (Internet Relay Chat)

The Internet protocol for chat, allowing one to converse with others connected to the Internet in real time. While similar to America Online chat rooms, there are many differences — America Online's chat rooms are more intuitive and user-friendly, while IRC chats offer greater control over the environment. See "Chatting with Internet Relay Chat" in Chapter 7 for more information. *See also* Internet; *contrast with* chat room.

IP (Information Provider)

See partner.

ISDN

Acronym for Integrated Services Digital Networks. ISDN is a relatively new type of access offered by local telephone companies. You can use an ISDN to connect to other networks at speeds as high as 64,000 bps (single channel). *See also* TCP/IP; *contrast with* packet-switching network.

ISP

Acronym for Internet Service Provider. An ISP generally provides a point to which you can connect and access various Internet-based services such as Web sites, FTP, e-mail, Gopher, and newsgroups. Some ISPs also provide more advanced services that range from hosting Web sites and servers to wide area networking. For more information see "Using Internet Access Providers" in Chapter 1. *See also* FTP, Gopher, newsgroups, *and* World Wide Web.

Java

A computer language developed by Sun Microsystems. Java is similar to C++ and is used to develop platform-independent applications commonly known as *applets*. Java programs are safely downloaded to your computer through the Internet and immediately run without fear of viruses or other harm to your computer or files. You may encounter a JavaScript error while browsing the Web; if you do, this simply means your browser was unable to successfully run the Java applet for one reason or another.

K56flex

One of two competing implementations for 56 Kbps modem data delivery. K56flex was conceived by Lucent Technologies and Rockwell, and competes with U.S. Robotics' X2 technology. Neither X2 nor K56flex is an international standard; look for a finalized 56 Kbps standard. America Online has begun field testing this technology; appropriate access numbers can be located at keyword: ACCESS. *See also* X2.

Keep As New

An America Online e-mail system feature that allows you to keep mail in your New Mail box, even after you've read or ignored it. To use, simply select and highlight the piece of mail you wish to keep [in either your "New Mail" or "Old Mail" list (a.k.a. "Mail You Have Read" list)] and then click the

Keep As New button at the bottom of the window. Returning read mail to your **New Mail** box with the **Keep As New** button will not change the time and date that appears in the **Status** box of the sender. *See also* e-mail.

keyboard shortcuts

The AOL software provides us with keyboard command equivalents for menu selections. For example, rather than selecting **Instant Message** from the **People** button on the toolbar, you can type **Control+I** on the PC (Windows AOL software or Geos AOL software), or **Command+I** on the Mac to achieve the same results. More information is available in "Taking Keyboard Shortcuts" in Chapter 3.

keyword

1. A fast way to move around within America Online. For example, you can "beam" directly to the Star Trek Forum by using the keyword: TREK. To use a keyword, type it directly into the entry field in the toolbar (the long, white box) and click the **Go** button. You can also press **Command+K** on the Mac or **Control+K** on the PC, type the keyword, and press the **Return** or **Enter** key. Keywords are communicated to others in a standard format: *Keyword: NAME*. The name of the keyword is shown in all caps to distinguish it from other words around it, but it does not need to be entered that way. Currently, there are more than 10,000 public keywords. An updated list of *most* public keywords is available online at keyword: KEYWORD. There is also a book listing all the keywords, including several hundred left out from the online list. It is titled *AOL Keywords* and was authored by yours truly (Jennifer Watson). See "Traveling with Keywords" in Chapter 3 for more information on keywords.

2. A single word you feel is likely to be included in any database on a particular subject. A keyword is usually a word that comes as close as possible to describing the topic or piece of information you are looking for. Several of America Online's software

libraries, mainly those in the AOL Computing channel, can be searched for with keywords.

lamer

A colloquial term for someone who follows others blindly without really having a grasp on the situation. Used frequently within the hacker culture. *See also* hacker.

library

An area online in which files may be uploaded to and downloaded from. The files may be of any type: text, graphics, software, sounds, and so on. These files can be downloaded from America Online's host computer to your personal computer's hard disk or floppy disk. Some libraries are searchable, while others must be browsed. You may also upload a file that may interest others to a library. A library is the best way to share large files with other America Online members. To search libraries available for your platform, go to keyword: FILE SEARCH and click **Download Software**. *See also* file, download, upload, search, *and* browse; *contrast with* FTP.

line noise

Extraneous noise on telephone lines that is often heard as clicks or static. While line noise is usually only a nuisance to voice communications, it means trouble for data being transmitted through modems. If you are having problems remaining connected, it may be the result of line noise. Signing off, redialing, and getting a new connection will often help this problem.

link

A pointer to another place that takes you there when you activate it (usually by clicking it). America Online has literally thousands of links that crisscross the service, but they can't compare to the millions of links on the Web (often called "hyperlinks") that can cross continents without you knowing it. *See also* address, browser, Favorite Place, page, site, URL, *and* World Wide Web.

LISTSERV

An automated mailing list distribution system, which allows a group of e-mail addresses to receive (and often send) e-mail to one another as a group. You can subscribe to a LISTSERV mailing list as a member of America Online. More information and a database of available mailing lists are available at keyword: LISTSERV. See "Subscribing to Mailing Lists" in Chapter 7 for more details. *See also* e-mail *and* mailing list.

Lobby

Often seeming more like the Grand Central Station of America Online rather than a sedate hotel foyer, the Lobby is the default chat room of the People Connection. When you first enter the People Connection, you will most likely enter a Lobby where any number of members are also gathered. Some prefer the bustling atmosphere of the Lobby, while others use it as a waystation for other rooms in the People Connection. To get to the Lobby, go to keyword: LOBBY. If you'd rather avoid the Lobby, see "Bypassing the Lobby" in Chapter 5. *See also* chat, chat room, *and* Guide.

LOL

Shorthand for "Laughing Out Loud," often used in chat areas and Instant Messages. Another variation is ROFL, for "Rolling On Floor Laughing." A complete list of shorthand is available in Appendix B. *See also* shorthands, abbreviations, *and* chat; *contrast with* body language *and* emoticons.

lurk

To sit in a chat room or read a message board, yet contribute little or nothing at all. Hamsters are known lurkers. *See also* chat *or* conference room.

lurker

One who lurks in a chat room or message board.

Mac AOL software

The Apple Macintosh version of the AOL client software. The current version is 4.0. May also be referred to as MAOL. *Contrast with* Geos AOL software *and* Windows AOL software.

macro

A "recording" of keystrokes or mouse movements/clicks on a computer that allows you to automate a task. Macros are usually created with shareware and commercial software and can be initiated with a single key. They may contain something as simple as your signature for an e-mail note or a complex sequence that opens an application, converts the data, saves it in a special format, and shuts down your computer. Online, macros are most useful for sending large amounts of text to a chat area or for automating tasks such as archiving a message board or saving e-mail. Unfortunately, only Mac and Windows users can run macros; the Geos America Online environment doesn't allow macro use. Macro programs that work with your AOL software are described in Chapter 8.

mail controls

A set of preferences that enable the master account holder to control who you receive mail from. It can be set for one or all screen names on the account. Changes can be made by the master account screen name at any time. To access controls, go to keyword: MAIL CONTROLS. You can also block junk mail from your e-mailbox at keyword: PREFERRED MAIL. For more information check "Blocking Mail" in Chapter 4. *See also* e-mail.

mailbomb

What you have when one person sends you an excessive amount of e-mail, usually done in retaliation for a perceived wrong. This is a serious offense, as it not only inconveniences you but occupies mail system resources. If you receive a mail-bomb, you can report it at keyword: NOTIFY AOL and consider turning your e-mail off temporarily at keyword: MAIL CONTROLS. *See also* e-mail, snert, *and* TOS.

mailing list

A group of e-mail addresses that receive e-mail on a regular basis about a topic in which they have a mutual interest. Mailing lists can be as simple as a few friends' addresses that you often e-mail, or as complex as a daily digest of news delivered to the e-mailboxes of millions of addresses. More information is available in "Sending Mail to a Group" in Chapter 4 and "Subscribing to Mailing Lists" in Chapter 7. *See also* address, e-mail, *and* LISTSERV.

massmail

The act of sending a piece of e-mail to a large number of members. Also used as a noun. See "Sending Mail to a Group" in Chapter 4. *See also* e-mail, cc, *and* bcc.

megabyte

1,048,576 bytes of data.

member

An America Online subscriber. The term "member" is embraced because we consider ourselves members of the online community. There are currently over 12 million member accounts on America Online, each of which may be shared by up to five people. *See also* Online Community.

Member Directory

The database of America Online member screen names that have profiles. To be included in this database, a member need only to create a Member Profile. Note that profiles for deleted members are purged periodically; therefore, it's possible to have a Member Profile for a deleted screen name. You can search for any string in a profile. Wildcard characters and Boolean expressions also may be utilized in search strings. The Member Directory is located at keyword: MEMBERS. More information is available in "Searching the Member Directory" in Chapter 3. *See also* member, Member Profile, database, *and* searchable.

Member Profile

A voluntary online information document that describes oneself. Name, address information, birthday, sex, marital status, hobbies, computers used, occupation, and a personal quote may be provided. This is located at keyword: MEMBERS. More information is available in "Creating a Member Profile" in Chapter 2. *See also* member *and* Member Directory.

mcssage

A note posted on a message board for other members to read. Message titles are limited to 30 characters. Message text sizes have practical limits on each of the platforms — note that Geos AOL software users can only read 5,095 bytes of text in a message (with any additional text scrolling off the top); Mac AOL software and Windows AOL software can read any message in its entirety. There is no limit to the number of messages in a topic. A message may also be referred to as a post. *See also* message board.

message board

An area where members can post messages to exchange information, ask a question, or reply to another message. All America Online members are welcome and encouraged to post messages in message boards (or boards). Because messages are a popular means of communication online, message boards are organized with "topics," wherein a number of messages on a specific subject (threads) are contained in sequential order. Members cannot create new topics, so they should try to find an existing topic folder before requesting a new one. There are two kinds of message boards in use on America Online right now: regular and response-threaded. Message boards may be grouped together in a Message Center to provide organization and hierarchy. Message boards are occasionally called bulletin boards. *See also* cross-post, folder, message, Message Center, spam, *and* thread.

message board pointer

An automatic place-marker for message boards. America Online keeps track of the areas you have visited by date, allowing you to pick up where you left off upon your return. Once you've visited a message board, clicking the **List Unread** button will show you only the new messages that have been posted since your last visit. The pointers are updated each time you return.

Message Center

A collection of message boards in one convenient area. *See also* message board.

MHM (Members Helping Members)

A message board in the free area where America Online members can assist and get assistance from other members. Located at keyword: MHM.

Microsoft Internet Explorer

A popular Web browser that is also integrated into all America Online 3.0 and 4.0 clients. More information on Web browsers is available in Chapter 7. *See also* Netscape Navigator.

Microsoft Network (MSN)

An online service by the Microsoft Corporation. *See also* America Online, CompuServe, eWorld, *and* Prodigy.

modem

An acronym for modulator/demodulator. This is the device that translates the signals coming from your computer into a form that can be transmitted over standard telephone lines. A modem also translates incoming signals into a form that your computer can understand. Two modems, one for each computer, are needed for any data communications over telephone lines. Your modem speaks to a modem at America Online through a network of telephone lines provided by AOLnet or SprintNet, for example. For assistance with your modem, see "Troubleshooting Modems" in Chapter 1.

modem file

An information file that stores your modem settings for connecting to America Online. As modems differ, you often need to use a modem file configured specifically for your modem. Luckily, America Online software offers over 100 standard modem files that you can select from in the **Setup** window. If you cannot find a modem file for your modem, you can call America Online Customer Service, try the Modem Help area (keyword: MODEM HELP), or edit your modem file. *See also* CCL.

moderator

Typically a host who facilitates a discussion during a conference. The moderator usually manages protocol, if used. *See also* host, conference room, *and* protocol.

MorF

Acronym for male or female. To ask another member their sex. This happens frequently in Lobbies and chat rooms in the People Connection, but it is considered ill-mannered by most seasoned onliners. BorG (Boy or Girl?) is another manifestation of this virus that seems to infect some members. *See also* Lobby, chat room, *and* People Connection.

MSIE

See Microsoft Internet Explorer.

MSN

See Microsoft Network.

'Net

Abbreviation for the Internet. *See* Internet.

NetFind

See America Online NetFind.

netiquette

'Net manners. Cyberspace is a subculture with norms and rules of conduct all its own, understanding of these will often make your online life more enjoyable and allow you to move through it more smoothly. Online etiquette includes such things as proper capitalization (don't use all caps unless you mean to shout). Basically, the most important rule to keep in mind is one we learned offline and in kindergarten of all places: Do unto others as you'd have them do unto you (a.k.a. The Golden Rule). See Appendix B for a primer in America Online etiquette.

Netscape Navigator

An Internet browser produced by the Netscape Corporation. You can use Netscape Navigator in place of America Online's built-in browser with AOL software 3.0 or later. Details are available in "Using Alternate Web Browsers" in Chapter 7. *See also* Microsoft Internet Explorer, TCP/IP, *and* winsock.

network

A data communications system that interconnects computer systems at various different sites. America Online is a huge network.

Network News

America Online maintenance broadcasts and feedback that are displayed in a small window when transmitted. Network News can be enabled or disabled with the Windows AOL software (select the **My AOL** button in the toolbar, select **Preferences**, and click **General**).

newbie

Affectionate term for a new member (under six months). Good places for the new member to visit are keywords: QUICKSTART and AOL INSIDER. *Contrast with* wannabe.

newsgroups

Internet's version of a public message board. Available on America Online at keyword: NEWS-GROUPS. *See also* FileGrabber, header, *and* Internet; *contrast with* FTP, Gopher, WAIS, *and* World Wide Web.

node

A single computer or device accessible via a phone number and used by one or more persons to connect to a telecommunications network, such as America Online. Everyone signs on to America Online via a node, which is usually local to them and doesn't involve long-distance charges. Sometimes a bad connection is the result of a busy node and can be corrected by trying a new node. *See also* packet-switching network, 800 number, access number, AOLnet, *and* SprintNet.

online

The condition of a computer when it is connected to another machine via modem. Contrast with *offline*, the condition of a computer that is unconnected.

online community

A group of people bound together by their shared interest or characteristic of interacting with other

computer users through online services, BBSs, or
networks. Because of the pioneer aspects of an
online community, established onliners will welcome newcomers and educate them freely, in most
cases. On America Online, elaborate conventions,
legends, and etiquette systems have developed within the community. *See also* cyberspace.

OnlineHost

The screen name of America Online's host computer used to send information and usually seen in chat
rooms, conference rooms, and auditoriums. The
OnlineHost screen name may signal when a member
enters or leaves the room. On all platforms, the
OnlineHost screen name will give you the result of
dice rolled. *See also* chat room, conference room,
auditorium, *and* //roll.

Open-Apple key

See *Command key*.

OS (operating system)

The software that is used to control the basic functions of a computer. Operating systems are generally responsible for the allocation and control of a
computer's resources. Some common operating
systems are as follows: System 8, Windows, MS-DOS,
UNIX, and OS/2. *See also* DOS, System, UNIX, *and*
Windows.

Option key

A special function key commonly found on Mac keyboards. Usually located on the bottom row of keys
and labeled **Option**. Holding down the **Option** key
while another key is pressed will often activate a
special function. See "Taking Keyboard Shortcuts"
in Chapter 3 for more information.

OS/2

IBM's 32-bit operating system, which offers a
Macintosh-like interface for IBM PC and compatible

machines. The current release of OS/2 is called OS/2 Warp. It runs Windows 3.1, DOS, and OS/2 specific applications. *See also* operating system, DOS, *and* Windows.

P*

Shorthand for Prodigy Service. *See also* Prodigy.

packet-switching network (PSN)

The electronic networks that enable you to access a remote online service by dialing a local phone number. Information going to and from your computer is segmented into "packets" and given an address. The packets are then sent through the network to their destination much as a letter travels through the postal system, only much faster. America Online uses a variety of PSNs to supply local nodes (local telephone numbers) for members' access. *See also* access number, node, AOLnet, *and* SprintNet; *contrast with* ISDN.

page

A document on the World Wide Web, presented in the Browser window. Web pages can contain any combination of links, text, graphics, sounds, or videos. A set of pages is often referred to as a site. *See also* browser, Favorite Place, home page, html, link, site, URL, *and* World Wide Web.

palmtop

See PDA.

Parental Controls

Parental Controls enable the master account holder to restrict access to certain areas and features on America Online (such as blocking Instant Messages and chat rooms). It can be set for one or all screen names on the account. Once Parental Control is set for a particular screen name, it is active each time that screen name signs on. Changes can be made by the master account holder at any time. To access controls, go to keyword: PARENTAL CONTROL. See "Using Parental Controls" in Chapter 2 for more information. *Contrast with* $im_off/$im_on *and* ignore.

parity

A method of error correction at the character level, which is used in sending information via modems. Errors occur less frequently now — once every 1,024 characters isn't rare — so parity is almost a thing of the past.

partner

A person or party supplying material for use on America Online's services, and/or responsible for the content of an area on America Online's services. Also known as an information provider or IP. *See also* corporate staff *and* community leader.

password

The secret four-to-eight-character code word that you use to secure your account. Never reveal your password to anyone, even those claiming to be America Online employees. More information on passwords is available in "Protecting Your Password" in Chapter 2. *See also* phish.

password scammer

See phish.

PC/GEOS

See Geos AOL software.

PC-Link

A discontinued service for PC users that utilized a Deskmate-style interface with special support areas provided by the Tandy Corporation. PC-Link was phased out in late 1994. Abbreviated PCL. *See also* America Online *and* Q-Link.

PDA

Short for Personal Digital Assistant. A handheld computer that performs a variety of tasks, including personal information management. PDAs are gaining in popularity and variety. A limited version of the AOL software can be run on the Casio Zoomer and Sony MagicLink. The HP-100/200LX and Apple Newton can also access America Online mail. PDAs may also be referred to as palmtops. For more information, check out the PDA Forum at keyword: PDA.

People Connection (PC)

The America Online channel dedicated to real-time chat. Many different rooms can be found here: Lobbies, officially sanctioned rooms, member-created rooms, private rooms, the America Online Live area, and PC Plaza. You can access this area with keyword: PEOPLE. Feel free to surf PC, but please obey hamster crossing signs. More information on the People Connection is found in Chapter 5. *See also* channel *and* chat room; *contrast with* conference room.

Personal Filing Cabinet

A special feature of the AOL software that organizes your mail, files, newsgroup postings, and Favorite Places. Note that everything in your Personal Filing Cabinet is stored on your hard disk. You can set your Filing Cabinet preferences by choosing **My AOL** from the toolbar, selecting **Preferences**, and selecting **Filing Cabinet**. This feature is not currently available for those on Mac AOL software 2.7 and lower or Geos AOL software. See "Using the Personal Filing Cabinet" in Chapter 4. *See also* e-mail, Favorite Place, file, *and* newsgroup.

PKZip

A compression utility for PCs to compress one file, or multiple files, into a smaller file (called an archive), which will make for shorter up/downloading. The latest version is 2.04g. Windows AOL software 2.5 and Mac AOL software 2.6 (and higher) can automatically decompress 2.04 ZIP archives. More information is available in "Decompressing and Installing Files" in Chapter 6. *See also* archive, download, file, file compression, ARC, *and* StuffIt.

phish

The act of tricking members into revealing their passwords, credit card numbers, or other personal information. Phishers will often disguise themselves as America Online staff, but remember that America Online staff will never ever ask you for your password or credit card information while you are online. Phishers may also ask you to send certain files to them, or do something that seems odd to you. Phishers should always be reported to America Online so that they don't continue to prey on other, less-knowledgeable members. If you get an Instant Message from them, save the Instant Message, refrain from responding, and then report them at keyword: NOTIFY AOL immediately. *See also* hacker, password, *and* phisher.

phisher

One who phishes. *See also* cracker, hacker, phish, *and* snert.

polling

The act of requesting information from everyone in a chat room. For example, a member may ask "Everyone here who is cool, press 1" and the chat room will scroll with 1's for several minutes. This is considered disruptive and shouldn't be done in a public room. *See also* chat room.

post

1. The act of putting something online, usually into a message board or newsgroup.

2. A message in a message board or newsgroup. *See also* message board *and* message; *contrast with* upload.

postmaster

The person responsible for taking care of e-mail problems, answering queries about users, and other e-mail-related work at a site. America Online's post-master can be reached at, you guessed it, screen name: *Postmaster*. You can also reach other post-masters by simply adding the @ symbol and the domain name you wish to reach, such as *postmaster@msn.com*. *See also* domain *and* e-mail.

PPP

An acronym for Point-to-Point Protocol. PPP is one method of specifying how computers connect to the Internet through a dialup connection. *See also* SLIP.

private

The state of being in a private room. It is considered taboo by some members to be "seen" in a private room because this is often the communication channel of choice for "hot chatters." In reality, however, private rooms are a convenient way to meet with someone when IMs would get in the way. If you are private and another member does a search for your screen name, they will be told that you are "online, but in a private room." More information is available in "Creating Chat Rooms" in Chapter 5. *See also* private room *and* hot chat; *contrast with* chat room *and* conference room.

private room

A chat room that is created by a member via an option in the People Connection where the name is not public knowledge. Private room names have the same restrictions as chat room names: They may only contain up to 20 characters, must begin with a letter, and cannot contain punctuation. Some commonly named private rooms are rumored to be open 24 hours a day; AOLoholics have been known to make a hobby out of finding these "hidden" rooms. If you happen to stumble into a private room already occupied by other members, proper netiquette calls for you to apologize and leave. See "Creating Chat Rooms" for information on creating private rooms. *See also* chat room *and* hot chat; *contrast with* conference room *and* auditorium.

Prodigy

An information service founded as a joint venture between IBM and Sears. In the past, it was one of the larger competitors that America Online faced. *See also* P*; *contrast with* America Online, CompuServe, eWorld, *and* Microsoft Network.

profile

America Online allows each screen name to have an informational file (a profile) attached to it. A profile tells a bit about who you are, where you live, what your interests are — anything you want others to know about you. A profile can be created or updated at keyword: PROFILE. You can only modify the profile of the screen name you are currently signed on under, and each screen name has a unique profile. To read another member's profile, press **Ctrl+G** (in Windows) or **Command+G** (on the Mac), enter their screen name, and press **Enter**. Not all members have profiles. You may search profiles through the Member Directory. A little-known America Online fact is that a Member Directory search reveals that over 100 hamsters are lurking among profiles. More information is available in "Creating a Member Profile" in Chapter 2 and "Searching the Member Directory" in Chapter 3. *See also* member, Member Directory, *and* screen name.

protocol

On America Online, a system used in conference rooms to keep order and facilitate a discussion. When you have a question, you type **?**, when you have a comment, you type **!** and when you are finished, you type **/ga**. A queue of those waiting with questions and answers is displayed at regular points throughout the conference, and members will be invited to speak by the moderator or host. It is considered impolite and a breach of protocol to speak out of turn. More information on using protocol is available in Appendix B. *See also* conference room, host, *and* moderator.

public domain

A file that's completely free, uncopyrighted, and typically posted on services like America Online for distribution (via downloading) directly to the user. Since the producer (or programmer) usually posts this and the user downloads it, distribution is direct and nearly without cost. Users are generally encouraged to make copies and give them to friends — even post them on other services. Often little, or no, documentation is available for it, though. *Contrast with* freeware *and* shareware.

punt

The act of being disconnected from America Online often as a result of difficulties at America Online or interference on your node (such as line noise). Used as a noun or verb. *See also* bounce, node, *and* line noise.

punt pillows

Virtual "pillows" given, via chat or IMs, to cushion the posterior of a member who was punted. Often depicted as () () () () or [] [] [] []. *See also* chat, IMs, *and* punt.

push technology

A technology that allows online services to deliver content to your computer automatically during times when your computer is otherwise inactive. We expect America Online will implement push technology shortly to deliver content to your desktop within in a year of writing.

'puter

An affectionate abbreviation for one's computer; often employed by enthusiasts and AOLoholics.

Q-Link

A discontinued service for Commodore 64 and 128 users. *See also* America Online *and* PC-Link.

quoting

To include parts of an original message in a reply. One or two greater-than characters (>) is the standard method for setting off a quote from the rest of the message. They are usually placed to the left of the sentence, followed by a space, but may also be placed on the right as well. For example:

>Wow! That's great! How did
 you come by it? (Internet style)

<<Wow! That's great! How did
 you come by it?>> (AOL style)

>> Wow! That's great! How did
 you come by it?<<

Mac AOL software 3.0 and Windows AOL software 2.5 and higher members can quote text automatically in e-mail by first selecting it and clicking **Reply**. Mac AOL software 4.0 users can also add quoting to any text by first copying it and then pasting while holding down the **Option** key. *See also* << *and* >>.

Re:

Short for "regarding" or "reply." *See also* e-mail *and* message.

real time

Information received and processed (or displayed) as it happens. Conversations in Instant Messages and chat rooms happen in real time.

RealAudio

A streaming audio data format that allows Internet users and America Online members to listen to music and events in real time. The basic RealAudio player is available free for individual use from Progressive Networks at `http://www.realaudio.com`. More information is available in "Watching the World Wide Web" in Chapter 7. *See also* America Online Radio.

release

To make something available to the general public, such as a file in a file library. *See also* file *and* library.

remote staff

See community leader.

return receipt

A feature available with the AOL software that returns a piece of e-mail acknowledging that mail you sent to another America Online member (or members) has been received. Return receipts should be used sparingly as they can clutter up your mailbox. More information is available in "Getting Return Receipts" in Chapter 4. *See also* e-mail, carbon copy, blind carbon copy, *and* status.

revolving door

A chat or conference room has a "revolving door" when members are quickly moving in and out of the room. Lobbies and many popular chat rooms in the People Connection will often have "revolving doors." *See also* chat room, conference room, *and* Lobby.

rich text

Rich text can be considered the opposite of its less-formatted cousin: plain text, also known as ASCII. Rich text takes advantage of "html" tags to control positioning, size, color, and other attributes of appearance. America Online members using AOL software version 3.0 or later can use rich text formatting in e-mail and America Online's new-style message boards. See "Setting Your Style" in Chapter 2 for more information.

Road Trip

An AOL software feature which allows members to create "tours" of the World Wide Web and America Online, and then present these to others. For more information, see keyword: ROAD TRIP. *See also* World Wide Web.

savvy

To be knowledgeable or perceptive at something. Often seen as "computer savvy" or "online savvy." *Contrast with* newbie *and* wannabe.

screen name

The names (actually pseudonyms more often than not) that identify America Online members online. Screen names may contain no fewer than three and no more than ten characters, and must be unique. Any one account may have up to five screen names to accommodate family members or alter-egos, and each can (and should) have its own unique password. Either way, you cannot replace the original screen name created when you set up the account and the person that established the original screen name and account is responsible for all charges incurred by all five screen names. To add, delete, or restore deleted screen names, sign on with your master screen name and go to keyword: NAMES. More information is available in "Choosing a Screen Name" and "Creating More Screen Names" in Chapter 2. *See also* address, e-mail address, member, *and* uniform.

scroll

1. Refers to the movement of incoming text and other information on your computer screen. *See* scroll bar.

2. The act of repeatedly typing similar words onscreen or spacing out the letters of a word. For example, if a member typed the word "hello" seven times in a row, with returns between each, this would be scrolling. So would hitting **Enter** after each letter of a word. Polling also causes scrolling. Scrolling is prohibited in America Online's Terms of Service, and you may be given a warning for this if observed by a guide or host. Go to keyword: TOS for more information. *See also* polling.

scroll bar

The bar on the right-hand side of a window, which allows you to move the contents up and down, or on the bottom of a window for moving things to the left or right. The area on the scroll bar between the up and down arrows is shaded if there is more information than can fit in the window, or white if the entire content of the window is already visible. *See also* scroll (1).

search

Typically used in association with libraries and other searchable databases, the term search refers to a specific exploration of files or entries themselves. More information is available in "Searching with Skill" and "Finding Text in a Window" in Chapter 6. *See also* searchable, database, file, *and* library; *contrast with* browse.

searchable

A collection of logically related records or database files, which serve as a single central reference; a searchable database accepts input and yields all matching entries containing that character string. The Members Directory is an example of a searchable database. *See also* search, database, *and* Members Directory.

self-extracting archive

A compressed file that contains instructions to automatically decompress itself when opened; the software that decompressed it originally is not needed. On the Mac and the PC, these files can be decompressed simply by double-clicking the icon. Self-extracting archive files are usually identifiable by the `.sea` extension. On the PC, these are identified by an `.exe` extension. More information is available in "Decompressing and Installing Files" in Chapter 6. *See also* file compression *and* StuffIt.

server

A provider of resources, such as a file server. America Online uses many different kinds of servers, as do several of their partners, such as Dragon's Gate.

shareware

A fully functional file that is distributed with the promise of "try before you buy." Made available with the downloader's good conscience in mind, the authors of shareware ask that if you continue to use their product, you pay the fee requested in their documentation. Shareware is often made available in libraries of online services like America Online for downloading or is distributed via CD-ROM collections. There are shareware programs of exceptional quality and many are often comparable to commercially distributed software. There are a great number of variations of the shareware theme, such as demoware, which is often fully functional except for printing or saving functions or is only functional for a short period of time; postcardware, which requests a postcard sent to the author; contributionware, and so on. *See also* file; *contrast with* demoware, freeware, *and* public domain.

shorthands

The collective term for the many emoticons and abbreviations used during chat. These devices were developed by members over time to give information on the writer's emotional state when ASCII text only is available. A brief list of these is available online at keyword: SHORTHANDS, and a much more extensive one is in Appendix B. *See also* emoticons, abbreviations, *and* chat; *contrast with* body language.

sig

Short for signature. A block of text that some folks include at their end of newsgroup postings and/or e-mail. You can designate a sig for your own newsgroup postings through your newsgroup preferences. More information on using signatures in e-mail is available in "Creating a Signature" in Chapter 4. *See also* newsgroup *and* post.

sign-on kit

The free software, registration codes, and directions for creating a new America Online account. There are a number of ways to obtain sign-on kits. Online, go to keyword: FRIEND and follow the directions there to have a kit sent via snail mail. Offline, you can always find a "free offer" card in a magazine, particularly those magazines that have online forums like *Macworld* magazine. You may also find the sign-on kits themselves bundled with commercial software, modems, and computers. Sign-on kits can also be ordered via phone (1-800-827-6364). Of course, you can always purchase a book with the AOL software bundled in the back, such as *America Online For Dummies* by IDG Books Worldwide, Inc. If you simply need new AOL software but not an entirely new account, you can download the latest software for your platform—see "Finding AOL Software" in Chapter 1 for assistance.

sim

Short for simulation. A sim is a free-form game where participants role play in various scenarios. Sims are generally held in a chat or conference room, and may have rules associated with them. Check out the Simming Forum at keyword: SIM. *See also* //roll, chat room, *and* conference room.

simulchat

> A chat held simultaneously with a radio call-in broadcast. Online chat participants listen to the broadcast and discuss the same topics being discussed on the air. The radio broadcast takes questions and comments from the online chat as well as from callers. Simulchats are organized through the Digital City Chicago Online (keyword: CHICAGO) and Craig Crossman's Computer America (keyword: CROSSMAN). *See also* chat.

site

> A specific place on the Internet, usually a set of pages on the World Wide Web. *See also* address, link, page, URL, *and* World Wide Web.

slideshow

> *See* AOL Slideshows.

SLIP

> An acronym for Serial-Line Internet Protocol. The SLIP protocol specifies how computers connect to the Internet through a dialup connection. SLIP is used by some ISPs to connect their members to the Internet. *See also* PPP.

Smart Art

> A capability of the America Online v3.0 software that downloads system art to your computer progressively as you watch. You can stop the art download at any time by clicking a button or closing the window. Smart Art is a significant advantage over the old DOD style of art download, which forced you to wait for new artwork when you opened a window that required it. *Contrast with* download, DOD, *and* UDO.

smileys

> See Appendix A. *See also* shorthands *and* emoticons.

snail mail

Mail that is sent via the U.S. Postal Service. Not meant as derogatory, but to point out the difference between nearly instantaneous e-mail versus the delivery of tangible packages. Despite its relative slowness, snail mail will be used until matter transfer becomes possible. *See also* e-mail.

snert

Acronym for Sexually Nerdishly Expressive Recidivistic Trolls. A member who is disruptive or annoying. *Contrast with* cracker, hacker, phisher, *and* troll.

software file

See file.

sounds

See chat sounds.

Spam

1. A luncheon meat produced by the Hormel Foods Corporation. Spam is frequently the butt of many online jokes originally due to Monty Python's use of Spam as the topic of some of their skits. Lately, Spam jokes have taken on a life of their own online, and you may see many references to it. There is even a newsgroup dedicated to Spam, as well as at least one Web site. Fortunately, hamsters consider Spam a delicacy.

2. To barrage a message board, newsgroup, or e-mail address with inappropriate, irrelevant, or simply numerous copies of the same post (as in cross-posting). Not only is this annoying, but it is exceedingly bad netiquette. Members who "spam" will often have their posts removed (if in an America Online message board) or find their mailbox full of e-mail from angry onliners (if in a newsgroup). *See also* cross-posting, e-mail address, message board, *and* newsgroup; *contrast with* flame.

SprintNet

Formerly known as Telenet, SprintNet is a packet-switching network that provides members with 1200, 2400, 9600, 14400, and 28800 bps local access numbers to America Online. SprintNet networks are owned and operated by U.S. Sprint. To find SprintNet local access numbers, go to keyword: ACCESS or call 1-800-877-5045. *See also* packet-switching *and* access number; *contrast with* AOLnet.

Status (of e-mail)

An AOL software feature that allows you to check whether e-mail has been read and, if read, when. The status for an e-mail message may be "(not yet read)," "(ignored)," "(deleted)," or show the precise date and time when the mail was read. Status information includes recipients who were carbon copied (and even those who were blind carbon copied, if you were the sender). To check the current status of e-mail on the Mac platform, select and highlight the piece of mail you are interested in (either in the New Mail, Mail you have read, or Mail you have sent window) and then click the **Status** button at the bottom of the window. *See also* e-mail, carbon copy, blind carbon copy, *and* return receipt.

Stratus

America Online's host computer is known as the Stratus and is actually a collection of computers manufactured by outside companies, including the Stratus Corporation. These days America Online utilizes other types of computers for specific purposes, but Stratus continues to indicate the collective group of computing power. The Stratus features a fault tolerant system. This is achieved through "redundant" multiple processors, disks, and memory banks. The Stratus runs 365 days a year, 24 hours a day, and it's backed up by a standby diesel generator in case the power fails. *See also* host (1) *and* hamster.

streaming

A method whereby information, usually in the form of audio or video, is delivered to your computer and becomes available for immediate playback. Information that is delivered through streaming technology differs from normal file or download because you don't have to wait for the entire file to download before it becomes usable. *See also* America Online Radio, America Online Slideshows, downloading, *and* RealAudio.

StuffIt

A popular compression program for the Apple Macintosh currently published by Aladdin Software and written by Raymond Lau. StuffIt is the standard method of compressing Mac files for uploading to America Online's file libraries. With StuffIt, it's possible to combine several files into one archive, which is a convenient way of transferring several files at once. Stuffit files, also called archives, are often recognizable by the .sit extension to the filename. A file that has been compressed with StuffIt is said to be "stuffed." Files compressed with StuffIt can be automatically "unstuffed" when downloaded from Mac AOL software or when opened using the Mac AOL software. StuffIt is currently distributed both as a shareware product, StuffIt Lite, and a commercial product, StuffIt Deluxe. Programs to extract stuffed files are free and exist both for the IBM and Mac. More information is available in "Decompressing and Installing Files" in Chapter 6. *See also* archive, file compression, self-extracting archive, download, *and* shareware; *contrast with* ARC *and* PKZip.

surf

To cruise in search of information not readily evident in the hope of discovering something new. Usually paired with another word to describe the type of information being sought. Examples are room surfing and keyword surfing. The joy of surfing is only interrupted by the occasional "bump" when you forget to stop at the hamster crossing signs distributed randomly around America Online. See "Randomizing" in Chapter 3 for surfing through America Online. *See also* password scammer.

synchronous

Data communication technique in which bits are transmitted and received at a fixed rate. Used to transmit large blocks of data over special communications lines. Much more complex than asynchronous communication, this technique has little application for most personal computer users. *See also* asynchronous.

sysop

Abbreviation for system operator. The individual who operates and maintains a computer service, usually including a message board, a library or collection of libraries, and a chat room. Forum leaders are sometimes referred to as sysops, although that term isn't favored by many on America Online (pronounced "sis-op"). *See also* forum, host, *and* uniform.

system

Short for operating system, this refers to the software that controls the basic operations of a computer. System can also refer to the collection of components that have a functional existence when combined. Some examples of this include your computer system, the telephone system, or the America Online system. *See also* operating system, OS/2, *and* Windows.

TCP/IP

Acronym for Transmission Control Protocol/ Internet Protocol. The protocol language that Internet machines use to communicate. Windows AOL software 2.5 and Mac AOL software 2.6 and higher allow you to sign on via TCP/IP, and you can use other TCP/IP-capable applications through Mac

AOL software 3.0 and higher at the same time. *See also* Internet.

Tech Help Live

Sometimes also known as CS Live, this is a free area where you can ask questions of America Online staff live. The Tech Help Live is open from 7 a.m. to 2:45 a.m. Eastern Time, seven days a week. Here you can get live help from experienced customer relations staff working in-house at America Online headquarters or remotely. This service is available in the Unlimited Usage (free) area through keyword: TECH LIVE. *See also* Customer Relations.

Telnet

An Internet protocol that lets you connect to another computer without hanging up your modem and dialing again, using the connection you've already established with your local provider. Bulletin boards, online stores, and multi-user games are a few items you can tap into using Telnet. Telnet is accessible at keyword: TELNET. More information is available in "Traveling with Telnet" in Chapter 7. *See also* Internet.

thread

In general terms, a discussion that travels along the same subject line. More specifically, a thread refers to a group of posts in a message board under the same subject and (hopefully) topic. *See also* message board.

thwap

To hit someone upside their screen name; a virtual slap. For example, you may be ::thwapped:: for requesting an age/sex check in a chat room.

timeout

1. This happens when you've got two computers connected online and one gets tired of waiting for the other [i.e., when the hourglass (PC) or beach-

ball (Mac) cursor comes up and the "host fails to respond"]. You can report problems with frequent time outs at keyword: SYSTEM RESPONSE.

2. The result of remaining idle for a certain amount of time while signed on to America Online. This timeout time is about ten minutes or so, but may vary at different times of the day. In this case, America Online's computers are tired of waiting for you. It's also protection against staying signed on all night when an AOLoholic falls asleep at the keyboard.

title bar

The portion of a window where the name of the window is displayed. On the Mac the title bar also may include the close box and the zoom box. *See also* close box, window, *and* zoom box.

toast

Something totally ruined or unusable. For example, "Well, that file is toast." Also used as a verb.

toolbar

The row of buttons in the AOL software, usually found at the top of your screen. In AOL software version 4.0, many of the buttons have menus and portions of it are customizable. Navigational buttons and a keyword-entry box are also a part of the 4.0 toolbar. See the tip "Using the Toolbar" in Chapter 3.

topic

Groupings of messages by subject within message boards are termed "topics" on America Online. You cannot create topics. *See also* message *and* message boards.

TOS

Short for America Online's Terms of Service — the rules everyone agrees to when registering for and becoming a member of America Online. These terms apply to all accounts on America Online. You can read these terms at keyword: TOS. Also included are avenues of reporting TOS violations to America Online. *See also* TOSAdvisor *and* TOS warning.

TOSAdvisor

In days of olde, this was the screen name to which all TOS violations observed by members were sent. These days, if you feel something violates TOS, you should go to keyword: TOS to report it. Note that there is no longer a screen name: *TOSAdvisor*. Folks may still refer to *TOSAdvisor* as the deciding body in TOS deliberations, however. *See also* TOS, TOS warning, *and* OSW.

TOSsable

The state of being likely to receive a TOS warning. For example, a TOSsable word is one that a TOS warning could be given to if typed online. *See also* TOS *and* TOS warning.

TOS warning

An onscreen warning given by a trained Guide or Host for violating America Online's Terms of Service. These warnings are reported to America Online who takes action (or not, depending on the severity of the breach). *See also* TOS.

Trojan Horse

A destructive program that is disguised within a seemingly useful program. For example, one Trojan Horse was a file called AOLGOLD, which claimed to be a new version of AOL software, but actually corrupted files if it was executed. A Trojan Horse is only activated by running the program. If you receive a file attached to e-mail from a sender who you are not familiar with, you are advised not to download it. If you ever receive a file you believe could cause problems, forward it to screen name: *TOSEmail* and explain your concerns. More information is available in "Understanding Trojans" in Chapter 4. *Contrast with* virus.

troll

An online wanderer that often leaves a wake of disgruntled members before crawling back under their rock. It is unclear why trolls find America Online a popular watering hole, but it could be because they consider hamsters a delicacy. *Contrast with* cracker, hacker, password scammer, *and* snert.

typo

1. A typographical error. Some keywords would seem to fit this definition.

2. A dialect that many onliners have mastered with the advent of keyboreds and late nights. (Yes, there is a typo there.)

UDO

An older method of receiving updates to the AOL software. Upon signing on to America Online, the UDO sends all the necessary updates to your computer before you can do anything else. Rumor has it UDO stands for Unavoidable Delay Obstacle, but we haven't been able to verify it. *Contrast with* DOD *and* Smart Art.

uniform

The screen name that's often "worn" by a staff member, either in-house or remote (community leader), when working online. The screen name usually consists of an identifiable prefix and a personal name or initials. Uniforms aren't usually worn when the member is off duty. *See also* guide, host, *and* screen name. Some current uniforms include the following:

AFL	Apple/Mac Forum Leader
AFA	Apple/Mac Forum Assistant
AFC	Apple/Mac Forum Consultant
FCA/FCC	Family Computing leader
Guide	General System Guide

HOST	People Connection Host
MHMS	Members Helping Members Staff (Tech Live)
On Q	onQ Forum Leader
PC	PC Forum Leader
PCA	PC Forum Assistant
PCC	PC Forum Consultant
PCW	PC World Online
Rnger	People Connection Ranger
REF	Reference Desk Host
QRJ	RabbitJack's Casino Leader
VGS	Video Game Systems Leader

UNIX

An important operating system developed by Ken Thompson, Dennis Ritchie, and coworkers at Bell Laboratories. Because it also has superior capabilities as a program development system, UNIX should become even more widely used in the future. America Online does not currently have software for the UNIX platform. *See also* operating system; *contrast with* DOS, Windows, *and* system.

Unsend

An America Online e-mail system feature that allows you to retrieve mail that has been sent but not yet read. To use, simply select and highlight the piece of mail you wish to unsend from the Mail Sent window and click the **Unsend** button at the bottom of the window. The mail will be permanently deleted and cannot be retrieved. Note that only mail sent to other America Online members can be "unsent" or retrieved; Internet e-mail cannot be retrieved. *See also* e-mail.

upload

1. The transfer of information from a storage device on your computer to a remote computer, such as America Online's host computer. This information

may be uploaded to one of America Online's file libraries or it may be uploaded with a piece of e-mail as an attached file. Generally, any file over 16K (with the exception of text files) should be compressed before uploading to make the transfer faster and save money. Approved compression formats are ZIP, ARC, SIT, and SEAs. Important note: When uploading to America Online file libraries, be sure that the library you wish to upload to is the last one that you've opened after clicking the **Upload** button; there is a bug that sends your file to the last opened library, regardless of whether or not it was the one in which you initially pressed the **Upload** button. More information is available in "Uploading Files" in Chapter 6. *See also* file, file compression, *and* library; *contrast with* download.

2. The file or information that is sent or uploaded.

urban legend

A story, which may have once started with a kernel of truth, that has become embroidered and retold until it has passed into the realm of myth. It is an interesting phenomenon that has spread to the Internet and America Online. You may come across several urban legends, such as the $250 Neiman-Marcus Cookie Recipe legend or the Get Well Cards for the Sick Kid legend. A popular one on America Online these days is the America Online is Taking Away Free Chat legend (untrue). But never mistake hamsters for legends — we've really seen 'em.

URL

An address for an online resource, such as a World Wide Web site or an America Online page. URL stands for Uniform Resource Locator. You can enter a URL address directly into the keyword box in the toolbar or the keyword window. There is no list of URL addresses as they are constantly changing and growing, but you can save your favorites by clicking the heart in the upper right-hand corner of a window. America Online's home page URL is http://www.aol.com. More information is available in "Finding URL Addresses" in Chapter 3. *See also* address, browser, Favorite Place, page, site, *and* World Wide Web.

USENET

See newsgroup.

Virtual Places

An Internet-based chat room system that used avatars to represent the chat participants and allowed people to collectively tour the World Wide Web. Virtual Places was created by Ubique Ltd., which was later purchased by America Online. Virtual Places was beta tested on America Online for several months before disappearing from the service. Do not be surprised to see the technology surface again, but this time as a surcharged service.

virus

Computer software that has the ability to attach itself to other software or files, does so without the permission or knowledge of the user, and is generally designed with one intent — to propagate themselves. They may also be intentionally destructive; however, not all virus damage is intentional. Some benign viruses suffer from having been poorly written and have been known to cause damage as well. Virus prevention software and information may be found at keyword: VIRUS. See "Preventing Viruses" in Chapter 6. *Contrast with* Trojan Horse.

WAIS

Acronym for Wide Area Information Server, a database that allows you to search through huge amounts of information on the Internet, similar in some respects to a Gopher. WAIS databases are now widespread through the Internet. More information is available in "Digging with Gophers" in Chapter 7. *See also* Gopher *and* Internet; *contrast with* FTP, newsgroups, *and* World Wide Web.

wannabe

> Someone who aspires to something. Wannabes are often spotted by their obvious enthusiasm or their frustration at not being able to acquire a skill. Most wannabes are self-proclaimed and are considered a stage above newbies. For example, "He's a guide wannabe." See keyword: WANNABE and "Becoming a Community Leader" in Chapter 5. *Contrast with* newbie.

Web or WWW

> Abbreviations for World Wide Web. One of the more popular aspects of the Internet, the Web is actually an overarching term for the many hypertext documents that are displayed and linked together via a special protocol called Hypertext Transfer Protocol (or HTTP). World Wide Web information is available on America Online, using URL addresses to get to various Web sites or pages, much like you use keywords on America Online. Chapter 7 has several tips on using the Web. *See also* browser, Favorite Place, home page, Internet, page, site, *and* URL.

window

> A portion of the computer screen in which related information is contained, usually with a graphical border to distinguish it from the rest of the screen. Especially important in graphic user interfaces, windows may generally be moved, resized, closed, or brought to the foreground or sent to the background. Some common America Online windows include the chat room window, e-mail windows, and IM windows.

Windows

> Originally a graphical extension to the DOS operating system used on IBM PCs and compatibles, Windows has evolved into two sophisticated operating systems: Windows 95/98 and Windows NT. The former is used by 90 percent of the personal computers. The latter is a fully 32-bit operating system designed for networking environments. Developed

by Microsoft, the Windows environment offers drop-down menus, multitasking, and mouse-oriented operation. *See also* DOS, system, *and* UNIX.

Windows AOL software

The PC platform's Windows version of the AOL client software. The current version is 4.0. To learn how to check your revision number, see "Checking Your Version" in Chapter 1. *Contrast with* Mac AOL software *and* Geos AOL software.

winsock

Short for Windows Socket. Winsock is a standard that specifies how applications should support TCP/IP. Using winsock, AOL software versions 3.0 (or later) for Windows allow other applications such as RealAudio to take advantage of your connection to America Online and the Internet. *See also* RealAudio *and* TCP/IP.

X2

One of two competing implementations for 56 Kbps modem data delivery. X2 was conceived by U.S. Robotics and competes with Rockwell and Lucent Technologies K56flex technology. Neither X2 nor K56flex is an international standard; look for a finalized 56 Kbps standard in 1998. America Online has begun field testing this technology; appropriate access numbers can be located at keyword: ACCESS. *See also* K56flex.

ZIP

See PKZip.

zoom box

The zoom box is the small box in the upper-right corner of the window. Clicking the **zoom** box causes a reduced window to zoom up to fill the entire screen; clicking the **zoom** box of a maximized window causes it to zoom down to its reduced size. *Compare with* close box.

Index

Symbols and Numbers

CONTACTING IDG BOOKS WORLDWIDE

For general information on IDG Books Worldwide's books in the U.S., please call our Consumer Customer Service department at 800-762-2974. For reseller information, including discounts and premium sales, please call our Reseller Customer Service department at 800-434-3422.

For information on where to purchase IDG Books Worldwide's books outside the U.S., please contact our International Sales department at 650-655-3200 or fax 650-655-3297.

For information on foreign language translations, please contact our Foreign & Subsidiary Rights department at 650-655-3021 or fax 650-655-3281.

For sales inquiries and special prices for bulk quantities, please contact our Sales department at 650-655-3200 or write to the address above.

For information on using IDG Books Worldwide's books in the classroom or for ordering examination copies, please contact our Educational Sales department at 800-434-2086 or fax 317-596-5499.

For press review copies, author interviews, or other publicity information, please contact our Public Relations department at 650-655-3000 or fax 650-655-3299.

For authorization to photocopy items for corporate, personal, or educational use, please contact Copyright Clearance Center, 222 Rosewood Drive, Danvers, MA 01923, or fax 978-750-4470.